AF806964

Reconsidering Stagnation in the Brezhnev Era

Reconsidering Stagnation in the Brezhnev Era

Ideology and Exchange

Edited by Dina Fainberg
and Artemy Kalinovsky

LEXINGTON BOOKS
Lanham • Boulder • New York • London

Published by Lexington Books
An imprint of The Rowman & Littlefield Publishing Group, Inc.
4501 Forbes Boulevard, Suite 200, Lanham, Maryland 20706
www.rowman.com

Unit A, Whitacre Mews, 26-34 Stannary Street, London SE11 4AB

Copyright © 2016 by Lexington Books

All rights reserved. No part of this book may be reproduced in any form or by any electronic or mechanical means, including information storage and retrieval systems, without written permission from the publisher, except by a reviewer who may quote passages in a review.

British Library Cataloguing in Publication Information Available

Library of Congress Cataloging-in-Publication Data

Names: Fainberg, Dina. | Kalinovsky, Artemy M.
Title: Reconsidering stagnation in the Brezhnev era : ideology and exchange / edited by Dina Fainberg and Artemy Kalinovsky.
Description: Lanham : Lexington Books, 2016. | Includes bibliographical references and index.
Identifiers: LCCN 2016002159| ISBN 9781498529938 (cloth : alkaline paper) | ISBN 9781498529945 (electronic)
Subjects: LCSH: Soviet Union--Politics and government--1953-1985. | Brezhnev, Leonid Il?ich, 1906-1982--Political and social views. | Brezhnev, Leonid Il?ich, 1906-1982--Influence. | Stagnation (Economics)--Social aspects--Soviet Union--History. | Soviet Union--Economic conditions--1965-1975. | Soviet Union--Economic conditions--1975-1985. | Ideology--Social aspects--Soviet Union--History. | Political culture--Soviet Union--History. | Soviet Union--Relations--Western countries. | Western countries--Relations--Soviet Union.
Classification: LCC DK277 .R43 2016 | DDC 947.085/3--dc23 LC record available at http://lccn.loc.gov/2016002159

∞™ The paper used in this publication meets the minimum requirements of American National Standard for Information Sciences Permanence of Paper for Printed Library Materials, ANSI/NISO Z39.48-1992.

Printed in the United States of America

Contents

Introduction

Stagnation and Its Discontents: The Creation of a Political and Historical Paradigm

Dina Fainberg and Artemy M. Kalinovsky

> "Marxism is a theory of movement, not of stagnation."[1]
> —Leon Trotsky

The purpose of this volume is to test the by now well-established impression that the period in Soviet history between Nikita Khrushchev's ouster in 1964 and Mikhail Gorbachev's election as General Secretary in 1985 was one of stagnation. Accepting the stagnation paradigm generally means seeing the period as one where resistance to change, corruption, moral decay, and other negative trends were combined with a rise in the standard of living and foreign policy successes abroad (at least until the Soviet intervention in Afghanistan in 1979). The failure to confront systemic problems, this view holds, led the Soviet Union to a near crisis point by 1985. The "stagnation" label, we argue, created an impression of the period as one endless monolith, and therefore glossed over political, social, and cultural developments, as well as the state's attempts to lead and initiate change. The assumption that the period as a whole was characterized by rampant cynicism and decline of faith in the socialist creed obscured the persistence of popular engagement with the socialist ideology and the power it continued to wield within the Soviet Union.

It was Gorbachev who gave the era its appellation. At the XXVII Party Congress in 1986 he spoke of the leaders' failure to deal with mounting problems in the country:

> Over the course of many years, and due not just to objective factors but also to primarily subjective ones, the practical work of party and state organs fell behind the demands of the times, of life itself. Problems in the country's developments were growing rather than solutions. Inertia, freezing of forms and methods of management, declining dynamism in work, growth of bureaucratization—all of this did significant damage to our work [delu]. Phenomena of stagnation began appearing in the life of society.[2]

Gorbachev, of course, was setting the stage for a major political shake-up, a step in his search for a cure for the country's ills that would be possible only once the disease was properly identified. Nearly a year into his tenure, he already became frustrated with the friction his proposals for reform faced within the party, government, and security structures. The stagnation label was an important tool in drawing the line between those who supported the party and country's renewal, and those who opposed Gorbachev's program:

> Our party is a healthy organism, one that refines the style and methods of its activity, roots out formalism, bureaucratism and red tape (kazenschinu), cuts out everything stagnating and conserving that impedes movement forward, frees itself from those who have compromised themselves with poor work or unworthy behavior.[3]

In representing stagnation as alien to the true spirit of the Communist Party, Gorbachev was attempting to justify his future reforms, and to mobilize the party's rank and file to join the effort. To do so effectively, he positioned his reforms as a return to the true principles of Leninism, as a rallying cry to heal the party after a long period of degeneration.

In evoking the binaries of stagnation and revival, Gorbachev embarked on a well-travelled historical and intellectual path. On more than one occasion, concerns with corruption, stagnation and degeneration had arisen as a prelude to campaign for the transformation of Soviet society. In the 1920s these concerns were at the heart of the debate over NEP. As early as 1922 Lenin stressed the potential of the Bolsheviks' degenerating by adopting "bourgeois culture." Trotsky warned that "bureaucratization" in the state and party apparatus "under certain social conditions, might sap the basis of the revolution."[4] Students of the French revolution, the Bolsheviks worried that a new Thermidor was just around the bend. By the end of the 1920s fears of this double stagnation had pushed various factions in the party to support a break with NEP, even if they disagreed about how to move toward the next stage in development.[5]

After Stalin's death, critiques of bureaucratization and stagnation were mobilized to support a break with the Stalinist past. As in the late 1920s, Khrushchev positioned his reforms as a return to the true principles of revolution and Leninist methods. Attacks on bureaucratization and elitism, as well as stagnation in the construction of socialism became the central components of the culture of the Thaw and Khrushchev's attacks on Stalin.[6] Sometimes the term stagnation was used in a more limited sense. Thus, speaking at the 20th Party Congress, Mikhail Suslov used it to intervene in the debate over priorities in development, criticize "ill-starred economists who were spreading anti-Marxist views on the need to slow down the pace of developing heavy industry, [and thus] spread a theoretical justification for stagnation and conservatism in technology."[7]

Gorbachev's attempts to mobilize the party and the public for new reform by means of attack against bureaucratization and stagnation thus built on well-established Soviet traditions. Moreover, Gorbachev did not invent the stagnation label for the Brezhnev era. It had already been used in more limited ways, particularly in economic debates. In 1970, the term figured in Gosplan's research institute warning that the eighth Five Year Plan (1966–1970) was going to lead to "all basic indicators [to] decelerate, deteriorate or stagnate." The report was criticizing an emerging imbalance between state resources and the needs of national economy and between the output of consumer goods and monetary income of workers. In other words, Gosplan warned that with nothing to buy, monetary incentives would no longer be enough to stimulate workers.[8]

The diaries and memoirs of Gorbachev's advisors suggest that among at least some mid-ranking party officials, the sense that the Soviet Union was in a period of stagnation had also taken hold in the 1970s. Such themes are found in the memoirs of Georgii Arbatov, Anatolii Chernyaev, Karen Brutents, Aleksandr Yakovlev, and other "reformers" who played an influential role in the making of *perestroika*.[9] Arbatov, for example, calls the period from 1975 to 1982 the "apogee of stagnation."[10] He explains that while other periods had seen ups and downs, until the mid-1970s "movement did not stop, and the search [for solutions] did not stop. And thus it was not yet stagnation in the true sense of that word." However, by the mid-1970s, according to Arbatov, "the leadership...did not even look for paths of renewal. And in economics the reforms [of the 1960s] lived only a short time and were soon replaced with the most flamboyant bloom of familiar command-administrative, bureaucratic styles and methods of management."[11] Similarly, Aleksandr Yakovlev, known as the "architect of Perestroika," was unequivocal in his writing about the period, though he speaks about "crisis" rather than "stagnation": "Theft, mismanagement, plugging of endless holes by eating through national resources more and more clearly signaled a crisis in the system. Everywhere there was deception and ostentatiousness. . . . Deception permeated the system through and through."[12]

Many sentiments expressed in these texts were grafted in the need to explain the memoirist's role in the reforms unleashed by Gorbachev, associated as they are, with the ultimate collapse of the Soviet Union. The opinions found therein (echoed in interviews, excerpts published in newspapers, and other articles drawing on these memoirs) helped solidify the negative perception of this period in the USSR and abroad. However, that does not mean that their ideas about the period emerged only after 1985, though they may have crystallized then. The most valuable source for a contemporary view is Anatoly Chernyaev's diary for the Brezhnev years, since it makes it possible to distinguish between Chernyaev's opinions at the time and his writings after 1985.

Chernyaev's diary reveals no shortage of frustration with the country's economic condition and the leadership's inability to do anything about it. Although Chernyaev did not use the word "stagnation" (zastoi) in his diary entries, the impressions he recorded at the time convey a general sense of decline and immobility. Chernyaev expresses frustration with his boss in the international department, Boris Ponamorev, and with other members of the Politburo, who often seemed unwilling to even admit the very existence of problems. "Things are bad," he wrote in November 1978, "and there's no one willing to look facts in the face. They don't even want to know. Everything is great. Everything is wonderful. All successes and achievements . . . for five years we have been talking about raising quality and efficiency, but nothing moves. And we have not found a solution."[13] At a Central Committee discussion on labor-saving technology in August 1979, Chernyaev observed the spectacle of ministers being chided for failing to meet their quotas; but the ministers replied that they lacked the resources and the ability to meet their own targets: "The main thing was that the Central Committee was unable to offer any measures to improve the situation—not in terms of reapportioning resources, not [in terms of providing] new resources, nor anything else."[14]

Chernyaev's diary suggests that such feelings were not uncommon among the more liberally inclined party members as well as the more conservative ones, or among the cadres in the KGB and the military, who felt that corruption had gone too far. Valerii Boldin, Gorbachev's chief of staff who ultimately turned on him, supported the August 1991 putsch, and wrote a scathing memoir of his time working with Gorbachev, describing the period in roughly the same terms as Chernyaev and Arbatov. Boldin referred to "stagnation and degradation" in the economy as well as pervasive corruption in the party ranks.[15] These critical party apparatchiks supported Yuri Andropov's elevation after Brezhnev's death in 1982, and Gorbachev's election in March 1985. The "liberals" alone would not have made it possible for either of these men to take the helm, let alone institute any kind of serious agenda. It is plausible that there was a coalition that saw the late Brezhnev period as one of stagnation and supported this label as a necessary prerequisite to broader reform efforts and a major campaign against corruption.[16]

Foreign observers of the Soviet Union in the Brezhnev era also evoked the idea of stagnation, albeit without naming it so. Travellers and journalists from North America and Western Europe frequently described the Soviet people as cynical and devoid of hope. Publications based on first-hand experience in the Soviet Union emphasized such things as shortages of consumer goods in the Soviet stores, swollen bureaucracy, problems of housing and health care, and the widespread "second economy" of favors and theft. They stressed that while the simple people spend their days queuing for basic foods and goods, their leaders enjoy unimaginably luxurious lifestyles. One glance at the everyday life of the Soviet people was enough to know that the USSR failed to provide an alternative to capitalism, suggested one American journalist:

> Above the clouds circled Soviet space capsules and killer satellites. In their remote bunkers sat ICBM missiles. Down on earth, in the capital city of Communism itself, which is allocated the best food and consumer goods in the country, soldiers and mothers stood in the slush for thirty minutes or more to buy candy available in even the most ordinary shops in most of the rest of the world.[17]

These observations were marshaled to support the conclusion that Soviet socialism failed to deliver its promises and strengthened the impression that the USSR is on the downward spiral of ideological decline. Thus in 1983 *New York Times* correspondent David Shipler began his book about the Soviet Union stating that the Russians "have lost their heroes and their faith, their faith in their ideology and in their future."[18] This picture of hopelessness for Russia's future was a sharp contrast to Western observers' exuberant treatment of Gorbachev and his reforms. Adopting Gorbachev's terminology, Western observers began to use the label of "stagnation" in their references to the Brezhnev era. "Stagnation" became the world that separated the hopeless past from the exciting present: finally Russia reformed itself and converged with the West.

By contrast, contemporary Sovietologists often had a much more nuanced view of the period than popular commentators. H. Gordon Skilling, T. H. Rigby, and others saw the Brezhnev regime as managing a rapidly changing and increasingly complex society with different interest groups. Others noted that Soviet society was increasingly educated and urbanized—a phenomenon, it should be noted, not limited to central Russia, but perhaps even more noticeable in some of the republics. The "convergence" model, in its various forms, saw the social-economic transformations going on in the USSR and the capitalist West making them increasingly alike.[19] In a 1978 volume, the dean of Soviet economics in the West, Alec Nove, noted a generally improving situation in agriculture in the period since Khrushchev's ouster, while Archie Brown observed the regime's seeming ability to negotiate among various groups and maintain a "limited institutional or bureaucratic pluralism."[20] Writing after Brezhnev's death, the Sovietologist Seweryn Bialer described the years 1976–1982 as a period of "domestic stagnation, resistance to change and foreign adventures with dubious long range consequences and clearly negative short-range effects." At the same time, he chided other observers for missing impressive Soviet achievements, particularly, the rising standards of living, the successful co-optation of intellectual elites and non-Russians into the Soviet order, and the system's ability to provide upward mobility and engagement in local politics and administration without inviting challenges in the sphere of high politics.[21]

If there was a relatively broad agreement that the late 1970s and early 1980s had witnessed some sort of stagnation, it is doubtful that all the people in the "anti-stagnation" coalition could agree on the precise definition of that term. For example, Boldin notes that for all of the problems of the period, it was also one of significant growth and improvements in some sectors, including residential construction. More generally, he writes, "in many fields of knowledge, science had achieved impressive results, culture was developing, education continued improving."[22] For others, the increasingly critical tone taken in Soviet film and literature of the period, and the abilities of those genres to defy censorship, was a cause for celebration. Chernyaev, for example, praised Soviet literature and the arts for "liberating themselves from the dictum of politics (and politicians) and acquiring a logic of their own, a logic of critical and independent reflection of reality."[23] It is unlikely that the KGB or others would have agreed.

Likewise, the economist and writer Nikolai Shmelyov, who was calling for a transition to market reforms by 1987, told Stephen Cohen and Katrina Vanden Heuvel that he had "always found ways to express [himself] honestly" during the Brezhnev years. He went on to insist that while it was sometimes hard to speak, write, and publish honestly:

> In very reserved and disguised ways, you could express almost everything, if you were skillful enough. There may have been peace and quiet in the press, but some intellectuals and even ordinary people found useful ways to say what had to be said. Even a few leaders raised the real questions that faced the country in their speeches and memorandums.[24]

Evoking the image of a fetid swamp may have been a stroke of political genius on Gorbachev's part, but was it an adequate description of the USSR's political, economic, cultural, and social development in the two decades before he came to power? As one starts to add up the exceptions, the accuracy of the term "stagnation" begins to crumble. A period of strictly enforced ideological conformity also saw incredible creativity in the arts, and not just at the underground or samizdat level, but often in the most public venues. As numerous scholars have shown, a conservative backlash against liberal-minded intellectuals in the early 1970s was nevertheless followed by a period of unprecedented creativity and engagement with ideas from within and beyond the socialist bloc, facilitated by international détente in fields like economics, sociology, and political science.[25] Although the policy ideas generated by thinkers in this field would not find a reception in leadership circles until after Brezhnev's death.

If we accept that stagnation is not an accurate label for what was happening in culture, science, and intellectual life, the most difficult aspect of the paradigm to challenge is that pertaining to the party-state apparatus. All of the memoirists listed above complain about the unwillingness of the Brezhnev era leadership to confront problems, to cede power to a younger generation, or to hear reform ideas. It is hard to dismiss these claims outright—for there was clearly a certain paralysis of decision-making caused in part by Brezhnev's physical decline. The historian Moshe Lewin identified stagnation primarily with the failing of the party apparatus: "'Stagnation' was marked by the impossibility of extracting anything from the bureaucracy and a lack of will and ideas at the top about how to stop the rot. All attempts to reduce the size of the bureaucracy, or force it to change its habits, were so many losing battles."[26] Similarly, Stephen Kotkin wrote that "People with initiative, independent judgment, and integrity who had joined the party to lead politically active lives or to better their countries were generally weeded out or beaten down."[27]

There is certainly plenty of evidence to support this view, but the exceptions are crucial as well. Big decisions were taken, especially on matters of foreign policy, often with Brezhnev's active participation. And if the system was too rigid in the late 1970s to support truly creative and dynamic people, how did someone like Gorbachev rise through its ranks, let alone the many bright and heterodox intellectuals and technocrats that supported him? It is worthwhile in this regard to note the words of Yegor Ligachev, an early Gorbachev ally who came to see *Perestroika* going too far, too fast, and who challenged the emerging portrayal of the previous era:

> In the years of stagnation, I lived and worked in Siberia—a harsh but truly wonderful land. I am often asked what I was doing during that time. I answer with pride: I was building socialism. And there were millions like me. It would be an act of betrayal if I did not mention those with whom I linked my fate and shared joys and sorrow. Many of them have left this life. Not everything turned out as we wanted . . . but we worked without looking over our shoulders, perhaps because we knew they couldn't send us farther away in Siberia. We worked in order to give the people a better life, to give the state more, and to protect the interests of the province.[28]

These nuanced views of the period are important because they help us understand the stakes that contemporaries invested in the stagnation debate before and after the collapse of the Soviet Union. While the Brezhnev elites thought of the period as "Developed Socialism," Gorbachev and his allies evoked the narrative of stagnation as a justification of the radical transformation of the Soviet Union that they initiated.[29] By 1991, however, Gorbachev's liberal rivals began to use the label of stagnation to justify their turn against perestroika. Yeltsin publically attacked Gorbachev and clamed that he was trying to return the USSR to the era of stagnation, thus turning Gorbachev's own definition of the Brezhnev era against him.[30]

The popularity and the convenience of the term stagnation helped it become an important narrative describing the Brezhnev era. However, the political, public, and scholarly debate over this period in Soviet history is often wedged over the lines of "pre-crisis" or "pre-renewal." When the Soviet Union collapsed despite Gorbachev's reform and attempts to modernize the country, "stagnation" became the primary explanation of the failure of the Soviet socialist project. Even today, the questions in the stagnation debate are informed by retrospective view of the events. Therefore the debate over the "stagnation narrative" whether or not it was possible to reform Soviet socialism or whether the crisis was inevitable. Had the Soviet state already missed its chance for reform by 1982, or were the conditions and resources for reform in place?[31]

The purpose of this volume is to push the discussion of the Brezhnev era beyond the debate over the possibility of reform. We do not seek to replace the stagnation narrative with a new story, but to examine the Brezhnev era on its own terms and to situate it on the continuum of Soviet history. The chapters that follow focus on developments in politics, society, and culture as well as the state's attempts to lead and initiate change, which are mostly glossed over in the stagnation narrative. We would like to challenge the assumption that the period as a whole was characterized by rampant cynicism and decline of faith in the socialist creed and to study the persistence of popular engagement with the socialist ideology and the power it continued to wield within the Soviet Union.

In doing so, we are building upon other recent attempts to re-evaluate the Brezhnev era. One of the earliest notable efforts in this regard is the 2002 volume edited by Edwin Bacon and Mark Sandle, *Brezhnev Reconsidered.* Though focusing more explicitly on Brezhnev himself, a number of the essays nevertheless challenge some common perceptions about the period.[32] The volume calls for a reevaluation of the dichotomy between the "thaw" and "stagnation," highlighting the intellectual space available in the Brezhnev era and the creativity that existed within the intellectual establishment and beyond. Rather than viewing the Brezhnev period as "stagnation" devoid of independent thinking, Sandle suggests approaching intellectual life under Brezhnev as "heterogeneity, struggle, conflict and creativity."[33]

Since the publication of Bacon and Sandle's volume more and more scholars began to turn their attention to the Brezhnev era, taking Sandle's suggestions to heart. In 2013 and 2014 *Cahiers du Monde Russe* and *Russian History* published special editions dedicated to the Brezhnev era with articles spanning a variety of topics such as state institutions, ideology, collective memory, everyday life, nationalities policies, and the cultural world. More and more scholars now use the term "late socialism" to describe the period between late 1960s and mid-1980s in socialist countries, including the Soviet Union in the Brezhnev era. The term "late socialism" transcends the negative image of the 1970s as the downward spiral usually associated with the idea of "stagnation." Instead it focuses on the long 1970s as a period of diversity, mobility, and innovation in politics, society, and culture.

Alexei Yurchak's seminal study, *Everything Was Forever Until It Was No More,* demonstrated that the increasingly formulaic and frozen discourse of state ideology had actually allowed a creative and meaningful engagement with its institutions. While many people viewed the official Komsomol meetings as boring functions, they saw their own day-to-day work within the organization as fulfilling and important.[34] Scholars such as Svetlana Boym, Susan Reid, David Crawley, and Lewis Siegelbaum have re-evaluated the categories traditionally used to analyze the Soviet system and have stressed the flexible and the interchangeable nature of the boundaries between the private and the public in late socialism and their mutual coexistence.[35] They argue that it was through these semiprivate, semipublic icons of "materialism" like the dacha, the car, the décor of one's flat or room in a communal apartment that people negotiated their relationship with the state and carved personal meaning that was also closely connected to the public realm.

Taking the Brezhnev era on its own terms challenges other dichotomous categories of analysis. For example, in a recent volume, *Soviet Society in the Era of Late Socialism, 1964–1985,* the editors Neringa Klumbyte and Gulnaz Sharafutdinova propose to transcend the binaries of socialism/liberalism and domination/resistance that were often used to characterize the Soviet society.[36] Instead, the volume focuses on "multiple circulation of power" and daily experiences of the Soviet people. In exploring such diverse spheres as consumption, literature, football, and humor, the volume offers a new picture of Soviet life during the Brezhnev years, which highlights the interplay between the agenda of state institutions and the citizens' individual agency.

Our volume contributes to this growing re-evaluation of the Brezhnev era, shaping a new historiography that gives us a much richer and nuanced picture of the time period. It shows us the importance of challenging the labels and descriptions given by politicians to an era, and the value of looking at a given historical period from many directions at once. The multifaceted prism reveals a dynamic society and a political and intellectual class that remained committed to the ideological foundations of the state, recognized the challenges that the system faced, and embarked on a creative search for solutions.

Natalia Chernyshova's chapter in this volume explores people's routine encounters with the state system in their capacity as consumers. Chernyshova suggests that the central place of personal consumption in people's lives, identity, and perceptions of success in the long 1970s does not automatically translate into unqualified withdrawal from the public sphere and shutting off from the state. On the contrary, Soviet consumption had a strong public aspect, and Soviet consumers had to engage actively with the existing system of retail, customer services, and even the black market. Chernyshova challenges the traditional image of a disengaged and a disappointed Brezhnev era consumer. The rising standards of living increased the aspirations of Soviet consumers and their personal investment in the system, she argues. Taking the regime's promises with utmost seriousness, Soviet consumers demanded that the state fulfills its commitments for better living and held it responsible when it failed to do so.

Simon Huxtable's contribution to this volume reveals how the Soviet press—an important pillar of Soviet ideological establishment—continued its attempts to engage and mobilize the citizens. The years that followed Khrushchev's ouster, Huxtable points out, saw a concerted attempt to reform Soviet society along technocratic lines, which heavily involved the press. Huxtable demonstrates how the economic reforms of 1964–1965, which placed increased importance on profits and introduced quasi-market conditions to the Soviet press, necessitated gathering of information on readers. As a result, almost all leading newspapers employed sociologists to conduct quantitative studies of their audience. These sociologists revealed journalists' ignorance of their readership, and showed that readers responded to the content of the press in ways that were entirely unexpected. Influenced by the findings of the sociologists and by the need to secure subscribers, the journalists began to conceive of their audience not just as individuals to be enlightened but also as potential consumers—and adjusted their content accordingly. The result, Huxtable suggests, was a fracturing of notions of the Soviet public as a cohesive whole, something that has relevance to our understanding of the social dynamics of private and public in the Brezhnev era.

Lewis Siegelbaum's chapter on migration from rural areas to Soviet industrial centers shows how young people in the kolkhozes took their fates in their own hands and embarked on life-changing journeys to study, work, and settle in the cities. The central inspiration for these monumental changes, according to Siegelbaum, was the idea of a good life, which was actively promoted by socialist culture and institutions. Movement and transformation are also the subjects of Christian Noack's contribution to this volume. Noack's examination of tourism in the Soviet Union points out that Soviet private and public spheres were entangled in leisure as in work. During the Brezhnev era, Noack contends, Soviet tourism became a "middle ground" where the state and the people negotiated their competing ideas about the relationship between the family and the collective. As a result of these negotiations, the Soviet concept of leisure was transformed, resulting in the emergence of family vacations and motor-tourism—both previously unseen in the Soviet context.

As these contributions suggest, a close examination of practices and institutions that were central to Soviet everyday life challenges the view of the Brezhnev era as a period of stagnation. In contrast to the conception of a cynical population, we see how socialist culture and the hopes for a better life that it propagated permeated the daily activities of Soviet citizens, as well as their engagements with the world around them.

It is perhaps one of the most interesting phenomena of the Brezhnev era that officially sanctioned socialist culture offered ample opportunities to criticize the Soviet regime and to express popular grievances and discontent. Andrey Shcherbenok's article examines how certain segments of the public came to terms with the shortcomings of the Soviet system through the medium of film. The article aims to complicate Alexei Yurchak's notion that Soviet citizens perceived late socialist reality as quite stable and as sure to last for many more decades. Shcherbenok demonstrates that a number of films, which enjoyed cult status precisely among urban intelligentsia studied by Yurchak, depicted Soviet reality as crumbling away, full of insoluble problems and undergoing deep crisis—in short, incompatible with a notion of longevity and stability. Most importantly, these films demonstrate the crisis of deep-seated values and cohesive communities of "normal people" that Yurchak viewed as the cornerstones of late Soviet stability. Shcherbenok also outlines several possible explanations of how the popularity of crisis films could coexist with the perceived stability and speculates about possible psychosocial drives that made late Soviet audience invest in subversive cinematic phantasy.

The Cold War and the relationship between the Soviet Union and what we call the West loom large in the challenge to stagnation narrative. Several scholars have recently pointed out that the Soviet relationship with the outside world featured imaginative policies and radical departures with strategies from the past.[37] Sari Autio-Sarasmo's contribution on East-West economic cooperation and technological exchange against the backdrop of the Cold War demonstrates how dominant initiative and innovative thinking in Soviet engagement with the outside world were. Focusing on exchanges of technology and scientific know-how between the Soviet Union and Western Europe, Autio-Sarasmo points out that these exchanges peaked precisely in the period usually associated with high stagnation (1973–1982). This essay offers an important corrective to a traditional view, which pitted the allegedly backward Soviet science and technology against "Western advancement."[38] By contrast, Autio-Sarasmo contends that Soviet leaders were eager to import foreign technology as one of the means to promote and facilitate modernization and development at home. Soviet leaders' continuous emphasis on development and modernization accounts for the efforts they invested in establishing, cultivating, and promoting business relationships and exchange with the West.

Continuing these themes, Anna Geltzer explores the dynamics of Soviet relationships with Western scientists and points out the challenges and achievements of cooperation in the realm of development of anticancer drugs. Not only was Soviet science engaged with international developments, Geltzer shows, but the perception that Soviet science suffered from underfunding and lack of professional autonomy is largely wrong. On the contrary, the system, though flawed, provided much room for individual initiative as well as de-ideologized debate about scientific methodologies.

An important pillar of the stagnation narrative emphasized the decline of a competitive drive to "reach and surpass the West" on the one hand, and the Soviet public's infatuation with Western commodities and cultural artifacts on the other. For example, in his celebrated book on globalization, renowned *New York Times* columnist Thomas L. Friedman wrote that the Iron Curtain collapsed because the people wanted things that were on the other side—McDonald's, IBM, and Mickey Mouse.[39] Scholars of U.S. "soft empire" often echo Friedman's view and depict the globalization of American culture as a one-sided, uninterrupted flow from the West to the East.[40] However, the picture changes significantly if we consider East-West relations as a system of exchange rather than of one-sided influence, and emphasize the dynamics of mutual imagination that informed transnational interactions. Such a perspective on Soviet relations with the outside world allows scholars to move beyond the seemingly contradictory features of the late Soviet period, like participation in party-sponsored institutions on the one hand, and listening to Western rock bands on the other.[41]

The final papers in this volume explore the different forms of Soviet engagements with the world, addressing imagination of the Soviet self and the Western other as well as exchange and appropriation of ideas, commodities, and symbols. Julianne Fürst's essay on hippies examines how this essentially Western cultural phenomenon was appropriated and transformed in the Soviet context. In fact, she argues, the social and cultural climate of the Brezhnev period enabled the development of the hippies into an unofficial subculture. The Soviet hippies could lead colorful, carefree lives precisely because the state now provided them the security and (relative) freedom to do so.

Courtney Doucette explores the dynamics of unofficial cultural exchange through a case study of the relationship between a prominent Western art collector, Norton Dodge, and Lianozovo group, a collective of unofficial Soviet artists. Doucette's essay challenges the traditional narrative, which constructed dissent in the Brezhnev era as "a bastion of Western liberalism in a sea of communism." She argues that transnational collaboration between unofficial artists and Western collectors shaped the "political and politicized" image of unofficial Soviet artists, which plays such an important role in contemporary narrative of the Brezhnev era. While the mutual expectations of Dodge and the Lianozovo Group converged in many ways, it was *not* because the artists and the collector shared political values. Western collectors viewed the work of unofficial artists as political acts of resistance to the Soviet regime. By contrast, the artists themselves "saw their art as a site not of political but of deeply individualistic activity." Doucette points out that the artists began to fashion themselves as dissidents and political opponents of the Soviet regime only after 1974, following the Bulldozer exhibition and the subsequent exodus of artists into emigration.

Simo Mikkonen examines the operations of the Soviet-Finnish society and reveals how cultural and personal relations that were established during the Thaw kept expanding after Khrushchev's ouster. People from all walks of life, not just professional elites, participated in official and semi-official delegations, exchange programs, and organized tours, constantly expanding the flow of ideas and people across the borders. Mikkonen points out that it was in this period, which is usually associated with stagnation, that individual initiatives complemented the Party agenda as the defining factor in transnational connections.

The rethinking of the stagnation narrative is important not only for our understanding of the Brezhnev era and its consequences. It also helps to explain why the Brezhnev era is so central to public discourse in Russia today. On the one hand, we have the nostalgic view of the Brezhnev era, a time that many contemporary cultural figures and political pundits experienced as young men and women. These result in loving representations of the Brezhnev period in glossy TV series and programs dedicated to the Soviet past. While the comic-nostalgic images of Brezhnev parade on the Russian screen, the specter of Brezhnev's stagnation haunts Russian leadership and its relationship with the world.

Since 2011, when Vladimir Putin announced that he will seek reelection for Russian presidency, liberal bloggers and publications on Ru-Net draw parallels between Putin and Brezhnev, arguing that the country is stagnating, as it did in the Brezhnev era.[42] Russian streets and the Internet were inundated with a famous portrait of Brezhnev, in which the latter's head was replaced with an older version of Putin. The caption on the poster was "Brezhnev reloaded."[43]

At the same time, the term stagnation also informs the analyses of foreign observers, who often draw implicit and explicit parallels between Putin's Russia and Brezhnev's USSR. Binary categories that functioned as the central pillars of stagnation narrative in the past, such as oppression/resistance, authoritarianism/democracy, or propaganda/free press, are slipping into American and European assessments of Russian politics and society. As Andrey Tsygankov recently observed, "The U.S. media sustains and promotes the binary narrative that juxtaposes and contrasts the vision of a morally inferior neo-Soviet Russia with that of a superior American system."[44] Yet, if the challenges to the stagnation narrative teach us anything, it is that a meaningful engagement with Russia requires taking it on its own terms. The present day uses of stagnation and its continuous presence in contemporary cultural and political life suggest the power and the prominence of this idea, and the timeliness of this volume. The main purpose of this volume is to reconsider the meaning and the validity of the idea of "stagnation" and its constitutive components. We hope that readers will be stimulated to do so with the help of the interdisciplinary array of scholars assembled here.

NOTES

1. *Socialist Appeal*, vol. 1, no. 7, September 25, 1937.
2. *XXVII Party Congress of the CPSU*, vol. 1 (Moscow: Politizdat, 1986), 24–25.
3. Ibid.
4. Leon Trotsky, *The New Course* (1923), Chapter 4. http://www.marxists.org/archive/trotsky/1923/newcourse/ch04.htm
5. Stephen F. Cohen, *Bukharin and the Bolshevik Revolution: A Political Biography, 1888–1938* (Oxford: Oxford University Press, 1971, 1980), 129–132, and Sheila Fitzpatrick, *The Russian Revolution*, 3rd ed. (Oxford University Press, 2008), 93–119; see also David Priestland, "Stalin as Bolshevik Romantic," in *Stalin: A New History*, ed. Sarah Davies and James Harris (Cambridge University Press, 2005), 181–201.
6. In his seminal speech to the 20th Party Congress Khrushchev charged: "Our nation bore forth many flatterers and specialists in false optimism and deceit. . . . Due to the numerous arrests of Party, Soviet and economic leaders, many workers began to work uncertainly, showed over cautiousness, feared all which was new, feared their own shadows, and began to show less initiative in their work. [Party and Soviet resolutions] were prepared in a routine manner, often without considering the concrete situation. . . . All this produced the danger of formalizing the Party and Soviet work and of bureaucratizing the whole apparatus." Khrushchev address to the 20th party congress, http://www.marxists.org/archive/khrushchev/1956/02/24.htm
7. Mikhail Suslov, Speech at the 20th Party Congress (London: Soviet News, 1956), 13–14.
8. Moshe Lewin and Gregory Elliott, *The Soviet Century* (London: Verso, 2005), 370–371.
9. Anatoly Chernyaev, *Sovmestnii iskhod: dnevnik dvukh epokh, 1972–1991* (Moscow: ROSSPEN, 2008).
10. Georgii Arbatov, *Chelovek sistemy* (Moscow: Vagrius, 2002), 279–280.
11. Ibid., 279–280, and 309–346 for more detail.
12. Aleksandr Yakovlev, *Sumerki* (Moscow: Materik, 2005), 320.
13. In a telling turn of phrase, he contrasts the country's economic condition to its insistence on maintaining a strong showing on the world stage: "We need a complete restructuring (*perestroika*) of the whole structure, we need to kick out all the planners and find new ones, and we need money, i.e. at least as much as SALT-2 costs." Chernyaev, *Sovmestnii iskhod*, 341.
14. Chernyaev, *Sovmestnii iskhod*, 373.
15. Valerii Boldin, *Krusheniia Pedestala: shtrikhi k portretu M.S. Gorbacheva* (Moscow: Respublika, 1995), 29–31.
16. Yet it is also clear that there was a vanguard in this process, i.e., people whose articulation of "stagnation" was forming before 1982, and those who got there later. Thus Marshal Sergei Akhromeev, who became a crucial supporter of Gorbachev's nuclear and Afghan strategies, though they would later part ways, admits that while he was troubled by some of the things happening in the Soviet economy of the late 1970s, from his position the country seemed to be functioning quite smoothly; it was

only after 1985 that he realized how difficult the situation had become. Georgii Kornienko and Sergei Akhromeev, *Glazami Marshala i Diplomata* (Moscow: Mezhdunarodnye otnosheniia, 1992).

17. David K. Willis, *Klass: How Russians Really Live* (New York: Avon Books, 1987), 2.

18. David Shipler, *Russia: Broken Idols, Solemn Dreams* (New York, New York: Times Books, 1983), 5.

19. Edwin Bacon, "Reconsidering Brezhnev," in *Brezhnev Reconsidered*, ed. Edwin Bacon and Mark Sandle (New York: Palgrave Macmillan, 2002), 15–18.

20. Alec Nove, "Agriculture," Archie Brown "Political Developments: Some Conclusions and an Interpretation" and "Political Developments, 1975–77," in *The Soviet Union since the Fall of Khrushchev*, 2nd edition, ed. Archie Brown and Michael Kaser (London: Macmillan, 1978), 1–5; 218–175; 299–329.

21. Seweryn Bialer, *U.S.S.R. after Brezhnev* (New York: Foreign Policy Association, 1983), 7–10.

22. Boldin, *Krusheniia pedestala*, 29.

23. Chernyaev, *Sovmestnii iskhod*.

24. Stephen F. Cohen and Katrina Vanden Heuvel, *Voices of Glasnost: Interviews with Gorbachev's Reformers* (New York: Norton & Co., 1989) 144–145.

25. Robert D. English, *Russia and the Idea of the West: Gorbachev, Intellectuals, and the End of the Cold War* (New York: Columbia University Press, 2000), 117–158.

26. Lewin and Elliott, *The Soviet Century*, 371.

27. Stephen Kotkin (with a contribution by Jan T. Gross), *Uncivil Society: 1989 and the Implosion of the Communist Establishment* (New York: Modern Library, 2009), 14.

28. Ligachev at 1988 party conference, cited in Stephen F. Cohen, *Soviet Fates and Lost Alternatives: From Stalinism to the New Cold War* (New York: Columbia University Press, 2009) 68–69.

29. Viktor Afanas'ev, *4-iia vlast' i 4 Genseka: Ot Brezhneva do Gorbacheva v "Pravde"* (Moscow: Izd-vo Kedr, 1994), 14–28.

30. Francis X. Clines, "The Thin Red Line: Gorbachev Fails to Stop the Forces He Set in Motion," *The New York Times*, March 31, 1991, p. E1.

31. Stephen Kotkin, *Armageddon Averted: The Soviet Collapse, 1970–2000* (Oxford University Press, 2001), 1–9.

32. Ben Fowkes's essay on "the national question" seems to confirm the perception that the Brezhnev era saw "many national grievance . . . quietly nursed until in the late 1980s they were able to come to the surface," and that "Brezhnev preserved the USSR in aspic for a couple of decades." By contrast, Mark Sandle's essay on intellectual life and John Gooding's on the "Roots of Perestroika" provides a more nuanced view, highlighting the intellectual space available in the period and the creativity that existed within the intellectual establishment and beyond. Ben Fowkes, "The National Question in the Soviet Union under Leonid Brezhnev: Policy and Response," in *Brezhnev Reconsidered*, 82; Mark Sandle, "A Triumph of Ideological Hairdressing? Intellectual Life in the Brezhnev Era Reconsidered," in *Brezhnev Reconsidered*, 135–164; John Gooding, "The Roots of Perestroika," in *Brezhnev Reconsidered*, 188–102.

33. The volume editors also stress the important role of establishment intellectuals. This group, writes Sandle, is usually represented as careerists who took the party money, status, and security and wrote what they were told without qualms. Their "real" views are usually presented as suppressed or nonexistent. The fact that many members of the establishment advanced in the party ranks during Khrushchev's reforms suggests that some attempts to rethink Soviet values continued into the Brezhnev era. Sandle, "A Triumph of Ideological Hairdressing?," 136–140.

34. Alexei Yurchak, *Everything Was Forever, Until It Was No More: The Last Soviet Generation* (Princeton University Press, 2006), 13–14, 24–28, 78–125.

35. Svetlana Boym, *Common Places: Mythologies of Everyday Life in Russia* (Cambridge: Harvard University Press, 1994), 121–167; David Crowley and Susan E. Reid eds., *Socialist Spaces: Sites of Everyday Life in the Eastern Bloc* (Oxford: Berg, 2002); Lewis

H. Siegelbaum ed., *Borders of Socialism: Private Spheres of Soviet Russia* (New York: Palgrave Macmillan, 2006).

36. Pp. 1–11.

37. One such example is presented in Vladislav Zubok's examination of Brezhnev's personal commitment to the US-Soviet détente and his role in promoting it. Vladislav M. Zubok, *A Failed Empire: The Soviet Union in the Cold War from Stalin to Gorbachev* (Chapel Hill: University of North Carolina Press, 2007), 191. Dima Adamsky has shown just how dynamic Soviet military science and strategic thought was with regard to developing the Revolution in Military Affairs in the 1970s. Dima P. Adamsky, "Through the Looking Glass: The Soviet Military-Technical Revolution and the American Revolution in Military Affairs," *Journal of Strategic Studies*, volume 31, issue 2, 2008 (257–294), and *The Culture of Military Innovation: The Impact of Cultural Factors on the Revolution in Military Affairs in Russia, the US, and Israel* (Stanford: Stanford University Press, 2010), 24–57.

38. David Reynolds, "Science, Technology and the Cold War," in *The Cambridge History of the Cold War. Volume III, Endings*, ed. Melvin P. Leffler and Odd Arne Westad (Cambridge University Press, 2010), 378–399. Reynolds argues that while the American capitalist system and consumer society fostered a vibrant development of new technologies, the rigid state control over research and the absence of market in the USSR blocked technological innovation. In another example, Jeremy Suri argued that the conservative Soviet leadership sought to copy technology from the West, because it was unwilling to invest in its own developments. "'Developed Socialism' was socialism that depended on capitalism. It fostered broad commercial exchange, technology transfer and financial borrowing for the preservation of communist institutions." Jeremy Suri, "The Promise and Failure of 'Developed Socialism': The Soviet 'Thaw' and the Crucible of the Prague Spring, 1964–1972," *Contemporary European History*, 15, 2, 2006, 133–158.

39. Thomas L. Friedman, *The Lexus and the Olive Tree* (New York: Anchor Books, 2000), 389.

40. See, for example: Victoria De Grazia, *Irresistible Empire: America's Advance through Twentieth-Century Europe* (Cambridge: Belknap Press, 2005); Walter L. Hixson, *Parting the Curtain: Propaganda, Culture, and the Cold War, 1945–1961* (New York: St. Martin's Press, 1997).

41. Yurchak, *Everything Was Forever*, 158–206.

42. "Ischem Vykhod: Evolutsiia Vladimira Putina," *Radio Echo Moskvy*, April 25, 2012, http://echo.msk.ru/programs/exit/881866-echo/; "Putin Brezhneva Dogonit? Kommersant Vlast," October 3, 2010, http://kommersant.ru/doc/1785754; "Delu Brezhneva Verny," Gazeta.ru, October 5, 2011. http://www.gazeta.ru/comments/2011/10/05_e_3790830.shtml

43. Isabel Gorst, "Putin spokesman: Brezhnev rules ok," The Financial Times blog, October 5, 2011, http://blogs.ft.com/beyond-brics/2011/10/05/putin-spokesman-brezhnev-rules-ok/#axzz1xxKA1svp

44. http://blogs.lse.ac.uk/europpblog/2015/08/17/nobody-loves-russia-how-western-media-have-perpetuated-the-myth-of-putins-neo-soviet-autocracy/

Part 1

Ideology between Public and Private Spheres

ONE

Consumers as Citizens

Revisiting the Question of Public Disengagement in the Brezhnev Era

Natalya Chernyshova

What could be a more fitting metaphor for the Soviet "stagnation" period than a shopping queue? The long, slowly moving line of people epitomizes the very lack of progress, waste of time and resources, and remoteness of the final goal, all of which are associated with the Brezhnev-era stagnation. Queues were a favored target for foreign observers and a source of embarrassment for Soviet ones. They pointed toward the continued lag behind Western consumer societies at a time when neither war nor industrialization could explain it away, and they undermined the country's claims to a superpower status.

At the same time, queues for consumer goods are often associated with another aspect of Brezhnev-era stagnation: Soviet consumerism. This has been interpreted by some scholars of mature socialism as an expression of popular disenchantment with the communist project as a whole. Indeed, various developments of the long 1970s, such as the curtailing of de-Stalinization, economic problems, the increasingly geriatric leadership, and corruption led to the perception of citizens living under developed socialism as growing publicly passive and detached from the workings of the state, and as being increasingly withdrawn from the public world of ideology into the private world of family concerns, friends and lovers, career advancement, and personal pursuits. Consumption of material goods was highlighted as one such pursuit. Notably, Vladimir Shlapentokh has argued that late Soviet consumerism was a manifestation and a product of what he called the "privatization of Soviet life."[1] The apparent popular interest in consumption has thus fed into the notion of stagnation as a catch-all interpretation of the Brezhnev decades. The Soviet shopper standing silently in a long queue and thinking only of the material rewards awaiting her at the end of the line seemed the very embodiment of the passive and disengaged citizen living in a disillusioned society.

The metaphor and the concept it evokes may have been made more convincing by the events that followed: perestroika and eventually the collapse of the Soviet communist project. Yet, a re-examination of urban shopping practices in the Brezhnev decades, which this chapter undertakes, suggests that both are misleading because they gloss over a number of important aspects of everyday life under mature socialism, which do not sit easily with the paradigm of a dormant society in crisis. For one, the emergence of Soviet consumerism as a mass phenomenon points in the direction of important socioeconomic changes that took place over the long 1970s. Consumer revolution, rather than consumer stagnation, was taking hold of society at the time. Secondly, the central place of personal consumption in people's lives does not automatically translate into unqualified withdrawal from the public sphere and shutting off from the state. On the contrary, Soviet consumption had a strong public aspect, and Soviet consumers had to engage actively with the system. Far from being a passive occupation, obtaining consumer goods required energy, a variety of skills, and most importantly, close interaction with the state and society. Indeed, it was impossible for consumers to avoid the state. They engaged with the state when they shopped in the state retail system, when they wrote letters to trade agencies and other party-state organizations, and when they were making decisions about how to dispose of their state income. This might not seem a very political form of engagement, but in the Soviet Union consumption was inherently political—not least because, by the Brezhnev period, it was a cornerstone of the Communist Party's legitimacy. Improving living standards meant that the scope of such engagement expanded rather than shrank.

To support these arguments, this chapter will focus on three key areas. Firstly, it will highlight the participatory character of Soviet shopping and show how it was a collective, rather than individual, experience. Secondly, it will argue that the expansion of the black market in the long 1970s should not detract from the fact that it was closely linked to the official sphere in a multitude of ways, suggesting that even when consumers chose to shop through unofficial channels, they were not completely disconnected from the state. Finally, the chapter will briefly comment on the fact that urban residents engaged with the state retail system and the authorities directly as citizens when they wrote letters to officials and mass media about problems in trade. Before discussing these points, however, it is useful to outline briefly what exactly changed for Soviet consumers in the Brezhnev era.[2]

To a casual observer, it may seem that not much did change. The appearance and quality of many mass-produced goods from clothes to furniture seemed inferior to their Western counterparts and even so, queues and shortages persisted. All sorts of ordinary things could be in short supply in the 1970s. Ailing Soviet agriculture, afflicted by droughts in the first half of the decade, caused interruptions in provision of various kinds of groceries.[3] Popular memory testifies, for instance, that good cuts of meat were hard to get in provincial state shops in the mid-1970s; they could be bought at the market, but at double the price. Visitors flocked to the cities at weekends hoping to buy decent salami and cold meats, giving suburban trains the nickname of "salami trains."[4] Dairy products, eggs, fresh vegetables, and sugar during the jam-making season regularly disappeared without warning, and other foodstuffs required some searching and queuing. A whole host of minor household goods could pose a challenge to a shopper, although not everywhere simultaneously. At various times and in various places, people complained of not being able to buy rubber boots, cotton towels, gloves, cheap cups and saucers, small pots, and other basic necessities.[5]

These shortages, however, were not nearly as endemic as in the earlier decades of the Soviet regime: everyday life had improved even in comparison with the Khrushchev years, not to mention the 1930s.[6] Wages were raised regularly. The average monthly wage of workers and office employees (*sluzhashchie*) went up from just over 80 rubles in 1960 to 122 rubles in 1970, and to over 168 rubles in 1980, with raises occurring annually.[7] In 1984, the average worker or office employee received 184 rubles a month, more than double what their parents would have earned in a comparable job in 1960.[8] Families now had more disposable income: in 1981 half the country's population had an income of 100 rubles or more per family member as compared to only 4 percent in 1965.[9] The state also offered more goods on which to spend the money. Partly thanks to the 1965 economic reform and partly thanks to growing imports, urban shops had more quality goods to offer its customers. As a result, consumption of food and commodities rocketed under Brezhnev. The basic structure of personal consumption had changed: people were spending more on clothes, furniture, electric durables, and other items rather than just food. For instance, during 1976–1980 sales of noncomestible goods grew twice as fast as food sales. That plates had shifted was reflected in popular culture: a famous comic sketch on shortages performed in the 1970s by the king of Soviet stand-up comedy Arkadii Raikin described *defitsit* (the shortage item) as something that "melts in the mouth," has "special taste," and "no-one else has it."[10] Such a description is telling. In the 1930s, scarce goods had meant bread, meat, milk, butter, and vegetables as well as shoes, clothes, pottery, baskets, thread, needles, and even buttons—to name just a few.[11] In the 1970s, it seems, scarce goods implied a delicacy.

Of course, things far more ordinary than a delicatessen could be in short supply, and late Soviet society was by no means a rich society, but urban consumption was no longer simply a question of survival and fulfilment of basic needs. As a result, people's relationship with material goods changed. It can be argued that they were more interested in consumption not only because of shortages, but also because such interest now had greater chances of being satisfied for more urban residents than ever before in Soviet times. Material well-being assumed a significant role in making people feel good about themselves and society. Soviet sociologists in the early 1980s found a strong link between material prosperity and one's perceptions of self and others. One study showed that over 70 percent of those respondents who negatively assessed their current life situation and prospects were those who found fashionable clothes largely beyond their means. On the contrary, among those who were happier with the way their life was going only a quarter had financial difficulties when buying clothes, and over 60 percent experienced no such difficulties and could even make savings.[12] Other polls revealed that prosperity assumed a top place in many people's hierarchy of values; market surveys told the story of rising consumer expectations; and enough survey respondents and letter writers were vocal in defending their entitlement to decent living to make sociologists and the authorities uncomfortable. Over the long 1970s, Soviet urbanites emerged as modern consumers, comparable sometimes in their behavior to their Western brethren and yet shaped by the peculiar marriage of improving living standards on the one hand, and shortages, bad shops, and rude service, on the other. On this fertile soil grew late Soviet consumerism, which may have been rejected in principle but was widely practiced in daily life.

Ironically, it was state economic policies and their failures that helped fan its spread. It was official policy to raise wages and keep prices artificially stable; and it was also official policy to encourage consumers to seek living standards on a par with the capitalist West.[13] The authorities wished for the advent of modern consumption, and even if they feared its individualistic effects, they took steps to usher it. Consumers gained new importance for the Party-state when the Brezhnev administration launched economic reform shortly after assuming office. To improve labor efficiency, the government was offering workers, among other things, material incentives in the form of increased wages and bonuses, and it was understood that for these incentives to work, better incomes had to be matched by better-stocked shops. In this late Soviet version of Fordism, happy consumers would translate into more productive workers. Prime Minister Aleksei Kosygin himself indicated the importance of accumulating reserves of consumer goods when he introduced the reform at the Party's September Plenum in 1965.[14] It became necessary to know what kinds of goods consumers wanted. The government and specialists insisted that consumer preferences should be studied properly and systematically.[15] The Brezhnev era saw the establishment of the first dedicated national agency for consumer research when the All-Union Scientific Research Institute for Studying Demand for Consumer Goods and the State of Trade (VNIIKS) was set up under the auspices of the State Committee for Trade and opened branches in the union republics.[16] The purpose of VNIIKS was to oversee and consolidate the gathering of information on consumer demand across the country and to advise both trade and industry. It was helped in its tasks by local agents of consumer intelligence: shops, department stores, and warehouses. Employees of wholesale trading firms were to visit shops to see which models of shoes or designs of fabrics were popular; stores held consumer conferences to gauge opinions; exhibitions of consumer goods kept track of which wares sold and which did not. Industry also had its own 'spies' surveying the market: factories had their own brand stores (*firmennye magaziny*), which sold only their products and fed back to the factory the analysis of sales. Such attention to consumers spread beyond retail: as Simon Huxtable's chapter in this volume demonstrates, even the press were drawn into studies of their readers, and journalists began to conceive of their audiences as potential consumers rather than mere plasticine for shaping the New Man.

All of these developments suggest somewhat unsettled, instead of stagnant, social waters. The impact of rising material aspirations in the contradictory ideological circumstances was manifold. Consumption gave expression to generational conflicts; it played a key role in redefining social hierarchies and notions of prestige; it offered opportunities for personal fulfilment in an environment where politics was formalized and open to a selected few, while creative careers had their limitations. Consumption also constituted a field where people responded to state policy by writing to the authorities as well as through daily practices of obtaining consumer goods. Let us now turn to those practices for what they can tell us about the relationship between the state and the Soviet urban citizen of mature socialism.

Shopping in Western societies has been described by historians as a form of individualistic leisure,[17] and Soviet ideologues warned their captive audiences of its isolationist character, but they needed not fear: obtaining consumer goods in the USSR was very much a social activity. To have access to quality things, it helped to be energetic and socially active. A Soviet consumer was a dynamic and skillful social operator, not a loner browsing boutiques or department stores at leisure. Shopping in state retail required a range of skills, the most important of which were "people skills": charm, sociability, persuasiveness, persistence, and so on. In short, consumption was a way to engage with the Soviet collective rather than isolate oneself from it.

A queue was one form of such a collective.[18] But there was more to Soviet queuing than standing in line with a group of other strangers for an hour or two on one's way from work or during a lunch break. Collectives born out of queues could be much more lasting and closely knit. Queuing could mean holding a night vigil by the store to keep the place in the queue and keep out the cheats, or deploying one's organizational skills to put together and enforce unofficial waiting lists. In one impressive, but not unusual instance, customers wanting to buy furniture in the Crimean city of Khersones organized a two thousand-strong waiting list at one of the city furniture stores. The store ignored their queue, and after three years, they resorted to more decisive measures and instituted night watches to prevent unregistered people forming a live queue at the shop before its morning opening. They also checked the lists to make sure no additional names were sneaked in. But these night shifts began to take their toll. "After sleepless nights at the shop we return in the morning to the factory floor, to the teacher's desk, to the shop counter, and to our posts by the hospital beds. Many of us fall ill more often and have to miss work, which damages the production process," complained one hundred representatives of the Khersones waiting list to the editors of the newspaper *Sovetskaia torgovlia* (Soviet Trade) in 1971.[19] In the protracted and exhausting process of shopping for furniture these Khersones residents ended up creating a collective of people who shared not only a common purpose of obtaining furniture but also a sense of entitlement. According to the newspaper editors, there were many similar cases. In the absence of a legal organization to defend their rights, consumers formed their own ersatz organization, where membership and duties were regulated. This also gave them an opportunity to convey their grievances to the authorities as a collective body with legitimate demands.

If these customers tried to bring fairness and order to queuing, others deployed creative strategies to beat the queue: one female profiteer specializing in shortage goods from the Moscow GUM invested in a couple of crutches to guilt-trip the crowds gathered for the morning opening of the store to let her enter first. It always worked: people unfailingly stepped aside to allow "the invalid" get to the front of the queue, but as soon as the doors opened and she got in, the profiteer dropped the crutches and dashed to the counter. Luckily for her, the GUM had many entrances, so she could avoid being recognized.[20] Unlike the Khersones shoppers, this profiteer was acting alone to maximize her chances of a successful shopping expedition, and yet in both cases the consumer had to find the right way of interacting with others: either by emotional blackmail (in the case of the profiteer) or by openly co-opting them in the efforts to obtain the goods (as with the Khersones shoppers).

Queuing is but one illustration of the social nature of Soviet shopping. *Blat*, the informal exchange of favors, is another. Also a product of shortages, its widespread existence meant that to be successful the Soviet consumer had to be firmly plugged into a social grid. The value of having a wide network of friends and contacts has been well documented by contemporaries and historians, and the famous Russian proverb advised that "it is better to have a hundred friends than a hundred rubles" (*ne imei sto rublei, a imei sto druzei*).[21] Soviet shopping was a magnificent illustration of the truth of this dictum. Befriending sales clerks in shops or second-hand stores (*komissionki*) gave one an advantage over other customers. The former Soviet fashion expert Iren Andreeva recalls that in the late 1950s she spotted an under-the-counter transaction taking place in a shoe shop and confronted the shop assistant involved. By confronting, however, she did not mean calling the police: instead she told the salesgirl with a smile and a wink that she, too, wanted such a pair and was ready to pay extra. The result of her quick thinking and charm attack was a years-long relationship whereby the girl rang Andreeva up every time the shop received a batch of fashionable footwear, and Andreeva paid her for this service.[22] As we can see, this practice was not unique to the Brezhnev era, but when in the late 1960s and during the 1970s shops began to receive desirable goods more often and money became less of a problem for customers, such contacts were bound to become more common. *Blat* transcended social boundaries, and every social group was involved in it, often seeing nothing particularly immoral about it.[23] As one concerned citizen N. P. Korolev from the town of Orel described the situation to the *Pravda* editors in 1972: "To the question where they obtained a nice thing the only answers one gets [from people] are: through *blat*; I gave five or ten [rubles]; relatives got it for me, etc. Unfortunately, such answers are also given by communists."[24] These practices were also depicted as commonplace in cinema and literature of the 1970s.

Salesclerks were not the only kinds of friends that mattered. Hairdressers, beauticians, masseurs, and bathhouse workers could be sources of desirable goods or connections, thanks to their extensive clientele.[25] Dental and medical practices, nurseries, bars, and other kinds of service points got plugged into the unofficial network of consumer goods circulation. Those who serviced the elites and thus had access to closed shops and warehouses, were especially important, but well-informed friends, regardless of their profession, served one well; for instance, they could point in the direction of a promising and little-known outlet or facilitate access to a "closed" shop. Andreeva recalls taking a friend to a shop specializing in unusual and foreign furniture in Moscow, the existence and address of which were revealed to her by another friend.[26] The ability to develop and maintain a wide circle of friends and acquaintances was, therefore, an important consumer asset as much as anything else. In the early 1980s, almost half of the respondents in a national poll said connections with "useful" people were important to succeed in life, and 63 percent also named family connections in that regard.[27]

Not everyone was keen on this way of shopping, of course. N. V. Kiselev, visiting Moscow from Khanty-Mansiisk in Siberia, was shocked by his experience in the GUM, where a salesclerk offered him an excellent suit from a rack hidden in the back room and demanded a commission fee of fifteen rubles. "I have to labor for two days to earn this money," fumed the visitor. "That means working in the taiga, in freezing temperatures of minus 40, and living in a tent. And this rascal, living in the capital, in a comfortable flat, makes 15 rubles in seven minutes!"[28] Besides the social resentment to which this letter gives expression, it also demonstrates that even the ultimate model store of the Soviet Union was plugged into the network of the grey economy.

The widespread presence of *blat* and the expansion of the black market in the long 1970s may seem to suggest privatization of shopping: consumers tended to abandon the state-controlled sphere of retail and sought to fulfil their material aspirations through private channels. But in fact the state economy was never completely separate from its informal counterpart. Although during the Brezhnev decades the second economy grew, it relied on the official economy for the supply of goods, facilities, contacts, resources, and the cooperation of many state agents at various levels, from top *nomenklatura* to shop assistants and local OBKhSS officers (economic police). If anything, these links between the legitimate and illicit economic spheres brought Soviet urbanites more tightly into the orbit of the existing system. In fact, where the state system ended and society or the black market began was often unclear.

The very existence of the 'second' economy was due to the fact that the state economy failed to function smoothly. In that sense, the 'second' economy was, willy-nilly, an essential part of the Soviet system. Its expansion during the Brezhnev years was fuelled not so much by the shortages—that was nothing new for the Soviet Union—but, paradoxically, by the improvements in living standards which took place during this period. The unprecedented increases in wages, more quality goods on the market, the influx of foreign items and the sanction to material prosperity given by the authorities through limited economic measures and public declarations all resulted in much higher consumer aspirations. These aspirations clashed with the declining rates of economic growth from the mid-1970s onward and worked to make alternative practices omnipresent. They also helped change both the popular attitudes and official approaches toward them. The substantive reduction in the use of state violence reflected this state of affairs. *Fartsovshchiki* have been called "economic dissidents" and "rebels against totalitarianism" for their flouting of the prescribed legal and social norms,[29] but in the long 1970s profiteers came to be treated more leniently than in earlier decades and not nearly as harshly as the political dissidents.[30] Despite the calls to step up the fight against economic crimes and a number of official campaigns to that effect, a range of milder penalties for the most common types of economic crime, including profiteering, was adopted by the police and courts during the late 1970s and early 1980s.[31]

A number of Western observers concluded that such tolerance of alternative economic practices by the government was perhaps intentional and constituted what James Millar has termed a "Little Deal." As the authorities turned a blind eye, citizens gained some leeway to use non-socialist methods of improving their personal material well-being, thereby filling the gaps left by the ailing economy and making the Soviet regime more sustainable. Millar's own experience during his stay in Moscow in 1979 suggested his "intentionalist" conclusions. Having observed and even used Soviet private services, he was struck by how little effort was made to conceal them, as when he watched how petrol was drained from state-owned chauffeured limousines right under the windows of a Moscow apartment block whose residents included high-ranking officials and Party members, as well as military and police officers.[32]

Recently, however, the emphasis on intentional flexibility has been questioned by an archive-based study of the late Soviet policing of economic crime, which finds little documentary evidence to support the idea that the failure to crack down effectively on the economic crime was the result of orders from above. The expanding black market may have helped the regime to muddle through, but not because the leadership sanctioned it to do so; rather because the authorities on the ground were unable to put a stop to it. The regime had been in denial about the persistence of economic crime in the Soviet Union for decades, because this was embarrassing for a society that was supposed to treat private property with indifference, but from the mid-1970s it was forced to start paying attention. The authorities took a number of measures against economic crime, from stepping up police campaigns to revamping research into its causes. Chronic offenders still faced harsh penalties. However, pragmatic considerations on the ground were winning the day: it was clearly becoming impossible for the penal system to accommodate the ever growing numbers of profiteers and other small-time perpetrators, and so both local courts and the police adjusted their approach. As Gilles Favarel-Garrigues argues, changes to the Criminal Code and to court practices made during the late 1970s and early 1980s, which brought in a range of more lenient definitions and punishments for economic crimes, reflected "tentative adaptations to obvious social changes," but also highlighted the inability of the system to cope due to the scale of the problem.[33] In fact, success in this struggle was impossible: alternative economic practices would persist as long as problems with consumer goods persisted. As the economic situation deteriorated further in the early 1980s, even the top leadership, namely Andropov, came to realize that combating underground practices through police action would have little impact without serious changes to the entire economic system.[34]

If some members of late Soviet officialdom wanted to see an end to alternative economic practices, others were less keen, or at least ambivalent. There is ample evidence to suggest a different kind of connection between the Party-state and the second economy: officials, from local elites to the most high-ranking members of the political establishment and their families, could be directly involved in its operations. Some within the *nomenklatura* acted as valuable suppliers to profiteers thanks to their own privileged access to desirable goods at home, via "closed" shops, and abroad, where they were not subject to the same constraints as their more ordinary comrades. The Soviet ballet star Maiia Plisetskaia saw her official tagalong on the dancing tour to Italy in the early 1980s push eleven large boxes through the Soviet customs "diplomatic exit" without any difficulties; she was later told they contained TV and video equipment.[35] Even the very top *nomenklatura* and their families seem to have participated in underground operations. Andropov's close associate I. E. Sinitsyn tells the story of Brezhnev's wife visiting a well-stocked military base store in Milovice during her holiday in Czechoslovakia: the shop had a special "Generals' Room" where privileged customers could choose crystal tableware and chandeliers, pieces made of the famous Czech glass, and jewelry; other rooms were well stocked with clothing, tights, and other goods. The First Lady allegedly filled a minibus with her shopping, taking everything she fancied without worrying about the limits of her admittedly generous allowance; she had no intention of paying at all.[36] It was unlikely that she needed all those goods for personal or even family consumption only. Brezhnev's niece Liuba claims in her memoirs that among the top elites "everyone who went abroad knew a black marketer who would pick up the merchandise and leave the money—very discreetly, of course. . . . The wives had their own buyers, who took dresses, cosmetics, socks, handbags, and brand-name diaphragms."[37]

Domestic sources were also used. There was speculation in Berezka checks. Brezhnev's daughter was implicated in a scandal over jewelry speculation in 1981.[38] Children of diplomats and other prestigious parents were frequent guests of *fartsovschiks*.[39] The links were not limited to Moscow-based elites or to trade in foreign goods only. As Favarel-Garrigues points out, underground workshops producing desirable consumer goods "could not have been organized without the support of administrative officials or members of the local elite, who could facilitate the provision, production and sale of goods at no great risk to themselves."[40] The Party-state establishment also fed the black market indirectly through the staff of its closed shops and distribution points, who used their proximity to valuable stock for their own enrichment and status-building.[41]

These top echelons were only the tip of an iceberg in the complex system of connections linking different social groups of consumers, the black market, and the state. Certainly, a number of black market dealers operated on a large scale and had ties with the criminal world; for instance, hard-currency prostitutes used their contacts with foreigners for *fartsa* (illegal trade in foreign goods) and currency speculation. There were several high-profile cases exposing corruption among trade workers and suggesting links to high-ranking officials.[42] But the black market was not limited to such "high-flyers." Many profiteers were pensioners or disabled who supplemented their incomes by combing stores during the hours when most other people were at work.[43] More importantly, a great many ordinary Soviets, who certainly did not make either profiteering or *fartsa* their full-time or even main occupation, routinely participated in transactions which were on the margins of or outside the legal retail system. One important consequence of the expansion of the grey area of the Soviet economy in the late socialist period was that it blurred the distinction between profiteers and ordinary consumers. People brought things to sell at their workplaces (most often in offices), offering colleagues the make-up, perfume, or garments they had bought in a shop or obtained through other channels. Friends sold each other shoes and clothes that did not fit; for instance, Andreeva's colleague sold her a pair of ultrafashionable knee-high boots which her father, an export organization employee, had bought for her in France but in the wrong size.[44] Shopping at workplaces, and even more exotically in women's toilets at workplaces, was a routine operation in the long 1970s, as is reflected in memoirs of contemporaries and many late-Soviet films.[45] Not only *fartsovshchiki*, but also regular passers-by could be caught accosting foreigners for their possessions. Andrea Lee, an American exchange student who spent 1978–1979 in Moscow, reported: "Wherever I go, people eye my ordinary outfits with rapacious interest and try to buy things off my back."[46] More than four thousand young people were detained in 1973 for harassing foreigners in Moscow and Leningrad—and around three hundred of them were Komsomol members.[47] In the 1970s, the newspaper *Komsomol'skaia pravda* openly called for the rapid completion of the first Soviet chewing gum factory in order to put an end to schoolchildren begging for chewing gum near hotels.[48]

Nor did foreign visitors to the USSR and even professional *fartsovschiki* hold a monopoly on extraretail trade in imported goods. They faced increasing competition not only from official imports, whose volume grew from the early 1970s onward, but also from the rising numbers of Soviet citizens going abroad, either for work or for pleasure. In 1965 almost 1.2 million tourists went abroad; in 1975 about 2.5 million travelled, and in 1985 the number of visitors exceeded 4.5 million.[49] These travellers brought back to the USSR not only things for their own personal consumption, but also for sale. Predominantly this applied to members of the *nomenklatura*, diplomats, specialists travelling on business, journalists, sports delegations, and the academic and cultural elite, who went abroad on a relatively regular basis. But tourists also took advantage of the opportunities presented by a short stint abroad, as subsequent reports from their tour leaders testify.[50] In 1969, the Commission for Foreign Travel at the Gorky regional Party committee complained about tourists and specialists engaging in excessive shopping or even speculation during their trips. Its report cited the case of G. F. Lbov, an engineer from a local factory, who was sent to France on business but "spent a large portion of the time shopping," while another example featured the shop assistant M. D. Kniazeva who illegally exchanged currency and took advantage of sales to purchase not one but fifteen pairs of shoes during her cruise along the Danube.[51] In 1976, the Gorky regional Party committee's report on foreign travel again cited examples of citizens caught exchanging currency or engaging in "speculative machinations" while abroad.[52] Given that the number of people travelling overseas increased significantly, it stands to reason that the number of such cases, and the quantity of goods the travellers brought back with them, grew noticeably since the 1950s and early 1960s.

Despite serious obstacles, travelling members of Soviet society added considerably to the pool of goods available to urban consumers in the Brezhnev era. Things brought from work trips and holidays could be sold though a chain of personal contacts or at work, as we have seen. They could also be turned into cash via secondhand shops, or the so-called commission shops (*komissionki*). Commission shops were known to sell foreign items even before the Brezhnev period—for instance, after the war when trophies brought by the Red Army officers returning from Europe could on a rare occasion turn up there.[53] But then it was unusual, whereas now the Bolshoi Theatre dancers, major orchestras and ensembles, circus troupes, or sports delegations in addition to journalists, diplomats, and sailors were expected to bring in new batches of things, with the dates of their return from abroad being duly noted by commission shops (and relayed to friendly customers) as if these were scheduled deliveries from reliable suppliers.[54]

The case of second-hand shops shows how the boundaries between legal and illegal economic practices might overlap in the late Soviet Union. *Komissionki* were a perfectly legitimate part of the state trade system, and those citizens who wanted to sell their personal possessions were entitled to use them as lawful intermediaries, for which the shops received a small commission. Using *komissionki* to sell things brought from overseas with the intention of making money was quite another matter and was condemned by the authorities, while tipping customers off about such deliveries or holding items back for them was illegal and implicated the shop assistants in this illicit business activity.

Berezka stores are another case in point. Officially they were off limits to ordinary consumers because they sold goods in exchange for special checks that could only be obtained with foreign currency. As such, they were outlets available only to foreigners or diplomats, international journalists, and other specialists spending long spells abroad and paid in foreign currency. But in reality access could be gained by others. Russian cardiologist Vladimir Metelitsa recalls getting a sum of dollars as payment for his participation in an international conference organized by the World Health Organization in Moscow in the 1970s: the money was given to him directly (literally, in an envelope) by the organizers, and Metelitsa rushed to the Berezka store with his wife in order to spend the money before the Soviet representatives could take it away.[55] Even less entitled to shopping in Berezka stores were *fartsovshchiki*, who nevertheless managed it indirectly, through a complicated chain of contacts, which sometimes included Westerners. But on occasion, Berezka checks and admission to the store could be gained by those who had nothing to do with foreign currency or visitors. Andreeva recalls getting such "currency" certificates through a friend and setting off for the Berezka. This was illegal: a guard at the door requested to see a document confirming that she was entitled to the checks. It may be that Berezka guards were experienced visual "readers" of social status, but the amount of Andreeva's ill-gotten checks was so small that the guard decided not to bother and let her pass.[56] What this example illustrates is that illegal access to a closed source of goods could only take place with the consent of those entrusted to keep people out. The cooperation of state retail agents—*komissionka* shop assistants, Berezka personnel, and so on—was required for the alternative sources of goods to function. Even the officers of the OBKhSS, the organization charged with combating theft of socialist property and speculation, were prone to taking advantage of their routine access to shops, their directors, and shortage goods.[57]

Such overlapping demonstrates that, in their capacity as consumers, Soviet urbanites engaged with the state system almost on a daily basis. They did not eschew state retail altogether but took initiative to adapt it to their needs, for instance, by persuading salesclerks to hold back high-demand goods for them, and to supplement it by acquiring things imported by individuals rather than official trade organizations, by buying from friends, colleagues, and profiteers. All of these channels linked back to the state system either through state shops and *komissionki*, or work-related trips abroad, or the allowances made by the customs officers, and so on. Consumers got increasingly enmeshed in a complex network of goods circulation that did not necessarily involve a simple visit to a shop but which was not, nonetheless, disconnected from state retail as well as other state institutions altogether.

Socialist citizens also engaged with the regime directly in their role as consumers when they complained to the authorities about problems with supply or quality. Partly, this was because the authorities were the ultimate arbiters in disputes between shops and customers, and partly because such engagement was invited by the state. Soviet shoppers were told not to obsess over fashions and washing machines, but they were also encouraged to be demanding and fussy consumers; indeed, they were encouraged to want more. The regime repeatedly promised good living to its citizens. Many took this seriously and held the state responsible for failures. Problems with consumer goods and trade services were at the forefront of citizens' grievances during the Brezhnev era. In a national survey of 1975, the absence of desirable items was the most common complaint about consumer trade.[58] Disgruntled customers wrote letters to trade departments, editorial offices of newspapers, and directly to the government, posing questions with political implications. In 1968, for instance, a report on citizens' letters to the Presidium of the Supreme Council of the USSR indicated that "weaknesses in trade . . . give rise to unhealthy moods and various rumors."[59] Hinting at the connection between economic issues and legitimacy, one dispatch from Moscow stated: "Soviet power has been around for 50 years. Much has been done, but not the most important thing—the quality of foodstuffs and manufactured goods remains very low."[60] P. M. Malinova from the town of Kemerovo asked the government in 1980: "Where have all kinds of necessary little things gone, from tooth brushes to radio sets? . . . All these seemingly trifling items give a reason for the people to grumble (*roptanie naroda*). . . . As a communist I feel embarrassed to listen to the various rumors . . ."[61]

Perhaps the most unexpected and convincing testimony to the new perceived precedence of consumer interests over everything else lay in some people's readiness to forgo even space exploration, the much-advertised pride and joy of the Soviet Union in the international arena. "We do not need 300 sputniks in space, flights to Mars, the Moon, and Venus; instead, make life better here, on your own territory," wrote one Muscovite only eight years after Gagarin's space flight.[62] Decisively brushing aside such celebrated criteria for government's popular legitimacy as scientific victories, B. Shvakuliak from the town of Roven'ki in the Voroshilovsk region declared: "If our social order has today many successes in . . . many directions and will further reach Venus, Mars, etc., but ordinary people in its own country on Earth will be half-dressed and half-starved, then I daresay this order is not worth an old song."[63]

These letters were, of course, critical of the regime, but the fact that people wrote actively to the state press and to the Party-state organs in order to complain about shortages, to ask for help in obtaining goods, and to expose what they saw as shortcomings or corruption in the trade system shows that they acted just as the state expected and encouraged them to act. Their authors behaved as concerned or frustrated citizens whose last resort, nevertheless, was to turn to the authorities.

CONCLUSIONS

The question of ordinary Soviets' engagement with the late socialist regime has been a subject of scholarly debate, and the image of the passive and disconnected citizen has not gone unchallenged. As early as in 1990, an article by Donna Bahry and Brian D. Silver drew attention to other forms of meaningful political engagement which could be observed in the Soviet Union.[64] Similarly, this chapter has proposed to look for engagement in less traditional places: in the field of consumption rather than in electoral politics. In the Brezhnev period, things like fashionable clothes, home furnishings, and music records occupied a central place in many people's lives, helping shape their sense of identity and perceptions of success. These may have been individual concerns, but to pursue them effectively, Soviet consumers had to be collective beings; furthermore, they were not only relying on friends and family for access to sought-after goods but also negotiating with strangers and forming new connections. But rather than detach them from the state, these rising material aspirations served to connect people to the state system in a number of ways. The relative prosperity of the Brezhnev years was state sponsored. The improved opportunities to acquire consumer goods were undermined by shortages, but they still meant that, as consumers, people had now more personal interest invested in the system than before. The Soviets might complain to the authorities about the shortcomings of industry and trade, but they still relied on them to provide the goods. Soviet citizens might have limited their involvement in political rituals to formality, but they interacted with the regime in earnest as consumers: by navigating state shops; by taking part in organized exhibitions, consumer conferences and state-sponsored marketing surveys; by writing letters to newspapers and party-state offices; by choosing certain goods over others; and finally, by choosing not to buy at all.

NOTES

1. V. Shlapentokh, *Public and Private Life of the Soviet People. Changing Values in Post-Stalin Russia* (New York and Oxford: Oxford University Press, 1989).
2. This chapter is based on a revised version of chapter 3 from N. Chernyshova, *Soviet Consumer Culture in the Brezhnev Era* (Routledge, 2013). It is used here with permission.
3. N. K. Baibakov, *Ot Stalina do El'tsina* (Moscow: GazOil press, 1998) pp. 175–77.
4. On shortages of meat and salami in the 1970s, see L. Parfenov, *Namedni. Nasha Era. 1971–1980* (Moscow: KoLibri, 2010) pp. 46, 93.
5. This is based on a score of letters to the authorities found in the archives.
6. A. A. Gumeniuk, "Chelovek i reformy v SSSR v 1953–1985 gody (po materialam Saratovskoi oblasti)," *Izvestiia Saratovskogo universiteta*, vol. 9, no. 2, 2009, p. 97.
7. RGAE, f. 1562, op. 63, d. 2631; *Narodnoe khoziaistvo SSSR za 70 let: iubileinyi statisticheskii ezhegodnik* (Moscow: Finansy i statistika, 1987) p. 9.
8. RGAE, f. 1562, op. 67, d. 2431.

9. *Narodnoe khoziaistvo SSSR, 1922–1982* (Moscow: Finansy i statistika, 1982) p. 418.

10. The monologue was written by Mikhail Zhvanetskii. See M. Zhvanetskii, "Defitsit," http://jvanetsky.ru/data/text/t7/defizit/ (accessed September 24, 2011).

11. S. Fitzpatrick, *Everyday Stalinism: Ordinary Life in Extraordinary Times* (Oxford: Oxford University Press, 1999) pp. 42–45.

12. I. T. Levykin and M. V. Pokrovskaia, "Problemy urovnia i kachestva zhizni sovetskikh liudei," in I. T. Levykin and A. A. Voz'mitel' (eds.), *Sovetskii obraz zhizni: sostoianie, mneniia i otsenki sovetskikh liudei* (Moscow: ISI AN SSSR, 1984) p. 35. Polls showed that welfare also affected family relations.

13. For examples of the efforts to keep prices low, see, for instance, "Iz postanovleniia biuro Gor'kovskogo obkoma KPSS i oblispolkoma Postanovlenie TsK KPSS i Soveta Ministrov SSSR ot 14 iunia 1971 g. 'O merakh po uluchsheniiu praktiki ustanovleniia i primeneniia roznichnykh tsen na tovary narodnogo potrebleniia i tarifov na uslugi, okazyvaemye naseleniiu,'" cited in A. A. Kulakov and A. N. Sakharov et al. (eds), *Obshchestvo i vlast'. Rossiiskaia provintsiia, 1917–1980-e gody (po materialam nizhegorodskikh arkhivov)*, vol. 5, 1965–1980 (Moscow: Institut Rossiiskoi istorii RAN, 2008) pp. 337–40; also "Zapiska V. Golikova L. Brezhnevu, 10 dekabria 1974 goda," in S. Kudriashov (ed.), *General'nyi sekretar' L. I. Brezhnev, 1964–1982* (Moscow: Arkhiv Prezidenta Rossiiskoi Federatsii, 2006) pp. 174–77. All pricing in the USSR was done artificially and reflected political priorities rather than the market value of a commodity.

14. "Doklad chlena Prezidiuma TsK KPSS, Predsedatelia Soveta Ministrov SSSR tovarishcha A. N. Kosygina," *Pravda*, September 28, 1965, p. 2. See also N. K. Baibakov, *Ot Stalina do El'tsina* (Moscow: GazOil press, 1998) p. 171.

15. RGANI, f. 1, op. 5, d. 28, l. 71. Also see A. Struev, "Torgovlia i proizvodstvo," *Kommunist*, no. 16, November 1964, pp. 44–45.

16. A. Struev, "Bol'she prav—vyshe otvetstvennost," *Sovetskaia torgovlia*, no. 6, 1965, p. 7.

17. See, for instance, G. Cross, *Time and Money* (London: Routledge, 1993).

18. On Soviet queuing as a cultural phenomenon, see V. Nikolaev, "Sovetskaia ochered' kak sreda obitaniia," *Rossiia i sovremennyi mir*, no. 3, 2000, p. 55–72.

19. RGANI, f. 5, op. 63, d. 290, ll. 204–205.

20. I. Andreeva, *Chastnaia zhizn' pri sotsializme: otchet sovetskogo obyvatelia* (Moscow: Novoe literaturnoe obozrenie, 2009) p. 153.

21. For a major study on *blat*, see A. Ledeneva, *Russia's Economy of Favours. Blat, Networking and Informal Exchange* (Cambridge: Cambridge University Press, 1998). For *blat* in the 1930s, see Fitzpatrick, *Everyday Stalinism*, pp. 62–66.

22. Andreeva, *Chastnaia zhizn'*, pp. 140–41.

23. A. A. Voz'mitel', "Normy i tsennosti sovetskogo obraza zhizni," in Levykin and Voz'mitel', *Sovetskii obraz zhizni*, pp. 55–57. See also Ledeneva, *Russia's Economy of Favours*.

24. RGANI, f. 5, op. 64, d. 275, l. 52.

25. On bath workers especially see an interesting discussion of the film *I Scratch Your Back, You Scratch Mine* (*Ty—mne, ia –tebe*, Seryi, 1976), where the main character is a bath worker, in A. Ivanova, "Izobrazhenie defitsita v sovetskoi kul'ture vtoroi poloviny 1960-kh—pervoi poloviny1980-kh godov," *Neprikosnovennyi zapas*, no. 3, 2011 http://magazines.russ.ru/nz/2011/3/iv18.html (accessed July 7, 2011).

26. Andreeva, *Chastnaia zhizn'*, pp. 88–89.

27. Voz'mitel', "Normy i tsennosti," pp. 55–57.

28. TsAGM, f. 346, op. 1, d. 2549.

29. P. Romanov and E. Iarskaia-Smirnova, "Fartsa: podpol'e sovetskogo obshchestva potrebleniia," *Neprikosnovennyi zapas*, no. 5, 2005, http://magazines.russ.ru/nz/2005/43/ro12.html (accessed March 1, 2006); Vasilii Aksenov, "Ostrov Krym," *Iunost'*, nos. 1–5, 1990.

30. Two Moscow profiteers Ian Rokotov and Vladislav Faibyshenko were executed in 1961: see "Dokumenty proshlogo," May 23, 2003, Radio Liberty, http://euro.svoboda.org/programs/hd/2003/hd.052303.asp. Only major corruption cases at-

tracted such severe punishments under Brezhnev, such as the Uzbekistan case of 1972 when Ismail Nurmukhamedov, former director of the Tashkent Cooperative Wholesale Firm, was sentenced to execution.

31. G. Favarel-Garrigues, *Policing Economic Crime in Russia. From Soviet Planned Economy to Privatisation,* trans. R. Leverdier (London: Hurst and Company, 2011) esp. pp. 23, 27, 61, and 94.

32. J. R. Millar, "The Little Deal: Brezhnev's Contribution to Acquisitive Socialism," *Slavic Review,* vol. 44, no. 4, 1985, pp. 694–706.

33. Favarel-Garrigues, *Policing Economic Crime,* pp. 23–99, esp. pp. 27, 94.

34. Favarel-Garrigues, *Policing Economic Crime,* esp. pp. 92–99.

35. M. Plisetskaia, *Ia, Maiia Plisetskaia* (Moscow: Izdatel'stvo 'Novosti', 1994) pp. 265–66.

36. I. E. Sinitsyn, *Andropov vblizi: vospominaniia o vremenakh 'ottepeli' i 'zastoia'* (Moscow: IIK 'Rossiskaia gazeta,' 2004) pp. 341–44.

37. L. Brezhneva, *The World I Left Behind: Pieces of a Past* (New York: Random House, 1980) pp. 346–58, cited on "Seventeen Moments in Soviet History" www.sovietHistory.org (accessed June 20, 2012).

38. Brezhneva, *The World I Left Behind.*

39. See Romanov and Iarskaia-Smirnova, "Fartsa;" M. Arbatova, *Mne 46: avtobiograficheskaia proza* (Moscow: Eksmo, 2004) p. 177. On links between black market sellers of music records and children of the elite in Dniepropetrovsk during the mid- and late 1960s, see S. I. Zhuk, *Rock and Roll in the Rocket City: The West, Identity, and Ideology in Soviet Dniepropetrovsk, 1960–1985* (Washington, D.C.: Woodrow Wilson Center Press, 2010) pp. 100–01, 170.

40. Favarel-Garrigues, *Policing Economic Crime,* p. 68.

41. O. Dorman, *Podstrochnik. Zhizn' Lilianny Lunginoi, raskazannaia eiu v fil'me,* Olega Dorman (Moscow: Astrel', 2010) p. 331.

42. See L. Duhamel, *The KGB Campaign against Corruption in Moscow, 1982–1987* (Pittsburgh: University of Pittsburgh Press, 2010).

43. Andreeva, *Chastnaia zhizn',* p. 153.

44. Ibid., p. 142.

45. Interview with G. P., July 2005, St. Petersburg, Russia.

46. A. Lee, *Russian Journal* (New York: Random House, 1979) p. 22.

47. RGASPI, f. 1, op. 31, d. 908, ll. 25–26.

48. A cutting from a newspaper cited in V. Slavkin, *Pamiatnik neizvestnomu stiliage* (Moscow: Artist. Rezhiser. Teatr, 1996) p. 126.

49. G. P. Dolzhenko, *Istoriia turizma v Rossiiskoi imperii, Sovetskom Soiuze i Rossiiskoi Federatsii: 1969 g.—sovremennost'* (Rostov-on-Don: Izdatel'skii tsentr MarT, 2010) p. 148. There is some debate about definitions of 'tourism', which might affect the numbers (see A. E. Gorsuch, *All This Is Your World: Soviet Tourism at Home and Abroad after Stalin* (Oxford: Oxford University Press, 2011) pp. 18–19, but this is not especially significant here, as what matters are the numbers of Soviets going abroad, whatever the declared purpose of their trip.

50. For example, "Otchet o poezdke gruppy sovetskikh turistov No. 1935 v Bolgariiu s zaezdom v Bukharest," cited in Kulakov et al., *Obshchestvo i vlast',* pp. 707–09; S. A. Shevyrin, "Proniknoven'e nashe po planete osobenno zametno vdaleke… Iz istorii zarubezhnogo turizma v SSSR," *Retrospektiva,* no. 1, 2010, pp. 15–18.

51. "Zapiska komissii po vyezdam za granitsu pri Gor'kovskom obkome KPSS 'O nedostatkakh v vybore i podgotovke lits, vyezzhaiushchikh v zarubezhnye strany,'" cited in Kulakov et al., *Obshchestvo i vlast',* pp. 696–98.

52. "Iz materialov k protokolu No. 6 zasedaniia sekretariata Gor'kovskogo obkoma KPSS," cited in Kulakov et al., *Obshchestvo i vlast',* pp. 730–32.

53. J. Fürst, *Stalin's Last Generation. Soviet Post-War Youth and the Emergence of Mature Socialism* (Oxford: Oxford University Press, 2010) p. 214.

54. See Andreeva, *Chastnaia zhizn',* pp. 138–39.

55. V. I. Metelitsa, *Stranitsy zhizni* (Moscow: Raduga, 2001) pp. 310–11.

56. Andreeva, *Chastnaia zhizn'*, p. 158.
57. Favarel-Garrigues, *Policing Economic Crime*, pp. 50–51.
58. RGAE, f. 1562, op. 55, d. 2406.
59. GARF, f. 7523, op. 101, d. 442, l. 1.
60. GARF, f. 7523, op. 101, d. 442, ll. 3–7.
61. GARF, f. 7523, op.136, d. 301, l. 104.
62. RGANI, f. 5, op. 61, d. 35.
63. RGANI, f. 5, op. 62, d. 266, l. 174.
64. D. Bahry and B. D. Silver, "Soviet Citizen Participation on the Eve of Democratization," *The American Political Science Review*, vol. 84, no. 3 (Sept. 1990), pp. 821–47.

TWO

The Life and Death of Brezhnev's Thaw

Changing Values in Soviet Journalism after Khrushchev, 1964–1968[1]

Simon Huxtable

In recent years, scholars have increasingly sought to challenge the equation of the Brezhnev era with stagnation. In particular, they have drawn attention to new modes of social organization and subjectivity and the Party's shift in legitimacy from politics to consumption and leisure as indicative of the term's inadequacy [2]. And yet within the intellectual sphere, the term stagnation seems more apt.[3] One can argue about the terminology and find exceptions to the general rule, but comparing the country's intellectual culture in 1964 with the situation a decade later is instructive. While the twists and turns of Khrushchev's cultural policy frustrated intellectuals, they were nevertheless granted a small but significant degree of freedom to express their viewpoints. By 1974, the country had seen trials of prominent intellectuals, a crackdown on suspect thought within the social sciences, and by September an exhibition of 'non-conformist' artists in Izmailovskii Park, Moscow, was literally crushed by the authorities, which gave it the name by which it is now known: the "Bulldozer exhibition." But if the Brezhnev era saw a "return to Stalinist orthodoxy" as one historian of the Soviet intelligentsia had suggested, then the key question was how that orthodoxy set in.[4] How does one get from the tendencies we associate with Khrushchev—romanticism, optimism, and voluntarism—to a Brezhnev era associated with conformity, pessimism, and stability?

This chapter will suggest that the brief interlude between 1964 and 1968, a period which is all but ignored in current histories of the Soviet press, provides the key to understanding this shift in emphasis.[5] Yet if we write the history of these four years merely from the point of view of the conservatism that subsequently took root, then this can blind us to the hopes and possibilities invested in this period. Reforms that at the time seemed like the future become blind alleys, while fiery discussion that once animated individuals is reduced to empty talk. By contrast, this chapter shows how the journalism of the early post-Khrushchev years was fuelled by an optimistic belief in the press's power to promote a new kind of technocratic governance, based on rational discussion of the country's needs through publicistic writing and criticism. Only in the latter years did these hopes evaporate as Party ideologues became concerned by the press's capacity to create unrest through criticism and discussion in a climate of international tension. From this point, Party figures demanded that the press play a stabilizing role which would ultimately overturn the Thaw consensus.

The chapter focuses on this period of change through the views of the journalistic profession, as they were expressed in Party and editorial meetings [*letuchki*] at *Komsomol'skaia pravda*, at the Union of Journalists, or on the pages of *Sovetskaia pechat'* and *Zhurnalist*. Examining those sources in detail illustrates the fundamental continuity between the ideas of the final years of the Khrushchev period and the first few years of the Brezhnev-Kosygin tandem. It also suggests that the creation of a professional ethos under Khrushchev, an ethos which included an innate sense of ethical responsibility and a shared sense of professional goals, was a shift that endured far beyond 1968. So rather than analyzing the changes taking place within the field of Soviet journalism after Khrushchev through the prism of liberalism and conservatism, this chapter seeks to place these shifts within the context of journalists' longer-term striving for intellectual and professional autonomy. Sometimes this desire was in harmony with the goals of the Party: as this chapter shows, calls to harness the expertise of intellectuals in the press chimed with elite journalists' own self-definition as "researchers of reality," and was reflected by an increase in the prominence of so-called 'publicist technologues' with expertise in economics, agriculture, and social science. However, journalists' hopes for a more balanced and nuanced press, which would be opposed to Stalin and Khrushchev-era exaggeration, were less easy to accommodate, as was their insistence on testing the limits of acceptable criticism. If we adopt Ronald Suny's terms and see the essential dilemma of Soviet ideological discourse as a battle between a dynamic and adaptable form of discourse ("discursive" or "cultural" to use Suny's terms) and an alternative which privileges symbols and orthodoxies ("dogmatic" or "doctrinal"), then this chapter suggests that this tension comes to the fore between 1964 and 1968.[6] As the regime's tolerance of "permitted dissent" began to diminish, a shift from discourse to dogma becomes ever more apparent as the press became a repository of the "authoritative discourse" of late socialism.[7]

CHANGING NORMS AFTER 1956

Before analyzing the post-1964 period, it is necessary to briefly sketch out the key changes that characterized the Soviet press after 1956, for it is the Twentieth Party Congress of 1956 that signaled a decisive and irreversible shift in the character of the Soviet press. For journalists, the Congress acted as a guarantee that the regime was serious about reform. By attacking Stalin's crimes, Khrushchev was simultaneously signifying that the repressions of the past were over. While in subsequent years the relationship between press and Party was frequently strained, journalists could nevertheless feel more confident that an era of violent reprisal had come to an end. Along with the decline in fear, journalists were also promised a more central role in the building of socialism.[8] Their enhanced prestige seemed to be confirmed by the creation of a Union of Soviet Journalists in 1956, a decision which also meant that journalists were finally able to discuss professional dilemmas.[9] Journalists now had a variety of spaces to discuss professional issues, whether at the Union, in *Sovetskaia pechat'*, the Union's official journal, or in semiprivate forums like editorial *letuchki*.

Journalists sought to exercise these newfound freedoms on the page, too. Under Stalin, journalistic quality had been defined by the ability to repeat canonical forms without error: V. Stepanov, editor of *Kommunist*, likened the newspaper of the period to a cow's second stomach, containing not fresh food, but what had already been chewed.[10] Now journalists were granted leeway (and indeed were expected) to express fresh ideas in print. While the regime still dictated much of the content of the press—in particular its editorials and propaganda articles—Party governance moved from pre-publication censorship to post-publication verification, opening up discrete areas of activity nominally free from Party supervision. A professional discourse of journalistic quality emerged which privileged literary skill and social resonance, as opposed to the ability to parrot the Party line.

A second long-term effect of the Congress was to focus journalists' minds on the social dimensions of their work. Correspondents saw the roots of the 'cult of personality' everywhere, and believed that by focusing more closely on readers' complaints about judicial willfulness, bureaucratic corruption, and misdeeds within industry and agriculture, they could aid the nation's reconstruction. The newspaper became a medium through which public officials could be called to account, and "socialist legality" established, though, over time, the Party became concerned that journalists' eagerness to criticize shortcomings in everyday life was threatening to Soviet power, and moved to curb journalists' "excesses."[11]

Journalists' concern for the public impact of their work also led to a rethinking of their connection with readers, which was the third key change brought about by the Congress. Journalists saw the newspaper as a means for educating and informing public opinion, and strove to make their articles more effective. But they were hamstrung by a lack of information. Under Stalin, sociological surveys had been effectively banned, and the peculiar structure of a Soviet press market where subscriptions were set by officials, meant that sales figures were a reflection of political calculation rather than reader interest. Despite this, journalists were able to include the public on the pages of the press more closely, with newspapers like *Komsomol'skaia pravda* at the forefront of attempts to involve readers on their pages through so-called "discussion clubs," and canvassing their readers' views on various questions through the creation of its "Institute of Public Opinion" in 1960.

But if this all suggests a certain degree of sobriety, the general atmosphere of the Khrushchev era veered toward utopianism. "Romanticism" became one of the keywords of the Khrushchev era, expressing as it did the optimistic belief that the country was overcoming the past, and building the future.[12] Journalists publicized voluntaristic campaigns such as the sowing of the Virgin Lands and the building of power stations in Bratsk and other locations with bombastic headlines and breathless reporting. Such optimism seemed especially well-placed at the beginning of the 1960s as Iurii Gagarin conquered space, and Khrushchev announced at the Twenty-Second Party Congress that the country would "catch up with and overtake" the United States by 1970, and build Communism by 1980. However, by the time of Khrushchev's ouster optimism was beginning to wane: after all, through readers' letters and their own *komandirovki*, journalists were well aware of how the public mood was taking a turn for the worse. By the last couple of years of Khrushchev's reign, Soviet newspapers' assertions of optimism, coupled with the abortive attempt to create a Khrushchev cult, were beginning to strain credulity, and thus threatened many of the positive advances that had de-Stalinized the Soviet press. Within the journalistic sphere voices began to advocate a different kind of press, which would enable the public to engage with the urgent tasks of building socialism. The roots of the post-1964 rethinking of Soviet journalism can therefore be dated to the Khrushchev era. As the following section will show, the changes that took place under Khrushchev—greater freedom for journalists and editors; the press's more intense focus on social issues; and the growing importance of readers' needs—would form the backbone of the Brezhnev era's rethinking of journalistic norms.

"VIVID IN FORM; SERIOUS IN CONTENT"

After Khrushchev's ouster in October 1964 there were immediate changes: a number of Khrushchev's Agit-Prop appointments were swiftly removed, and those editors thought to be closest to the former leader like *Pravda* editor Pavel Satiukov and Khrushchev's son-in-law, Aleksei Adzhubei, both of whom had accompanied Khrushchev on many of his foreign trips, were fired. Of Adzhubei's unofficial "Press Group," only one figure, *Komsomol'skaia pravda*'s Iurii Voronov, remained after October 1964—and his reprieve was only temporary.

It would be easy in retrospect to see Adzhubei's disappearance from the stage as a sign of the new leadership's desire for conformity, but it did not seem so at the time. The events of October 1964 were not lamented by the reformist sections of the intelligentsia, who saw Khrushchev's whims as too erratic a foundation upon which to build sustainable reform.[13] Rather, it seemed that the Brezhnev-Kosygin tandem might usher in a more collegial relationship between intellectuals and the Party, and a more rational approach to decision-making after Khrushchev's "harebrained scheming."[14] The appointment of the reform-minded Aleksei Rumiantsev to the editorship of *Pravda* provided no little justification for these hopes. An editorial published under his name in February 1965, entitled "The Party and the Intelligentsia," provided a programmatic statement of reform, which attacked both Stalin and Khrushchev, and lauded the virtues of "search, experimentation, free expression, and the clash of opinions."[15] The editorial, which advocated a more central role for the intelligentsia in constructing socialism, struck a chord with the cultural atmosphere of the Scientific-Technological Revolution, which envisioned the country being ruled by a technocratic elite.[16]

Within the journalistic sphere, it justified a sustained rethinking of the direction of the Soviet press after October 1964. And yet this search could be seen as representing a continuity, rather than a break with the Khrushchev era. As the romantic promises of 1961 gave way to greater sobriety after price rises on foodstuffs in 1962 and the poor harvest of 1963, calls for *publitsistika* to play a broader social role became more clamorous. In June 1964 a major 'creative meeting' of *publitsisty* was held at the Union of Journalists, which discussed how to reorient the press in light of the country's current challenges. While the press's 'romantic' orientation could not be explicitly criticized, there was general agreement that the press needed to allow for more of an exchange of viewpoints on important economical and agricultural questions. As the editor of Estonian newspaper *Tiesa*, Genrikas Zimanas said at the meeting, "Today we know that there is no science without a battle of opinions, just as there is no *publitsistika* without a battle of opinions. We need to create the conditions for such an honest battle of opinions."[17] That is not to say that the press abandoned its uncritical cheerleading of Soviet achievements—even the most cursory of glances at newspaper headlines illustrates this—but it is clear that journalists were increasingly beginning to ask critical questions, both in private and on the printed page.

Thus, we can see a continuity with journalists' and editors' calls for reform after October 1964, even if it meant toppling old idols. At *Izvestiia,* former editor-in-chief Adzhubei was subject to ritual criticism for, amongst other things, furnishing a cult of Khrushchev. However, the overall tone was reformist: new editor Vladimir Stepakov called for journalists to "find [a] rational path" which would "nourish the reader with the necessary complement of knowledge," and argued that journalists needed "to put together a newspaper which is vivid in form and deep and serious in content."[18] At *Komsomol'skaia pravda,* too, Deputy Editor Boris Pankin, called for the paper to become "more realistic, more sober, and more dialectical."[19] To do so, journalists would need to inculcate in themselves a sense of "conscious discipline" to reform the nation after the excesses of the Khrushchev era.[20] Both Stepakov and Pankin's views reflected a technocratic belief that if journalists were able to sweep away the bad habits of the past and place their work on a more "scientific" level, they would be able to contribute to the social and economic transformation of the country, alongside economists, sociologists, and cyberneticists.

Correspondingly, the content of newspapers became more sober, jettisoning the romanticism of the Khrushchev era and devoting increasing space to debates on economic and agricultural questions. Over the course of 1965, *Izvestiia* and *Pravda* traded blows on the subject of economics, with the former coming out in favor of introducing profit motives into industry, and the latter cautioning against the abandonment of "ideology."[21] Eventually, at the September 1965 Plenum, there was endorsement of the so-called "Kosygin reforms"—an attempt to render the Soviet planned economy more productive by introducing limited market principles and profit incentives into industry.[22] Newspapers sought to encourage public discussion about the future direction of the nation, devoting column space to such seemingly arcane issues as differential pay scales and the organization of *sovkhoz* labor. Rubrics with names like "On Economic Themes," "Calendar of Economic Reform," and "Workers' Planning Meeting" began to appear in newspapers, while economists such as Evsei Liberman and Leonid Kantorovich turned to the press to agitate for improving the efficiency of the Soviet productive apparatus.

A new breed of journalist with expertise in the fields of economics and agriculture was born: the so-called "*publitsist*-technologue." What journalists like Genadii Lisichkin and Otto Latsis was their attempt to communicate complex economic and agricultural problems to the general reader.[23] One such writer later recalled:

> There was a whole generation of journalists who were seriously interested in social problems and tried to give answers to the complex questions of social life. Those who learned to answer these questions and see the roots of a phenomenon in the person, in his/her position within the system of economic relations, became journalist-social scientists [zhurnalisty-obshchestvovedy].[24]

It was precisely this ability to see the human stories behind social processes that characterized the most prominent Soviet journalists of this period.[25] In doing so, journalists aimed to engage audiences who had become weary of the stock phrases of Soviet propaganda. The prominent economic *publitsist* Otto Latsis argued that it was "time to declare merciless war on words that absolve us from the necessity of thinking and analyzing. Today's readers do not believe in words, and are not convinced by epithets: they need arguments."[26] In Latsis's view, then, readers could not be won over by statements of orthodoxy and recitations of Party slogans; journalists needed to trust that readers were mature enough to sort through competing explanations.

Latsis's words were part of a wider discussion which aimed to place Soviet journalism on a new, more scientific footing. It is fitting that they were published in the professional journal *Zhurnalist,* because it was there that much of the debate over the future of Soviet journalism took place after October 1964. The title seems an unlikely forum for debate, since in the past it had been frequently criticized as "the most boring of all journals."[27] In a bid to reverse the decline, in mid-1966 the Central Committee took a bold decision to appoint Egor Iakovlev, formerly editor of the innovative daily newspaper *Sovetskaia Rossiia,* to the editor's chair. In double-quick time, Iakovlev succeeded in changing the journal from a title that mainly parroted Party orthodoxies to a journal for the intelligentsia, and subscriptions rose accordingly.

What is striking in the journalistic discussions that followed Khrushchev's ouster was the mixing of scientific and technocratic discourse with questions of professionalism and ethics. Soviet journalistic norms were defined with regard to moral criteria more often than they referred to the need for *partiinost'* (though perhaps this was simply taken for granted). The revamped journal often highlighted the damaging consequences of journalists' bad habits, and through this sought to redefine the meaning of journalistic responsibility and conscience. Iakovlev's first editorial at the journal, entitled "A Responsibility towards Readers" spoke of the existence of a code of journalistic "honor," and of the need to gain readers' trust by writing more truthfully. It attacked the platitudes of the Khrushchev-era press, and—most likely as a safe way of condemning certain recurrent practices that journalists found detrimental to progress—added that the Party had condemned the press's "ostentation, excessive, and unwarranted praise."[28]

Misgivings about the damaging nature of "unwarranted praise" were frequently voiced by journalists in private, but the arrival of Iakovlev at *Sovetskaia pechat'* allowed them a public forum.[29] An article by *Komsomol'sksia pravda*'s Svetlana Bol'shakova published in October 1966 illustrates this tendency. It discussed the social and personal damage that could be caused by journalists' creation of a black-and-white universe.[30] In the first part of her article, Bol'shakova discussed how journalists had created a superman out of nothing, making a poor worker into a hero simply to fulfil an editorial assignment. In the second part, she discussed the story of Lena from Kiev, who had written to Bol'shakova to complain about ill treatment by her parents. Bol'shakova's 'investigation' of the letter took the form of a leisurely conversation: "We were silent; we spoke about various things, but never about the main issue which had brought us together. But nevertheless, it was during those hours that we became closer as humans."[31] However, the local newspaper, having received a letter from the girl's parents, wrote a mocking article about her, calling her workshy. Bol'shakova wrote of the article: "They made this young girl worse than she was in reality. Everything that her agonizing history had to give, my colleagues took, and as for the rest—the real, living Lenka—they had nothing to do with it. I found such an exploitative relationship somehow sinister."[32] Bol'shakova wrote a more sympathetic article which reported on Lena's ultimately successful struggle to complete high school.

Therefore the article contrasted two approaches: one which treated the individual merely as fodder for a story, and another which sought to find the human behind the black-and-white heroes and villains. For Bol'shakova, Lena's story illustrated the need for journalists to observe a particular moral code: "We search for things differently. And, on the whole, we have different criteria for assessing journalistic success and failure. But, you will surely agree, there can only be one understanding of 'journalistic honor.'"[33] In this sense, journalism was not just about the social resonance of an article, but also a question of individual conscience. In contrast to the U.S. ideal of journalistic objectivity, in a Soviet case where journalists' ability to be objective was constrained, journalistic ethics became synonymous with constructive interpersonal interactions, and moral behavior toward subjects.[34] Bol'shakova's criticisms were echoed in a 1967 article by the well-known *publitsist* Anatolii Agranovskii, which was published in *Zhurnalist*. In it, he accused journalists of omitting information that contradicted their preconceptions: "We professionals know that one can talk to a hero so that he says only what you need him to say. . . . That which isn't needed we choose not to hear."[35] For Agranovskii, what was important was to overcome these preconceptions, and to represent reality truthfully, opening up a space for both journalists and readers to think through the problems of their society.

Whether practiced by figures like Lisichkin or Latsis, Bol'shakova or Agranovskii *publitsistika* was a journalistic form that sought to capture a changing society, generally doing so through the prism of the individual. For Thomas C. Wolfe, who devotes a chapter to the work of Agranovskii, *publitsistika* provided a means for investigating and representing the contours of Soviet life, and for painting a picture of how an individual might go about such an investigation.[36] But while for Wolfe *publitsistika* is synonymous with the Khrushchev era, interest in *publitsistika* as a means of social transformation in fact crosses the 1964 divide.[37]

One way of analyzing the rise of *publitsistika* in the 1960s is as a form of self-fashioning which positioned journalists as intellectuals, activists, and artists. This latter aspect explains the rise of the discourse of *masterstvo* [skill, craftsmanship] within professional discussions. Within Soviet journalism this did not simply signify a fine style, though this was part of it, but depth of thought. An article published in *Sovetskaia pechat'* at the start of 1966 provided a definition:

> In its widest sense, literary *masterstvo* includes above all a deep understanding of the subject we are writing about, mastery in taking care of facts and observations, mastery in searching for an original theme, mastery in acquiring from facts and phenomena the significance that they hold within themselves, and, of course, the ability to use all the riches of language, originality of style, the ability to compose your work.[38]

Thus, *masterstvo* was concerned both with knowledge (to the extent that journalists were expected to become experts in whatever field they covered) and also with literary qualities. It therefore doubly endorsed journalists' claims to be part of the intelligentsia, not just as creative artists but also as experts, who increasingly described themselves as "researchers of reality" or as "intellectuals."[39] In this sense, *publitsisty* seemed to be doubly privileged, both as *belletristic* writers, and also as potential academic experts.

Publitisistika also positioned journalists in a privileged position with regard to their public. Taking on the mantle of nineteenth century journalists like Herzen, Soviet publicists assumed a role both as activists and as public teachers. To the extent that they "showed their working" in coming to their conclusions, the role of the Soviet *publitsist* conforms to the position of the "decentering journalist" described by journalism scholar Géraldine Muhlmann. For her, such journalists lay bare their own partiality, allowing the reader to reflect critically on the epistemological foundations of journalism.[40] Resisting the temptations to artificially unify the public behind slogans or received wisdom, decentering journalists allow for a more progressive and more reflexive relationship between reader and text and a more questioning attitude to reality. But although the Soviet *publitsisty* did allow for a more reflexive form of journalism which included the reader to a far greater extent than traditional propaganda boilerplate, epistemological questioning had no place in the *publitsist*'s arsenal. Relativism had no place in Soviet journalism, and nothing could have been clearer than the idea that, through careful thought, both journalist and reader might arrive at objective truth. Moreover, although the emphasis in articles is on a collective enterprise of seeking after truth, the superiority of the journalist's analytical gaze over the reader's is clear. In 2000, Gennadi Lisichkin explained his journalistic mission by saying:

> To a certain extent we can help people if we manage to communicate to them: "Kids, there are reefs there, be careful." That's the most we can do. But people still swim and drown, they get tangled up in those reefs and then remember: "That voice was right. They warned us that there were reefs."[41]

So while *publitsistika* sought to position the reader in a more active role, journalists never entirely shed the infantilizing belief in their own intellectual superiority. That is not to denigrate the contribution made by these journalists in challenging existing economic *doxa* and their attempts to widen the acceptable parameters of Soviet journalistic discourse, but it is important not to somehow reduce this to caricatures in the good fight between liberals and conservatives, intellectuals and state. As this section has shown, *publitsistika* served a number of functions in Soviet society. It was a means for improving the economic system, and to that end it was endorsed by senior figures within the Party hierarchy. It was also seen as a way of overcoming the hackneyed representations of Soviet reality that had traditionally filled Soviet newspapers. To that end, it enabled journalists to speak truthfully about the world, and thus regain their lost "honor." Finally, it was also a means for widening the remit of the journalist, for showing their analytic and literary talent. To *that* end, it was a way of showing the centrality of the journalist in the revitalization of the Soviet project in an era where intellectuals sought to assume a more central role in constructing socialism. Such a belief in the transformative power of the press was similarly apparent in journalists' advocacy of criticism and self-criticism, as we will see in the next section.

CRITICISM AND ITS DISCONTENTS

In May 1965, *Komsomol'skaia pravda*'s popular columnist Arkadii Sakhnin published an article entitled "At Sea and Afterwards," a sensational exposé of Aleksei Solianik, the famed captain of a whaling fleet, Hero of Socialist Labor and three-time Cavalier of the Order of Lenin. The article related the Captain's misdeeds and corruption, which ranged from financial irregularities to cavorting with his young wife on deck. Most sensationally, the article claimed that Solianik was a slave driver, under whom many sailors were worked to death or driven to suicide.[42] The article was notable, not just for the scale of the misdeeds reported, but for the figure it attacked: a widely known, well-decorated Hero of Socialist Labor. The fact that the paper devoted so much column space to the issue showed that its editor believed that the case should be publicized as widely as possible.

For the paper's journalists, the article exemplified the social resonance of the Soviet press. In the editorial meeting that followed, journalists spoke of a "festive atmosphere," as journalist after journalist stood up to praise Sakhnin's exposé. One staff member, Sergei Goliakov, told colleagues that confronting social demons such as "bad management, indifference, bureaucratism, and a lack of principle" was of benefit to the population, and a sign of fidelity to Leninist principles. He continued:

> The things that we write about with a heavy heart will become the object of concern for a large number of people. And that means that every one of us will become more interested in what is happening in our own surroundings, and be more intent on looking in our hearts and more decisive in uprooting the shoots of injustice.[43]

By publicizing such cases, the press would contribute to improving Soviet society, and encourage citizens to fight shortcomings themselves.

Goliakov's views on the social importance of criticism chimed with the regime's official values. "Criticism and self-criticism" [*kritika i samokritika*] had always been considered one of the most fundamental responsibilities of the Soviet press. The third edition of the *Great Soviet Encyclopedia* from 1973 stated that it was "one of the motivating forces for the development of a socialist society."[44] Through attacks on corruption and injustice within the Party and industrial hierarchy, journalists were charged with ensuring not just the smoother running, but the "revolutionary transformation" of the Soviet system.

However, given the very real tension between revolutionary transformation and political stability, these stated aims were often contradicted. In 1956, *Komsomol'skaia pravda* journalists interpreted the Secret Speech as a sign that they needed to attack manifestations of the cult of personality throughout Soviet life, but by the end of the year the paper found itself unceremoniously upbraided for its apparent negativity.[45] Excessive criticism was thought to have destabilized the balance between the paper's "discursive" and "dogmatic" poles. This was a pattern which would recur over time.

Fuelled by the atmosphere of reassessment after October 1964, the early Brezhnev period witnessed frequent debates over the social role of criticism, which have echoes in Agranovskii and Bol'shakova's attacks on the Soviet press's tendency to squeeze reality into predetermined frameworks. In February 1965, when soldiers survived four weeks in a snowdrift on a mountain, their feat was celebrated on the pages of Soviet newspapers. But one *Komsomol'skaia pravda* journalist was furious about the celebratory tone of his newspaper's coverage, and claimed that journalists should have asked why the soldiers had not been rescued sooner: "The article should have been critical. The soldiers would have been a hundred times more grateful to us."[46] In their desire to praise the bravery of the Soviet hero, journalists had forgotten that their main task was to ensure the improved running of the system by attacking shortcomings. An article in *Zhurnalist* stated the problem bluntly: "It seems that to overpraise is better than to go overboard with criticism. But [the newspaper] is not a collection of legends. One really cannot know today's readers to believe that they require rose-tinted optimism."[47] At *Pravda*, too, journalists like Anatolii Blatin believed that it was important to criticize "without taking account of the individual," and criticized the paper's local correspondents for having "lost their taste for critical materials," despite numerous examples of "lawlessness and red tape."[48]

Just as in 1956, journalists after 1964 saw the traditional press role of *kritika i samokritika* as one of the most effective ways of overcoming bureaucratism, corruption, and red tape. In doing so, they were following the instructions of the Party, which continued to talk about its necessity, both after Khrushchev's ouster and into the 1970s. However, what the Party advocated in theory and what they wanted in practice were very different things. The reference in the editorial to "unpleasant explanations" to the Party illustrates the fact that criticism was a task fraught with dangers. To write a successful article often required journalists to survive a wave of investigations from the lowest levels to the very top, each seeking to find deviations from a truth which was always conceived in terms of *partiinost'*. A successful outcome was often to receive 'only' a reprimand, and to avoid having to print a retraction.

A 1966 editorial in *Sovetskaia pechat'* argued that it was time to bring to an end the hazardous practices of the past, and for newspapers to criticize what needed to be criticized. The editorial cited the hypothetical situation of a journalist who, when asked to write a positive story about a factory, uncovers a scandal:

> What to do? By all statistical indicators the factory is a leading one. How can it be subjected to criticism? After . . . agonizing wavering the article sees the light of day. Naturally, it isn't easy for the editors of the paper: there are unpleasant explanations at the obkom, at the sovnarkhoz, and the author and editor have to fight off attacks from the leaders of the factory. But nothing can compare with the wonderful feeling of satisfaction that the journalists of that paper experience in connection with the fact that they have not acted against their conscience before readers![49]

But it is worth noting here that the payoff is conceived not in terms of politics, but in terms of professional and personal satisfaction. Increasingly, there was a sense that "unpleasant explanations" were a fact of life that could not be changed.

One important factor, which would become increasingly central in turning back the course of reform, was the Party's sense of being under attack, particularly after the 1963 decision to end jamming of foreign radio stations.[50] Party circulars and reports were peppered with references to the threat from the West, and the need for Soviet journalists both to exercise vigilance to counter them. *Pravda* editor Mikhail Zimianin expressed this point of view at a Party Meeting in 1965:

> We cannot forget that we work beneath the gaze of our enemies. We cannot expose our flanks to their attacks. To criticize in order to turn things on their head—should that really be our goal? We must publish critical materials but we need to weigh up every word of criticism in order to write Party truth, but in a suitable manner, without exposing our flank to the enemy, without losing our Party-minded feeling of proportion.[51]

The reference to the need for "Party truth," coming from the Editor-in-Chief of the country's largest newspaper, suggested that, even if journalists' articles were factually correct, they should consider the domestic and international resonance of their coverage before publishing. Thus, the officially advocated value of criticism and self-criticism was subject to a number of caveats: journalists could expect to be attacked by local party bodies seeking to discredit them, and they should take into account the possible benefit to foreign governments. In other words, there was a very thin line that journalists had to toe with very little margin for error.

This becomes apparent when we return to the case with which we started this section: *Komsomol'skaia pravda*'s attack on the fishing captain Aleksei Solianik. As we saw, the article was celebrated by journalists at the paper. It was also lauded by readers, while British visitors to the country were shown the article as an example of Soviet press freedom.[52] However, the article enraged powerful figures within the party hierarchy, including the Ukrainian network grouped around Brezhnev, Petr Shelest, and Nikolai Podgornyi, who saw the Ukraine-based Solianik as "*svoi*." The affair set two Party factions off against each other. The Odessa Party Committee predictably criticized *Komsomol'skaia pravda* for its "lachrymose" and "philistine" article, and referred to the article's "misinforming of public opinion both within the country and abroad."[53] However, the paper found a powerful supporter in the Central Committee's Agitprop Department, headed by Aleksandr Iakovlev, which supported the article and censured both the Fisheries Committee and the local Party committee.[54] Because of the deadlock, the case was sent to the Central Committee Secretariat, where, once again, committee members could not agree on the correctness of the article: Podgornyi and Shelest were predictably against; Shelepin (a key ally of Voronov) and Suslov were in favor. However, editor Iurii Voronov's fate was sealed after the meeting, when Brezhnev called him and Iakovlev over and shouted: "Criticize all you want, but don't make a fuss!" [*Kritikovat' kritikuite, no ne podsvistyvaite!*][55] Voronov was censured for alleged inaccuracies and before long dispatched to Berlin to become *Pravda* foreign correspondent in the GDR, where he languished until Gorbachev recalled him in the 1980s.

As this case shows, a tension emerged between the need for the press to perform a watchdog function in the interests of social transformation and the need to maintain stability in the face of domestic and international tensions. Although politicians were committed to change in principle, when it came to their own fiefdoms, they were fiercely protective. All of this suggests that Soviet journalism operated not so much according to the officially stated values, which lauded the virtues of *kritika i samokritika,* but to unwritten rules owing much to the personalized forms of administration that were becoming increasingly central to Soviet life elsewhere. As the Solianik case shows, journalists and editors needed protection, but woe betide you if your opponent had more powerful ones. All of these 'wildcards' in the everyday processes of journalism—aspects that did not live up to the officially stated 'rules'—meant that journalists were increasingly unsure of where the ideological limits lay, and how seriously to take the regime's ideological prescriptions, which were so often contradicted in practice. Over time, it is not surprising that fewer journalists were willing to risk attacking entrenched bureaucracy and corruption, even if those remained the press's officially mandated tasks.

1968 AND THE OVERTURNING OF THE THAW CONSENSUS

When did Brezhnev's Thaw end? The previous section suggests that it did not last long. Indeed, it is possible to identify the start of a gradual shift toward conservatism and consolidation as early as autumn 1965, with the arrest of Siniavskii and Daniel'. Gradually, deviation from established truths were considered dangerous; "liberal" became a term of abuse.[56] By the end of the year, Aleksei Rumiantsev had been fired as Editor-in-Chief of *Pravda* for his editorial "The Party and the Intelligentsia," to be replaced by the ideologically orthodox Mikhail Zimianin. Voronov departed from *Komsomol'skaia pravda* in December, after which he would spend almost two decades in the political wilderness. The reformist articles on agriculture and economics which had been so fundamental to the journalistic landscape from 1964 to 1966 were by 1967 the subject of sharp criticism from members of the Central Committee, including Petr Shelest, who noted the resonance of Liberman's ideas in "imperialist and

Maoist propaganda," and urged the Central Committee to ensure that Liberman's ideas were no longer welcome in the press.[57]

Shelest's comments show not only that Kosygin's reformist path had been decisively defeated by 1968, but also the centrality of international concerns in the minds of Party officials. Fears about foreign incursion over the radio waves and political unrest in Eastern Europe were coupled with anxieties about heteronomous views within the intelligentsia, with *Zhurnalist* at the forefront. But the case of *Sovetskaia pechat'* and *Zhurnalist* to some extent counsels us against seeing the situation between 1964 and 1968 as a linear slide toward homogeneity. Of particular interest in this regard were the discussions taking place between 1965 and 1968 about the nature of Soviet news, with reformists advocating a faster-paced, more Westernized form of news in response to the challenge of Western incursions.[58] As we saw with our discussion of *publitsistika,* many reformist discussions continued to take place in 1966 and 1967, within editorial departments, the Union of Journalists, and especially on the pages of *Zhurnalist.*

Indeed, *Zhurnalist*'s editorial line became increasingly bold over the course of 1967. In February, the writer Aleksandr Bek called for a new law on the press, arguing that the 1917 law had become outdated, and needed to be updated in order that "the opinion of all citizens should be freely expressed in public."[59] He cited the recent example of the new Czechoslovakian press law, which to some extent loosened the shackles of censorship, as a model for the Soviet authorities to follow. In response to reader requests, the text of that law was published in *Zhurnalist* in June that same year.[60] In April 1967, critic Feliks Kuznetsov controversially argued for the primacy of specialist knowledge in judging artistic questions, something which journalists at *Pravda* interpreted (most likely correctly) as an attack on the expertise of ordinary workers or *kolkhozniki* in judging literary matters.[61]

Such discussions were not confined to the pages of *Zhurnalist*: two months later, two *Pravda* journalists, Len Karpinskii (who was an ally of Egor Iakovlev) and Fedor Burlatskii, published an article in *Komsomol'skaia pravda* attacking theater censorship, arguing that questions of censorship should be placed in the hands of experts.[62] At a closed Party meeting a week later, the pair was accused of advocating "'absolute' freedom of artistic creation" and attacking Party control over theater and drama.[63] Again, the most striking feature of the meeting was the frequent reference to the international climate: one journalist at the paper mentioned the fact that the article had been picked up by the BBC and the Voice of America, and concluded that "with their article in *Komsomol'skaia pravda* they have aided imperialist propaganda, the most bitterest enemies of our party, and our Soviet homeland."[64] For their incorrect ideological position, and also for publishing their work at a different paper to ensure publication, Karpinskii and Burlatskii were forced to leave *Pravda*; judgment of Kuznetsov's article would wait until a year later, but met with similarly baleful results.

Equally as worrying for the Party was the challenge from those intellectuals standing outside official structures. As is well known, there emerged in the mid-1960s a significant group of disaffected artists and intellectuals, whose disillusionment with the system saw them reject official culture. These "dissidents" developed their own channels of media circulation through *samizdat*, which included challenges to news media through titles such as the "Chronicle of Current Events," which began in 1968. Even before this, the close relationship between dissidents and Western journalists had caused problems for the regime: the careful orchestration of the Siniavskii-Daniel trial was derailed because of the ability of dissidents to speak to Western correspondents, whose stories reached the Soviet Union through Western radio stations such as the Voice of America.[65] There thus emerged a potentially damaging loop involving dissidents, Western reporters, and foreign radio stations that allowed unwanted messages to reach Soviet ears.[66]

It seemed that by 1968 the Soviet journalistic field had split into two distinct factions: one advocating a more central role for the intelligentsia, and greater intellectual freedom, and another seeking to maintain ideological stability in the face of international tensions. The situation was in many ways reminiscent of the situation in 1956, when fears over subversive moods within the intelligentsia, anxieties over youth (and its consumption of Western media), and the strained situation in Hungary led to a crackdown on the press. And so it came to pass in 1968. In late March, a hardline speech by Brezhnev at a conference of the Moscow *gorkom* was published in *Pravda*, in which he claimed that certain figures within the intelligentsia were aiding the forces of 'imperialism' with their "ideological immaturity."[67] At a Central Committee Plenum a few weeks later, he reiterated the importance of maintaining international communist solidarity and waging war on manifestations of "bourgeois" ideology, including heterodox tendencies within the art world.[68]

Only days later, a Central Committee resolution entitled "On serious shortcomings in the work of the journal *Zhurnalist*" was promulgated.[69] It stated that the journal had made "serious errors" in its work, and that it had "unsatisfactorily report[ed] on the practice of Party leadership over the press, radio, and television." It added that the journal had regularly published "ideologically weak materials" that had provided an "incorrect" orientation for journalists, and that it "irresponsibly" printed photographs and pictures of a "modernist" and "naturalist" character (one edition printed a picture of a woman in a swimsuit). It was using precisely these terms that *Zhurnalist* admitted its sins in an editorial of August 1968. The editorial further warned of the "enormous propaganda apparatus of imperialism" which aimed "using all ways and means, to undermine the position of socialism in the world, to weaken its influence and authority, to inflict losses on it, and, if it succeeds, defeat."[70] Iakovlev was not its author: he had already been removed from his position as Editor-in-Chief and from the Editorial Board of *Pravda*. Later that month, Warsaw Pact troops invaded Czechoslovakia, a move which was accompanied by the return of jamming. *Zhurnalist* before long returned to its former role as an organ of received truths about the practice of journalism, and the Soviet press began a decisive shift in emphasis.

Rocked by events in Prague, the Party sought to consolidate its hold on power by demanding constant transmission of the signs and symbols of Communist rule. In January 1969, a Central Committee resolution urged journalists and artists to exercise greater responsibility in speaking out against instances of "manifestations of bourgeois ideology" "in light of the intensifying ideological conflict between capitalism and communism."[71] *Partiinost'* was now to be the central criterion for judging literary quality, and for making personnel decisions. Between October 1964 and the end of 1965, *Pravda* and *Izvestiia* each had three editors in little over twelve months; in the eighteen years between 1966 and 1984 there were only two. Newspapers became ever more "doctrinal" in their quest to rally the Soviet public around the symbols of the Soviet past.[72] In December 1969, *Komsomol'skaia pravda's* Editor-in-Chief Boris Pankin announced that the three main tasks of the paper in 1970 would be to cover the centenary of Lenin's birth, the twenty-fifth anniversary of victory in the Great Patriotic War, and Komsomol elections.[73] Newspapers would now concentrate on consolidation, rather than revolution.

But while the events of 1968 represented the unravelling of a Thaw consensus that had lasted for over a decade, there remained elements of continuity between the journalism of the 1970s and that of the 1960s. Not only did newspapers like *Literaturnaia gazeta* continue to publish controversial critical articles on the state of the nation, but the articles on moral and ethical questions that were so central to the Thaw press continued to be printed in great numbers into the 1970s and 1980s. Unlike the late Stalinist press, which was haunted by an atmosphere of citationalism and the dominance of the *kul't lichnosti*, there was still variety in the Brezhnev-era press.

Nevertheless, as opportunities for self-expression diminished, the prestige of journalism fell dramatically amongst younger generations. While in 1969 there were ten applications for ever place available in journalism faculties, this number had fallen by a half by the mid-1970s, and further still by the early 1980s.[74] But for the journalists who came of age in the 1950s and 1960s, social transformation continued to be the goal. For them, journalism continued to be a moral calling, to be spoken about in terms of one's responsibility to the wider society. Despite the punishment meted out to Voronov in 1965, his successor at *Komsomol'skaia pravda* Boris Pankin pushed ahead with criticism of the Party's plans to build a cord-cellulose plant beside Lake Baikal.[75] Despite the Party's annoyance,

Pankin saw criticism as crucial, not just for their social resonance, but also as giving the newspaper a *raison d'être*. As he explained to colleagues at an editorial review meeting (or '*letuchka*'):

> Such articles are an event in society, they set the tone in the press. Such things don't appear often. The article . . . shows the possibilities and the authority of the paper. These two weeks have been filled with humdrum days [*budni*], with a critique of our shortcomings. If we look only at that side, it could seem that there are nothing other than humdrum days at our paper. But then serious things like this come out of our humdrum days, that show that what we are doing is not in vain.[76]

The "humdrum" was provided by an endless cycle of more-or-less interchangeable articles on patriotic themes and anniversaries, but the serious was what journalists lived for.

Yet the fundamental irony here was that part of newspapers' "humdrum" work was to go on the attack against heterogeneous currents in society. Reformist-minded journalists were therefore victims of the cultural atmosphere that they themselves helped to create. This reveals the limitations of a strict state-society division in thinking about the press under Brezhnev. Journalists and editors, regardless of their political leanings, were not fully part of the Party apparatus, but nor can they be painted as fully outside it, either. As Natalia Roudakova has suggested, journalists were "simultaneously 'in' and 'out' of the state": they worked in ways that furthered the ruling ideology while at the same time positioning themselves as a force outside it.[77] If intellectuals are, to use Pierre Bourdieu's formulation, "the dominated fraction of the dominating class," then Soviet journalists were the most dominated fraction of that dominated fraction.[78] Though they had the freedom to air their own views—sometimes in public; almost always in private—they nevertheless lacked the professional autonomy to turn talk into practice.

But if we shift our gaze from the newspapers to the journalists who produced them, we see a shift from politics to ethics where acting according to one's conscience in the face of official obstacles became a marker of professional standing.[79] The memoirs of most journalists of the 1970s contain a story or two about a critical article they published, and the abuse they suffered from the authorities for doing so. Such stories may be embellishments, reflecting journalists' desire to be on the right side of history by emphasizing their own bravery in the face of intimidation, but the pitfalls were real enough. Into the 1970s, a low-level battle ensued, with journalists attempting to sneak critical materials into the paper and censors trying to keep them out—sometimes successfully, sometimes not and, most of the time, somewhere in between.[80] One could see this in Wolfe's terms as a battle between two visions of journalists' "governmental" role: a vision which emphasized the journalist's role in helping the public to understand their role within the socialist project, and an alternative which demanded that journalists create stability.[81] Yet the continuation of this low-level battle to place material in the paper provides proof of the durability of late socialist journalistic practices. While under Stalin newspapers were verified before printing, the Khrushchev era saw a move to post-publication verification. Once editors gained the censor's trust, they were expected to exercise their own judgment over the suitability of an article, knowing that if the *vertushka* didn't ring before 11 am, the previous day's paper had passed muster with the Politburo.[82] This allowed significant space for editors to take risks, and for journalists to engage in subterfuge to ensure that their articles would be published, ranging from misleadingly labelling material to sending two critical articles to print to guarantee that the 'lesser evil' would be printed.[83]

The necessity of diverting from the official rules in order to get things done is a hallmark of a Brezhnev period characterized by the widespread employment of "unofficial" social practices to compensate for the inadequacy of the official codes. In this sense, the trickery practiced by some Brezhnev-era journalists makes them model Soviet citizens. And yet the significance of such subterfuge should not be underestimated: it suggests that the collegial (if strained) relationship between journalists and the regime that had existed before 1968 was in the process of breaking down. In this sense, there really was a division between the state and the journalistic profession—or at least parts of it. Reformist journalists were increasingly acting according to their own consciences, basing their decisions according on their own (rather than the Party's) sense of the country's best interests: they saw themselves as a force for progress within the Soviet Union, but viewed the regime as impeding it. This was the paradoxical position of the socially minded journalist of the 1970s: their actions were not those of individuals who believed that the regime knew best, but neither were they the actions of dissidents. Rather, their actions embodied both a battle for intellectual autonomy, while simultaneously "fighting for [the system's] improvement, to uphold its ideals and understandings of ethical decency, of moral rectitude, of social equality," as Egor Iakovlev would later put it.[84] It would be these notions of equality and justice that would perform a far more explosive function during *perestroika*.

NOTES

1. The research for this chapter was funded by an Arts and Humanities Research Council doctoral grant.

2. *Soviet Society in the Era of Late Socialism, 1964-1985*, ed. Neringa Klumbyte, Gulnaz Sarafutidinova (Lanham, MD: Lexington Books, 2012).

3. The key text in this regard is Stephen F. Cohen, "The Friends and Foes of Change: Reformism and Conservatism in the Soviet Union," in *The Soviet Union since Stalin*, ed. by Stephen F. Cohen, Alexander Rabinowitch, and Robert Sharlet (Basingstoke: Macmillan, 1980), pp.11–31.

4. For example, M. R. Zezina, *Sovetskaia khoudozhestvennaia intelligentsia i vlast' v 1950-e—60-e gody* (Moscow: Dialog-MGU, 1999), pp. 329-380.

5. D.L. Strovskii devotes only one page out of two hundred seventy to the subject, and only two-and-a-half to the Brezhnev period as a whole. See D.L. Strovskii, *Istoriia otechestvennoi zhurnalistiki noveishego perioda* (Ekaterinburg: Izd. Ural'skogo universiteta, 1998), pp.187-188.

6. R.G. Suny, "On Ideology, Subjectivity, and Modernity: Disparate Thoughts about Doing Soviet History," Russian History/Histoire Russe 35/1-2 (2008), 253-255.

7. Alexei Yurchak, *Everything Was Forever, Until It Was No More: The Last Soviet Generation* (Princeton, NJ: Princeton University Press, 2006), pp.63-65. The term 'permitted dissent' comes from Dina R. Spechler, *Permitted Dissent in the USSR:* Novyi mir *and the Soviet Regime* (New York: Praeger, 1982).

8. Thomas C. Wolfe, *Governing Soviet Journalism: The Press and the Soviet Person after Stalin* (Bloomington, IN: Indiana University Press, 2005), pp. 33-70.

9. On the work of the Union see Mary-Catherine French, 'Reporting Socialism: Soviet Journalism and the Journalists' Union, 1955-1966'. Unpublished PhD Dissertation, University of Pennsylvania, 2014.

10. V. Stepanov, 'Vo vsekh zhanrakh', *Sovetskaia pechat'* 4 (1965), 8.

11. For more on this see Simon Huxtable, 'Shortcomings: Soviet Journalists and the Changing Role of Press Criticism after the Twentieth Party Congress', in *De-Stalinisation Reconsidered: Persistence and Change in the Soviet Union*, ed. by Thomas M. Bohm, Rayk Einax, Michel Abesser (Frankfurt-am-Main: Campus, 2014), pp. 209-222.

12. Petr Vail' and Aleksandr Genis, *60-e: Mir sovetskogo cheloveka. 2-e izd.* (Moscow: Novoe literaturnoe obozrenie, 1998), pp.127-138.

13. Zezina, p.329.

14. Steven V. Bittner, *The Many Lives of Khrushchev's Thaw: Experience and Memory in Moscow's Arbat* (Ithaca, NY: Cornell University Press, 2008), p.6; Vladislav Zubok, *Zhivago's Children: The Last Russian Intelligentsia* (Cambridge, MA: Harvard University Press, 2009), pp.273-278; Boris Kagarlitsky, *The Thinking Reed: Intellectuals and the Soviet State, 1917 to the Present*. Trans. Brian Pearce (London: Verso, 1988), pp.188-201.

15. A. Rumiantsev, 'Partiia i intelligentsii' *Pravda*, 21/2/1965, 2-3. See also 'O partiinosti i tvorcheskogo truda sovetskoi intelligentsii', *Pravda*, 9/9/1965, 2-3. On Rumiantsev, see Michel Tatu, *Power in the Kremlin* (London: Collins, 1969), pp.466-471.

16. Zubok, pp.277-278.

17. GARF, f.10124, op.1, d.243, l.19.

18. TsAOPIM, f.453, op.2, d.35, ll.14-15.

19. TsAOPIM, f.1968, op.1, d.40, ll. 19–20.

20. Ibid., l.21.

21. Tatu, pp.446-456.

22. These reforms also extended to the press, where newspapers' circulations were from 1965 based on demand rather than on the calculations of planners, leading journalists to conduct a wave of audience research and engage in intense questioning of their relationship with readers. See Simon Huxtable, 'In Search of the Soviet Reader: The Kosygin Reforms, Sociology, and Changing Concepts of Soviet Society, 1964-1970', *Cahiers du Monde russe*, 55/3-4 (2013), 623-642.

23. Kagarlitsky, pp.192-195. On Lisichkin see French, pp. 415-418.

24. A. Volkov, 'Iz publitsistov-tekhnologov my prevrashchalis' v obshchestvovedov' in *Pressa v obshchestve (1959-2000): Otsenki zhurnalistov i sotsiologov. Dokumenty*. Ed. by A. Volkov, M. Pugacheva, S. Iarmoliuk (Moscow: Moskovskaia shkola politicheskikh issledovanii, 2000), p.97.

25. Wolf, *Governing*, pp. 45-48. On this point see Dina Fainberg, 'Notes from the Rotten west, Stories from the Backward East: Soviet and American Foreign Correspondents in the Cold War, 1945-1985' Unpublished PhD Dissertation, Rutgers, 2012, pp.86-104.

26. Otto Latsis, 'Sila reformy i sila predrassudka,' *Zhurnalist*, 2 (1967), 28.

27. 'O zhurnale *Sovetskaia pechat"* in *KPSS o srestvakh massovoi informatsii i propagandy* (Moscow: Politizdat, 1987), pp.340-342; GARF, f.10124, op.1, d.242, l.32; E.V. Iakovlev, "Pressa ravna obshchestvennomu sostianiiu" in *Pressa v obshchestve*, p.263. The journal was entitled *Sovetskaia pechat'* from 1955 to 1966, before a name change to *Zhurnalist* in January 1967.

28. 'Otvetstvennost' pered chitateliam,' *Sovetskaia pechat'* 7 (1966), 1-2.

29. On these discussions see Huxtable, 'In Search,' pp.633-634.

30. See also Iu. Krikunov, 'Slozhna nauka chelovekovedeniia' *Sovetskaia pechat'* 7 (1965), 5-6.

31. S. Bol'shakova, 'Muzhestvo videt' to, chto est'' *Sovetskaia pechat'* 10 (1966), 10.

32. Ibid.

33. Ibid. See also Tat'iana Tess, 'Neskonchaemaia komandirovka v zhizn' . . .,' *Sovetskaia pechat'*, 1 (1965), 9-12.

34. On this moral economy see Natalia Roudakova, "From the Fourth Estate to the Second Oldest Profession: Russia's Journalists in Search of their Public After Socialism." Unpublished PhD disseration, Stanford University, 2007, pp. 106-176.

35. A. Agranovskii, 'Davaite dumat' *Zhurnalist* 4 (1967), 15-18. On this essay see Wolfe, *Governing*, pp.97-100.

36. Wolfe, pp.71-103.

37. Wolfe's analysis itself points to this: three of the four Agranovskii essays he cites were in fact published under Brezhnev.

38. E. Lazebnik, 'I talantu nuzhna nauka' *Sovetskaia pechat'* 1 (1966), 7.

39. Igor' Beliaev, Viktor Lisakovich, 'My—issledovateli' *Zhurnalist* 8 (1967), 16-18; Efim Lazebnik, 'Zhurnalist kak intelligent' *Zhurnalist* 9 (1967), 34-36.

40. Géraldine Muhlmann, *A Political History of Journalism* (Cambridge: Polity, 2008), pp.28-31.

41. G.S. Lisichkin, 'Plan i rynok: nauchnaia diskussiia dlia massovoi auditorii,' in *Pressa v obshchestve*, p.80.

42. A. Sakhnin, 'V reise i posle', *Komsomol'skaia pravda*, 21/7/1965, pp.2, 4.

43. RGASPI, f.98M, op.1, d.384, l. 25.

44. 'Kritika i samokritika', Bol'shaia Sovetskaia entsiklopediia. 3-e izd. Tom 13 (Moscow: Bol'shaiaSovetskaia entsiklopediia, 1973), p.452.

45. See Huxtable, 'Shortcomings'.

46. 24/2/65, d.382, ll.4-5.

47. Irina Dement'eva, 'Ot chernogo k rozovomu' *Zhurnalist* 2 (1967), 22.

48. TsAOPIM, f.3226, op.1, d.74, l.133.

49. 'Otvetstvennost pered chitatelem', 1.

50. Kristin Roth-Ey, Moscow Prime Time: How the Soviet Union Built the Media Empire that Lost the Cultural Cold War (Ithaca, NY: Cornell University Press, 2011), Ch.3; Maury Lisann, Broadcasting to the Soviet Union: International Politics and Radio (New York: Praeger, 1975), Ch.3.

51. TsAOPIM, f.3226, op.1, d.74, l.139.

52. Ilya Gerol, Geoffrey Molyneux, *The Manipulators: Inside the Soviet Media* (Toronto: Stoddart, 1988), pp.89-90.

53. Leonid Mlechin, Zheleznyi Shurik (Moscow: Iauza, 2004), p.409

54. Arkadii Saknin, 'No eto bylo tol'ko nachalo' Izvestiia, 23-24/9/88.

55. Mlechin, p.412.

56. See General'nyi sekretar', pp.60-67 passim.

57. Shelest to TsK KPSS in *Pressa v obshcheste*, pp.495-497.

58. On these discussions see Huxtable, 'Compass', pp. 124-139.

59. Aleksandr Bek, 'Shosse dokumentalista', *Zhurnalist* 2 (1967), 15.

60. 'Zakon o periodicheskoi pechati i o drugikh sredstvakh massovoi informatsii ot 25 oktiabria 1966 goda' *Zhurnalist* 6 (1967), 48–49.

61. Felkis Kuznetsov, 'Dvizhenie prozy i kritiki' *Zhurnalist* 4 (1967), 28-31.

62. F. Burlatskii, L. Karpinskii, 'Na puti k prem'ere' *Komsomol'skaia pravda* 30/6/1967, 4. See Zezina, pp.339-340. The article was published in KP because it had been rejected by the *Pravda* editorial board, which was part of the reason for their colleagues' anger.
63. TsAOPIM, f.3226, op.1, d.78, ll.118-119.
64. Ibid., l.121 (see also ll.122-125).
65. Lisann, pp.57, 91-92.
66. Barbara Walker, 'Moscow Human Rights Defenders Look West: Their Attitudes toward US Journalists in the 1960s and 1970s', *Kritika* 9/4 (2008), 905-27; Wol'fram Eggeling, *Politika i kul'tura pri Khrushcheve i Brezhneve, 1953-1970 gg.* (Moscow: Airo-XX, 1999), pp.217-218.
67. L. Brezhnev, 'Speech at 19th Conference of Moscow City Party Organization', *Current Digest of the Soviet Press*, XX/13 (April 17, 1968), 3-7 [6].
68. Frederick C. Barghoorn, 'Trends in Top Political Leadership in USSR' in *Leadership in East European Communism, 1945-1970*, ed. by R. Barry Farrell (Chicago: Aldine Publishing, 1970), p.71.
69. 'O zhurnale *Zhurnalist* i osvobozhdeniii E.V. Iakovleva ot dolzhnosti glavnogo redaktora' in *Pressa v obshchestve*, p.577.
70. 'Vsem serdtsem', *Zhurnalist* 8 (1968), 2.
71. 'O povyshenii otvetstvennosti rukovoditelei organov pechati, radio, televideniia, kinematografii, uchrezhdenii, kul'tury i iskusstva za ideino-politicheskii uroven' publikuemykh materialov i reperturara' in *Istoriia sovetskoi politicheskoi tsenzury. Dokumenty i kommentarii*, ed. by Tat'iana Goriaeva (Moscow: Rosspen, 1996), p.189.
72. Wolfe, p.20.
73. RGASPI, f.98M, op.1, d.492, ll.1-2.
74. Thomas Remington, *The Truth of Authority: Ideology and Communication in the Soviet Union* (Pittsburgh, PA: University of Pittsburgh Press, 1988), p.159, see also pp.176-177.
75. For more on this campaign see B.P. Lapin, *Slovo v zashchitu Baikala* (Irkutsk: Vostochno-Sibirskoe knizhnoe izdatel'stvo, 1987); Huxtable, 'Compass', pp.90-95.
76. RGASPI, f.98M, op.1, d.505, l.86.
77. Roudakova, 'Fourth Estate,' p. 53.
78. Pierre Bourdieu, *The Field of Cultural Production*, ed. by Randal Johnson (New York: Columbia University Press, 1993), p.378.
79. Roudakova, pp.158-170.
80. Ibid., pp.91-95; Olessia Koltsova, *News Media and Power in Russia* (London: Routledge, 2006), pp.25-28.
81. Wolfe, pp.104-105.
82. See the reminiscences of former KP editor Lev Korneshov, 'Ia ee liubil. A ona menia?' in Bol'she, chem gazeta: Chistosedechnye priznaniia komandy shestogo etazha, sluzhivshei "Komsomolke" v 60-70-e gody proshlogo veka, ed. by Liudmila Semina (Moscow: PoRog, 2006), p.154, 157; Interview with A. Iakovlev, Tat'iana A. Volkova, 'A.I. Adzhubei -- Redaktor i publitsist'. Unpublished PhD Dissertation, MGU, 2010, p.354.
83. Roudakova, pp.91-95.
84. Ibid., p.87.

THREE

People on the Move during the "Era of Stagnation"

The Rural Exodus in the RSFSR during the 1960s–1980s

Lewis H. Siegelbaum

> *But a bold peasantry, their country's pride,*
> *When once destroy'd, can never be supplied.*
> (Oliver Goldsmith, "The Deserted Village")

Oliver Goldsmith may have had it right, at least as far as the Oxfordshire village he dubbed Sweet Auburn was concerned. But if the destruction of peasantries is a near universal feature of the modern world, its chronologies, mechanisms, and experiential dimensions have differed a great deal since Goldsmith penned his pastoral poem in 1770. England paved the way, but paths to the city proliferated on the European continent during the nineteenth century and eventually elsewhere, transcending national as well as continental boundaries.[1] In the case of Russia, rural to urban migration proceeded in three discrete phases. The first, beginning not long after the Emancipation settlement and gathering pace toward the end of the nineteenth century, coincided with the great age of urbanization on the European and North American continents that brought millions of small town and village folk to cities rapidly expanding with industrial production and commercial activity. The second, in the late 1920s and through the1930s, involved some 23 million people departing from the countryside for construction sites, mines, and cities old and new. This figure excludes millions identified as kulaks and either sent to the gulag or forcibly resettled on inferior and remote land. Men vastly outnumbered women among migrants to cities, but toward the end of the

1930s, the gap closed somewhat as wives joined husbands who had departed earlier. This chapter is about the third phase—the emptying out of collective and state farm villages that began soon after the end of the Great Patriotic War (which itself had caused significant population decline) and persisted through the remaining forty-five years of the Soviet Union's existence. Part of a larger project on internal migration within Russia and the Soviet Union during the twentieth century, it will concentrate for the purposes of this study on the period of Leonid Brezhnev's tenure as General Secretary of the Communist Party and limit itself to the RSFSR.

MIGRATION—SO WHAT?

The purpose of this chapter is to inquire into who was involved in this third migration, why they left, and what were the consequences for them and those they left behind. I use census data, albeit sparingly. This is not only because I have no training in demographic history, but also because the qualitative and belletristic sources I employ seem more appropriate to responding to a question often left implicit or unaddressed, namely, why should we care? In the case of the first two massive migrations, the answer seems obvious. If migration to the cities in the late nineteenth and early twentieth centuries was part and parcel of the making of an industrial working class and thereby connected to the workers' revolution of 1917, the second, precipitated by collectivization, provided the muscle for Stalinist industrialization. Both migrations figure prominently in the grand narratives that Western historians have constructed about Soviet history.[2]

The same, however, cannot be said of the third migration. Perhaps this is because the dominant associations with the period in which most of this migration occurred are with the opposite of movement, namely stagnation and stability.[3] Yet another way of interpreting what was going on in the Brezhnev era—modernization—on the surface seems more receptive to integrating migration: peasants migrated because they had become sufficiently modern to want what their villages were not providing and had gained the wherewithal to move. But for at least the past twenty years, migration historians have been warning us against understanding mobility as a function of modernity.[4] Absent a transcendent master narrative, I fall back on the transhistorical principle that migrants to the city mattered because in seeking a better or at least a different life elsewhere their individual decisions, fraught with leave-taking tears and fears, had a collective weight on those they left behind. They also altered the demographic balance between town and country, changing patterns of employment, gender relations, and even the content of literary and cinematic output. "Ah, the town is ramming the village! / Ah, something is being demolished!" wrote the *derevenshchik* poet Nikolai Rubtsov (1936–1971) two centuries after Goldsmith's "Deserted Village."[5] Unlike Sweet Auburn, it was not the flourishing of "princes and lords" that caused Rubtsov's village (and by extension, a certain Russian identity rooted in rural life) to disappear. But somehow I think the two poets would have understood each other. Demographic data, letters from despairing kolkhoz officials, and admonitory stories appearing in journals intended for a rural readership deserve no less attention than Rubtsov's lament. These, at least, are the main sources on which this chapter relies.

GENDER IMBALANCES

According to the historian Liubov Denisova, some 4.4 million of the 7 million men demobilized from army service by September 1946 returned to the countryside. But, as she makes abundantly clear, no sooner did they arrive back on the state and collective farms they had left during the war, then they—and others—started to depart. In the Iur'ev-Pol'skii district of Vladimir oblast, 40 percent of the able-bodied collective farm population left in the years 1949–51; in Kostroma oblast to the north, 35,400 were recruited during the years 1945–47 as "permanent cadres" into nearby industry and construction, the FZO and artisan schools, or to more distant locations such as the recently annexed Kaliningrad oblast in the west and the southern part of Sakhalin Island in the east. Denisova stresses that state recruitment (*verbovka*) generally predominated over self-departure. Of the 768,000 who left kolkhozes in 1949 for permanent work in industry, 80 percent went through recruitment channels, a proportion that did not change appreciably in 1950. Throughout the Russian Federation (RSFSR) in 1950, 1,366,800 people were recorded as leaving rural regions, which, taking into account births, deaths, and the few who arrived in the countryside, meant that the rural population declined by some 540,000. In all, industry and other urban-based institutions recruited some three million from the countryside during the years 1945–50.[6]

Jiliana Selezneva was one of those returning from wartime service. Drafted shortly after the Nazi invasion, she spent the war years as a "dedicated nurse" first in Kyzyl, then in Magnitogorsk and Cheliabinsk before being transported to the Far East. At the end of the war, she returned to her native Izmaelovka, a tiny village located on the steppe south of Magnitogorsk near the border with Kazakhstan.[7] As we shall see, it would take another generation for most women leaving the village not to return. The preponderance of women in the countryside was not new to the war years. It already was present, as Barbara Engel and others have shown, during the first phase of rural to urban migration, and, thanks to the First World War, the Civil War, and industrial recruitment during the 1930s, it persisted thereafter.[8] The Great Patriotic War exacerbated the gender imbalance—by 1945 women outnumbered men in the Russian countryside by a ratio of 1.8:1—and a postwar economy that privileged male recruitment largely recapitulated the experience of the 1930s. For every one hundred men that the 1959 All-Union census recorded among the rural population of the twelve oblasts of the Central Economic Region, there were at least 127 (in Tula) and as many as 141 (Kalinin) women.[9] The disproportion was particularly striking for the age group of forty to forty-nine, 70 percent of whom were women. It has been estimated that even if all rural men aged eighteen to fifty-five had married, at least 40 percent of women in the countryside would lack a husband.[10]

But then the situation began to change and eventually reversed itself. Denisova partly explains the change in terms of older women whose lives were marked by hunger and a heavy burden of labor advising their daughters to avoid the same fate—the notorious triple burden.[11] Viktor Perevedentsev, the dean of Soviet demographers, made the same point a few years earlier: "The rural woman well knows that the life of her urban equivalent (*svertsnitsa*) is easier, more pleasant and more varied. . . What rational mother would want her daughter to live the same life that she herself lived? That is why she 'shoves' her 15-year old daughter to the city after the eighth grade."[12] There is undoubtedly something to this, as we shall see, but we also need to recognize the significant role that the expansion of education played in providing girls with a range of skills beyond those appropriate to farm work, the slim chances of finding a lifelong male partner close at hand, and the easing of restrictions on departures. When Izmaelovka's Nina Kozhevnikova espied her future husband at a dance in 1955, he had just arrived from a secret town in the Cheliabinsk region to take up a position as tractor driver.[13] Such encounters would be the stuff of some of Vasilii Shukshin's most memorable short stories as well as popular songs of the era, but they are less characteristic of the succeeding era than rural Ninas leaving for cities, secret and otherwise.

Between 1959 and 1978, cities absorbed 1.5 million rural migrants every year. Over the next census period (1979–88), the rate declined to nine hundred thousand. Sixty percent of those leaving the villages during these three decades were women, the vast majority of whom were young.[14] Perevedentsev discerned three distinct age cohorts among youthful rural-to-urban migrants: fifteen- to sixteen-year-olds who left after completing the eighth grade and entered vocational programs and high schools; seventeen- to eighteen-year-olds who, after finishing secondary school, entered higher education or jobs in the city; and twenty- to twenty-one-year-olds who, having completed military service, returned to the city to either study or begin working full-time.[15] While young men monopolized the third of these cohorts, young women outnumbered them in the first two. In 1984 according to one study, 62 percent of girls finishing secondary school in rural areas indicated their intention of changing their place of residence (most often, leaving the village for the city). Only 20 percent of them cited an agricultural profession compared to 48 percent of boys.[16] The 1989 census revealed the extent to which a great reversal had occurred: for every thousand men aged between twenty and thirty-nine living in the countryside, there were 886 women. In some parts of the RSFSR, such as Arkhangel'sk, Vologda, Pskov, and Mordovia, the ratio was more skewed still, falling below 800 women to every thousand men.[17]

The greater the educational attainment, the less tolerable conditions at home seemed. M. Osipov, chair of the Land of Soviets kolkhoz in Tambov oblast, reported his unsuccessful attempt in 1970 to persuade the mother of a high-school graduate that her daughter should stay put "rather than leaving for some alien place." "Liuba did not finish the tenth class so that she could work on the kolkhoz," the mother categorically replied, substantiating Perevedentsev and Denisova.[18] For girls, Denisova writes, "the beginning of an independent life was associated with moving to the city and entering a VUZ (higher educational institution)." She quotes one respondent as remarking ("with the pathos of a Chekhovian heroine") "Yes, to flee, to flee. To Moscow, to Moscow. . . . Everyone would be more educated, there would be museums, and everything if I were to leave the provinces for the capital of our country."[19]

Among rural youth seeking higher education, only a tiny minority was able to study in Moscow. Most, like Jiliana Selezneva's four children, matriculated closer to home. But strikingly, once having left Izmaelovka, they did not return. Her older son received his medical degree from the university in Cheliabinsk and was practicing medicine in Togliatti. Both daughters earned pedagogical degrees in Magnitogorsk. One remained there; the other, after returning briefly to Izmaelovka, moved to the Orenburg region to take up a position as a principal. And the younger son, following in the footsteps of his older brother, studied in Cheliabinsk where he stayed to work as a physician.[20] The journeys of Selezneva's sons were reproduced by countless village boys. Writing to *Sel'skaia molodezh* (Rural Youth) in the mid-1970s about a sheep-raising sovkhoz in Stavropol' krai, Vadim Kuropatkin reported on the dearth of shepherds. Over the previous five years, only one high school graduate had signed up, and he doubled as the veterinarian. As for the less well educated, "Every year we hire 200, but 200 leave by the end of the year." Of one hundred ten Komsomol members, only twelve were shepherds, "big progress" since 1968 when there were only three, but nobody was under twenty-five years old.[21] Osipov, the Land of Soviets kolkhoz chair, tried his best to talk Valentin Grigor'skii, a high school graduate, out of departing. "We need people desperately," he reports telling him. "There's more than enough work here." But Grigor'skii had been "hanging around with intelligent people" who made him ashamed of his job as a tractor driver, and so he requested a certificate (*spravka*) to leave. In the end, Osipov relented.[22]

The departure of young men such as Valentin meant fewer eligible bachelors for rural women. What were the women to do? That is what V. A. Shishliakov, chairperson of the Revolution kolkhoz in Vologda oblast wanted to know when he wrote to the Communist Party's central committee in the mid-1960s. Referring to the twenty milkmaids, aged eighteen to thirty, who worked on the kolkhoz's four farms, Shishliakov reported that only one lived with her husband. "Every normal person," he added, "dreams of and prepares oneself for family life and hopes to find personal happiness in conformity with social interests. But in our conditions such happiness doesn't smile on everyone." And just as "where there is a needle, there will be thread," girls will follow the boys to the city. "No passport regime or endless rhetoric," he concluded, "will stop young people whose personal lives are unsettled."[23]

Thus, it was not a matter of women leaving instead of men or vice versa; the out-migration of the one made it more likely the other would leave too. As a popular ditty (*chastushka*) from the Russian republic's non-black earth region had it,

Председателю сказала, To the chairman I said,
Заместателю скажу: To the deputy I will say:
«Если парня не найдете, If a lad you don't find,
Из колхоза ухожу». From the kolkhoz I will stray.[24]

Even when it was the "lad" who had stayed in the village, the woman was reluctant to return. Eighteen-year old Valerii Kravchenko and his girlfriend, another Liuba, also eighteen, are a case in point. As Valerii wrote in a despairing letter to *Sel'skaia molodezh,* he lived on a sovkhoz in the Chimkent oblast of Kazakhstan, while Liuba lived in the city. And even though they saw each other often, they decided they couldn't live apart any longer. But when he proposed that she come live with him, she replied, "Better if you come to me in the city."[25]

From 1959 to 1973 the rural areas of the Central Economic Region lost 4.1 million able-bodied people of whom 2.4 million or nearly two-thirds consisted of those between twenty and twenty-nine years old. Until 1970, the exodus of young women exceeded that of men. Among the region's twelve oblasts, eight recorded a relative decline in the population of women compared to men between the ages of twenty and twenty-four, and in the other four oblasts the proportions remained the same. Then between 1970 and 1973, the proportions were reversed, only to revert thereafter to the earlier situation of more departures by women than men.[26] Taking the thirty years between the censuses of 1959 and 1989, the steepest decline in rural population among the region's sixteen oblasts was in Kirov, which lost over 700,000 of its 1.2 million rural inhabitants, followed by Pskov whose rural population dropped from nearly 700,000 to 312,000. The smallest decline was in Karelia which lost "only" 40 percent of its rural population.[27]

RURAL DEPRIVATION

Plenty of evidence exists to suggest that young people were increasingly choosing the city because that is where the action was. Letters written to the journal *Sel'skaia Zhizn'* (Rural Life) in the 1960s by those left behind—primarily kolkhozniki who were too old or too encumbered to contemplate leaving—explained the departure of (or desire to depart by) so many youths as a function of not so much the countryside's lack of fulfilling and well-paying jobs as its relative poverty and dearth of amenities. "Youth live in boredom and want to leave," was how one letter-writer summed up the situation on her kolkhoz in Kirov oblast. "There is no spiritual life and daily life is primitive," wrote another from Krasnodar krai. The lack of electricity and telephones, badly supplied stores, the remoteness of medical facilities, and poor roads comprised some of the material elements about which letter-writers complained. What there didn't appear to be a shortage of was alcohol. "It remains for youth to drink, hooliganize, and think about where they can escape to," wrote a villager in Saratov oblast. "It is not surprising that we often have drinking bouts," stated a collectively written letter from Voronezh oblast. "Vodka is the only form of 'entertainment.'"[28]

This litany of despair needs to be contextualized. First, relative to the Stalin era, individual happiness—the desire to lead a more comfortable and fulfilling life in a personal sense—seems to have counted for more. Education and the enhanced awareness it provided of how lives were lived elsewhere played a major role in this respect, though Denisova's point about mothers reconciling themselves but not their daughters to the harshness of rural life should not be forgotten. Second, the Soviet project of overcoming "backwardness" proved to be a victim of its own success. People fled their native villages in the 1930s primarily as a means of physical survival, that is, to avoid starvation or being branded a kulak with the associated likelihood of deportation to a special settlement. From the 1950s onward, sheer physical survival was not nearly as difficult. It was then that people started to notice and complain about the lack of amenities. "One can speak of the formation of a strong association in mass consciousness," the historian Oleg Gorbachev has noted with reference to the early 1960s, whereby "without a club, youth leave the village."[29] But many people in the countryside—especially youth—soon adopted still higher standards. "We have attended to the material side of things," chairperson Shishliakov, whom we have met already, asserted somewhat self-servingly. "[We have] electricity, a radio in each house, ATS [automatic telephone dialing], internal roads, and two clubs."[30] Such items may earlier have signified the arrival of culture, but according to a veterinarian from Kirov oblast writing in 1965, they no longer did so:

> We are used to talking about culture in the village with words like radios, electricity, clubs, libraries, television, and so forth. But this is now already little. They have become items of first necessity. Nowadays it is an everyday occurrence for a zoologist, agronomist, veterinarian, engineer or teacher to have higher education. This doesn't surprise us, but try to find an artistic director of a House of Culture or the leader of a choir with higher education in the village. . . . I haven't heard of comrades after finishing the conservatory going to work as director of a club, say, in the village of Ardashi.[31]

REGRETS

Nevertheless, urban living did not fulfill every desire. Valia Arinova, the heroine of a short story that appeared in *Krest'ianka* more than a decade after the veterinarian wrote his letter, starts out thinking that "to remain in the village is to intentionally rob oneself." And so she left her village for Barnaul, the administrative center of the Altai krai. But working in the town, she "more and more often began to return in [her] mind to the little creek and the verdant bushes. I could smell the mushrooms and the fresh-cut branches of the birch trees; I could taste the blackberries and strawberries. More and more often, I thought of my classmates who had remained at home. Maybe I made a mistake," Valia began to think. Having cut herself off from her own, she had not managed to attach herself to her new surroundings. "What am I—rural or urban?" she wondered. After several months of such pondering, she returned to the village.[32]

Fictionalized though it was, Valia's story is indicative of a prominent theme in contemporary sources—the regret experienced by those who moved to the city. Denisova cites the following lament uttered by a female migrant:

Эх, куда я залетела, Where did I fly to,
Куда черт меня занес? Where has the devil taken me?
Лучше б я жила в деревне Better to have lived in the village
Работала на совхоз And worked for the sovkhoz.[33]

O. Lykhmanova, who had left her native village with her husband nine years earlier, might have identified with the lament. Writing to party officials, she complained of the lack of suitable accommodation, adding sarcastically that she expected to receive it "when our [yet to be born- LS] children will be mamas and papas."[34] But aside from difficulties with housing or other material deprivations, the lament evoked a common feeling among migrants of longing (*toska*). Writing to *Sel'skaia molodezh* in 1970, Neli Osipova, an eighteen-year-old student at a technical school in Novocherkassk, complained of a lack of friends that was in striking contrast to her former life in far-off Iakutia. "There, where I spent my childhood [I] had bosom friends with whom I shared secrets and knew all of theirs. But now it is difficult to adjust to new people."[35] Even older people expressed this feeling. "Until the end of my days," wrote the novelist Viktor Astaf'ev (1924–2001), "I will never stop longing for the village. . . . It's like that as well for Rasputin, Nosov and Belov—we never will stop being rooted in our hearts."[36]

Rubtsov acknowledged in the poem "Boundaries" cited above the desire to have it both ways—"to live somehow at once in the city and the village." But in the melodramatic stories that appeared in the journal *Sel'skaia molodezh,* the message was that "spontaneously" wandering off to the city would only lead to unhappiness and that it was better to earn the right to be sent by one's sovkhoz or kolkhoz. In one such tale, Val'ka, who illegally sells goods at railroad stops between her native village and Moscow, encounters Katia, who as the district's outstanding milkmaid is being sent to Moscow by her kolkhoz to study at an institute. "Don't go," she advises Katia. "In Moscow *blat* [deals to acquire goods and services, or to get ahead—LS] is everywhere." But Val'ka is only expressing her jealousy and by the end of the story abandons her wayward existence, intending to return to the village.[37] Another story with the same theme concerns Aleksei, who at the outset longed to escape from the squalor of his family situation. He imagined himself in the city with its broad asphalted avenues and holiday jollity, the kind of life described in novels and visible on television screens. "What he would do in the city Aleksei couldn't imagine, but he saw himself returning to the village on a visit surrounded by people looking at him respectfully and enviously." But upon acting on his impulses, Aleksei is disappointed. His aunt Marusia, who works as a cleaning lady, agrees to put him up but he has to sleep on the floor. After a week, he moves to a factory dormitory, but it is hot and uncomfortable. Wallowing in misery, he is too ashamed to write home and can't go home lest he face ridicule. But by chance, he sees a photo in the newspaper of Vasia Rogov, who having finished a course at the mechanics institute is being sent by his kolkhoz for further education. Vasia, it turns out, had lived in the same factory dormitory. If he could do it—earn the respect of the kolkhoz by hard work and study—so could Aleksei.[38]

LABOR NEEDS

The publication of such stories might lead one to conclude that Soviet authorities had become alarmed at rural depopulation and were trying to reverse it. This would be true as far as kolkhoz officials, the rural party *apparat,* and editors of journals with a rural readership were concerned. Their concerns prompted economists, sociologists, and other social scientists to undertake numerous studies of the causes and dimensions of the problem and to suggest a variety of measures to halt or even reverse it. Many recommendations revolved around increasing investment in rural infrastructure to raise the quality of life and expand opportunities for those with professional degrees to practice their professions on sovkhozes and kolkhozes.[39] But such efforts were swimming against a powerful ideological tide. The loss of rural population, far from being cause for alarm, only confirmed that the country was heading in the right direction toward modernity, that it was overcoming what Marx and Engels (in "The Communist Manifesto") had referred to as "the idiocy of rural life." Here, for example, is a typical statement from a collection of articles published by the State Committee on the Utilization of Labor Resources of the RSFSR Council of Ministers in 1973:

> The transfer of labor resources from the rural economy to other branches is the natural (*zakonomernym*) consequence of scientific-technical progress in agricultural production. Reduction in the absolute numbers of those working in agriculture and their share in the total number of those employed in the country's economy must be regarded as a progressive tendency, since it stimulates growth in labor productivity, and raises the technical quotient in agricultural production.[40]

To be sure, the "released labor power from agriculture" was "not always realized in a sufficiently planned manner."[41] In Cynthia Buckley's judgment, the *propiska* (residence permits) and passport systems to control migration flows to the cities proved to be an "illusion," a "mythical method," "a paper tiger of regulations that [officials] could not hope to completely enforce."[42] But at least rural migrants were helping to alleviate the shortage of—especially unskilled—industrial workers, a shortage endemic to the Soviet form of the planned economy. In the 1960s, authorities replaced the outright ban on new residents in "regime" cities with a system of time-restricted residence permits. The system engendered *limitchiki*, that is, workers who crowded into dormitories that labor-starved enterprises provided along with the permits. How many? Estimates understandably vary. In construction, they may have comprised as many as three of every four workers. They also worked in textiles, metallurgy, automobile production, and other industries performing "non-prestigious jobs which the indigenous urban population considers undesirable."[43] Overwhelmingly ethnic Russians, *limitchiki* otherwise resembled immigrants in other countries in the ways they were perceived by locals, the conscientiousness and diligence of their labor, and the techniques they adopted (overstaying "visas," marrying "legals," and otherwise finagling the system) to become permanent residents. As Victor Zaslavsky observed, "Any analysis of Soviet society and the Soviet working class which ignored the *limitchiks* would be as incomplete as an analysis of the

German working class which failed to consider the role of the *Gastarbeiter*."[44]

Moscow and Leningrad absorbed many but of course not all migrants. In the late 1960s, only 30 percent of the 640,000 people who were recorded leaving villages in the Central Economic Region settled in cities with a population of more than 100,000. Smaller cities took over 40 percent, and the remaining 28 percent remained within the countryside.[45] The numbers are a bit deceptive, however, for many migrants moved to suburban towns and villages within commuting distance of the major cities, especially Moscow and Leningrad. In census data, such moves counted misleadingly as rural-to-rural migration.[46] Summing up Soviet analyses of migration patterns by the mid-1970s, the American economists Robert C. Stuart and Paul Gregory noted that "these studies . . . have tended to settle on the same variables found important in a market economy context [among which] the most important explanatory variable [was] standard of living differentials (rural-urban wage differentials, availability of good quality housing, the provision of services, and so on)."[47]

For rural-based officials and others concerned about the depopulation of the countryside, the siren song of the city represented a challenge they could not meet. As Oleg Poptsov, editor of *Sel'skaia molodezh,* noted in a roundtable discussion of 1970 sponsored by the central committee of the Moscow oblast Komsomol, the problem was too urgent "to wait until the club, asphalt, housing, high wages, and mechanized farms appear." Other participants urged working more with parents "whose authority sometimes works in the opposite direction from ours." "But how?" someone asked. "A mother doesn't want her daughter to work in the fields. 'In [industrial] production,' she says, 'you earn your hours and then rest on Saturdays and Sundays.' And in truth, we find it difficult to argue with that." Perhaps journalists were at fault too, Poptsov opined, because in celebrating some harvester (*khleborob*) as a hero, they made others think, "Well, I'm no hero. Let me out of here. I'm going to the city."[48] The fact that kolkhozniki did not have access to passports, which urban residents above the age of fifteen were required to carry, did little to prevent rural-to-urban migration either via organized recruitment, marriage, or simply flight. The extension of internal passportization to collective farmers in 1976 made departures even simpler.[49]

"SETTLEMENTS WITHOUT A FUTURE"

While some rural settlements waited for the clubs, asphalt, housing, and other sociocultural services that had been promised to them, others were condemned as unviable or "settlements without a future (*neperspektivnye derevny*)," their residents correspondingly forced to become migrants.

This is what happened to thousands of communities across the country. In a study devoted to "the disappearing countryside in Russia," Denisova cites the elimination of some 10,000 settlements in Kirov oblast alone between 1950 and 1980, and the abandonment of 2,000 villages in Smolensk oblast between 1973 and 1988.[50] Over all, of 142,500 rural settlements in the non-black earth region, 61,000 (43 percent) were determined to have completely lost their productive functions and therefore as far as the state was concerned, their *raison d'etre*.[51]

The application of the policy of rationalizing the distribution of the rural population dates from the end of the 1950s and the early 1960s. An outgrowth of Khrushchev's earlier grandiose plans for "agro-towns" that had been thwarted under Stalin, the policy received the ideological imprimatur of the new 1961 Communist Party program which projected that the kolkhoz would provide for all its members' needs and that villages would be "gradually transformed into reinforced population points of an urban type with comfortable housing, municipal services, consumer enterprises, cultural and medical institutions."[52] This came at the time of tremendous optimism in ruling circles about their ability to effectuate transformations that would catapult the USSR to the forefront of modern societies.

Khrushchev's ouster in 1964 did not slow down the efforts of Gosstroi, Rosgiprozem, and other state organs to realize these dreams—between 1959 and 1970, the total number of rural population points in Russia declined from 294,000 to 216,000. In the non-black earth region there were a third fewer rural settlements by the end of the 1970s than in 1959. Some of the decline can be attributed to the reclassification of large villages into towns. The remainder, however, occurred because small villages shrank to the point of becoming *neperspektivnye* owing to outmigration. Denisova, citing the work of several sociologists, notes that people who remained in these settlements exhibited unusually high rates of anxiety, depression, and other psychologically unstable conditions.[53]

The process thus fed upon itself. Because of shrinking opportunities for decent jobs and fulfilling lives, young people were prone to leave the villages faster and in greater numbers than their parents. The fewer youngsters, the more vulnerable a settlement was to closure. Little wonder then that the entire rural population aged rapidly in the Brezhnev era. The proportion of the elderly population (i.e., those beyond retirement age) in the non-black earth region rose from 14.5 percent in 1959 to 21.6 percent by 1974. The trend continued relentlessly thereafter. By the end of the Soviet period, the share of pensioners in the rural population of the Central Economic Region stood at 30 to 35 percent, while women between the ages of fifteen to forty-nine comprised only 17 percent.[54]

CONCLUSION

I would be remiss if I did not mention that even the Khrushchev-era initiative that sent tens of thousands of predominantly young people from both urban and rural areas of European Russia and Ukraine to the Virgin Lands of northern Kazakhstan and southern Siberia—essentially an exercise in state-directed demographic relocation—threatened to succumb to reverse population flow already in the 1970s. "Twenty years already! Lord, it's like one year," Nina Ivanovna Bychkova exulted in an article in *Sel'skaia molodezh* from 1974. Clearly, in citing Nina's good cheer and recollections of initial hardships, the article intended to persuade readers that persistence paid off. "For many," the article continued, "deciding whether to stay or return to the 'homeland' was, if not a tragedy, then at least a drama. Some who lived here for ten years returned, but after a year or two, came back." Another article in the same journal described the Virgin Lands as "a whole social complex of world views, occupational qualities, and special properties of character," comparing their settlement to "advanced science, cosmonautics, or any quest involving the previously unexplored. . . ."[55]

Such depictions were probably no more successful in persuading young people to remain in their parched villages than those claiming, in conformity with the old Marxist dream, that the contradiction between town and country was being overcome. "We have done a lot to blur the difference(s)," boasted one kolkhoz chair who cited the existence of two libraries, a house of culture, a club, sports facility, dance hall, dramatic groups, choir, and an orchestra.[56] But for Vitia Alishin, a Moscow driver who had migrated to the capital with his young bride in 1970, the intrusion of urban ways into his native village was a mixed blessing. A skilled accordionist, Vitia would perform at weekend gatherings of rural folk (*piatachki*) in Moscow's Ismailovskii Park. On one occasion, though, he is captured on film performing back in the village. The problem, as he explains in Aleksei Khaniutin's haunting documentary from 1987, is that while the rural culture embodied in the *piatachok* has migrated to the city, it has died out where it originated. "When I go there, I'm embarrassed. I feel like I am disturbing their peace," he says. Meanwhile, the camera and sound segue from Viktor playing for a crowd of elderly women and crying babies to up the hill to where a younger crowd, dressed in spiffier clothes, is boogying to a pop tune emanating from a reel-to-reel tape.[57]

NOTES

1. Leslie Page Moch, *Paths to the City: (Regional Migration in Nineteenth-Century France* (Beverly Hills: Sage, 1983); Moch *Moving Europeans: Migration in Western Europe since 1650* (Bloomington: Indiana University Press, 2003); Paul-André Rosental, *Les*

sentiers invisibles: Espace, familles, et migrations dans la France du 19e siècle (Paris: Ecole des Hautes études en Sciences Sociales, 1999).

2. On the first rural-to-urban migration, see *inter alia* Robert E. Johnson, *Peasant and Proletarian: The Working Class of Moscow in the Late Nineteenth Century* (New Brunswick: Rutgers University Press, 1979); Joseph Bradley, *Muzhik and Muscovite: Urbanization in Late Imperial Russia* (Berkeley: University of California Press, 1985); Barbara Engel, *Between the Fields and the City: Women, Work and Family in Russia, 1861–1914* (Cambridge: Cambridge University Press, 1994). On the second migration, see Sheila Fitzpatrick, "The Great Departure: Rural-Urban Migration in the Soviet Union, 1929–33" and Stephen Kotkin, "Peopling Magnitostroi: The Politics of Demography," in *Social Dimensions of Soviet Industrialization*, ed. William G. Rosenberg and Lewis H. Siegelbaum (Bloomington: Indiana University Press, 1993), 15–40, 63–104; David Hoffmann, *Peasant Metropolis: Social Identities in Moscow, 1929–1941* (Ithaca: Cornell University Press, 1994); Gijs Kessler, "The Peasant and the Town: Rural-Urban Migration in the Soviet Union, 1929–40," 2 vols. Doctoral Dissertation, European University Institute, 2001.

3. The Anglophone literature on migration during this period thus remains that of social scientists writing contemporaneously or just after the end of the Soviet Union. See, for example, Peter Grandstaff, *Interregional Migration in the USSR: Economic Aspects, 1959–1970* (Durham: Duke University Press, 1980); Mervyn Matthews, *The Passport Society: Controlling Movement in Russia and the USSR* (Boulder: Westview, 1993); Cynthia Buckley, "The Myth of Managed Migration: Migration Control and Market in the Soviet Period," *Slavic Review*, vol. 54, no. 4 (1995): 896–916.

4. For a particularly trenchant analysis see Stephen Hochstadt, *Mobility and Modernity: Migration in Germany, 1809–1989* (Ann Arbor: University of Michigan Press, 1999), 19–37.

5. N. Rubtsov, "Grani," cited and translated in Philippa Lewis, "Peasant Nostalgia in Contemporary Russian Literature," *Soviet Studies*, vol. 28, no. 4 (1976): 564.

6. L. N. Denisova, *Zhenshchiny russkikh selenii, Trudovye budni* (Moscow: Mir istorii, 2003), 245–48.

7. Jiliana Selezna, "Dedicated Nurse," in *The Women of Izmaelovka, a Soviet Union Collective Farm in Siberia*, Alexey Vinogradov and Albert Pleysier eds. (Lanham: University Press of America, 2007), 32–39.

8. Barbara Engel, *Between the Fields and the City: Women, Work and Family in Russia, 1861–1914* (Cambridge: Cambridge University Press, 1994), 64: "By contrast with the rural women of France . . . who were more likely than their brothers to leave the village, Russian peasant women stayed at home." See also Roberta T. Manning, "Women in Then Soviet Countryside on the Eve of World War II, 1935–1940," in *Russian Peasant Women*, Beatrice Farnsworth and Lynne Viola eds. (Oxford: Oxford University Press, 1992), 210.

9. O. V. Gorbachev, *Na Puti k gorodu: sel'skaia migratsiia v Tsentral'noi Rossii (1946–1985 gg.) i sovetskaia model' urbanizatsii* (Moscow: MPGU, 2002), 117.

10. Denisova, *Zhenshchiny*, 253–4. Denisova cites Norton D. Dodge and Murray Feshbach, "The Role of Women in Soviet Agriculture," in *Russian Peasant Women*, 254, but they somewhat more vaguely refer to "the most depleted age groups."

11. Ibid., 262. On the triple burden, see Liubov Denisova, *Rural Women in the Soviet Union and Post-Soviet Russia*, ed. and trans. Irina Mukhina (London: Routledge, 2010), 143–50. On its perpetuation into the post-Soviet years, see Hilary Pilkington, "'For the Sake of the Children': Gender and Migration in the Former Soviet Union," in *Post-Soviet Women from the Baltic to Central Asia*, ed. Mary Buckley (Cambridge: Cambridge University Press, 1997), 131.

12. V. I. Perevedentsev, *Molodezh' i sotsial'no-demograficheskie problemy SSSR* (Moscow: Nauka, 1990), 123.

13. Nina Kozhevnikova, "Unhappy Wife," in *Women of Izmaelovka*, 72.

14. "Novaia informatsiia Goskomstata SSSR," *Vestnik statistiki*, no. 8 (1991): 52. Of the 13.9 million people who were classified as migrants in the 1970 census, females

slightly outnumbered males. See Blaine Ball and George J. Demko, "Internal Migration in the Soviet Union," *Economic Geography*, vol. 54, no. 2 (1978): 96.

15. Perevedentsev, *Molodezh'*, 93.

16. "V pomoshch' agitatoru i propagandistu," *Vestnik statistiki*, no. 9 (1984): 65.

17. V. Brui and E. Mikhailov, "Nekotorye osobennosti demograficheskoi obstanovki v RSFSR," *Vestnik statistiki*, no. 7 (1991): 21; T. Levina, "Demograficheskaia situatsiia v sel'skoi mestnosti," *Vestnik statistiki*, no. 1 (1992): 15.

18. Mikhail Osipov, "Ia smotriu na molodezh' nastoiashchuiu," *Sel'skaia molodezh*, no. 6 (1970): 1. Another mother put in more piquantly: "Her father and I spent our whole lives in muck and filth, let Zina do some other work. There's nothing for her to do in the country." Quoted in Susan Bridge, "Soviet Rural Women: Employment and Family Life," in *Russian Peasant Women*, 290.

19. Denisova, *Zhenshchiny*, 265.

20. *Women of Izmaelovka*, 39.

21. Vadim Kuropatkin, "Duma o zolotom rune," *Sel'skaia molodezh*, no. 8 (1974): 3.

22. Osipov, 1.

23. Rossiiskii Gosudarstvennyi Arkhiv Sotsial'no-Politicheskoi Istorii (RGASPI), f. 591, op. 1, d. 164, 11. 131–33.

24. L. N. Denisova, *Ischezaiushchaia derevnia Rossii: Nechernozem'e v 1960–1980-e gody* (Moscow: Institut Rossiiskoi istorii RAN, 1996), 141.

25. "Vam pis'mo," *Sel'skaia molodezh*, no. 8 (1970): 27.

26. Denisova, *Ischezaiushchaia derevnia*, 141; Gorbachev, *Na puti k gorodu*, 120.

27. Tsentral'noe statisticheskoe upravlenie pri Sovete Ministrov SSSR, *Itogi vsesoiuznoi perepisi naseleniia 1959 goda RSFSR* (Moscow: Gosstatizdat, 1963), 24–27; Tsentral'noe statisticheskoe upravlenie pri Sovete ministrov RSFSR, *Narodnoe khoziaistvo RSFSR v 1989 g. Statisticheskii ezhegodnik* (Moscow: Gosstatizd., 1990), 59–61.

28. RGASPI, f. 591, op. 1, d. 58, ll. 1, 3, 9, 15, 113 (February 11–April 12, 1969); d. 172, l. 8 (1966).

29. Gorbachev, *Na puti k gorodu*, 97.

30. RGASPI, f. 591, op. 1, d. 164, l. 133.

31. RGASPI, f. 591, op. 1, d. 22, l. 115 (October 1965). Ardashi is a village in Kirov oblast located about 60 km to the southeast of the city of Kirov.

32. L. Butkovskaia, "Kak Valia romantiku iskala," *Krest'ianka*, no. 7 (1978): 1–3.

33. Denisova, *Zhenshchiny*, 252.

34. RGASPI, f. 591, op. 1, d. 164, l. 174.

35. "Vam pis'mo," *Sel'skaia molodezh*, no. 8 (1970): 27.

36. Cited in Denisova, *Zhenshchiny*, 252. These were all, like Astaf'ev, village prose writers (*derevenshchiki*) whose most active period was during the 1960s and '70s.

37. Tat'iana Riabikina, "Val'kina doroga," *Sel'skaia molodezh*, no. 3 (1962): 22–24.

38. Roman Kharitonov, "Mif Alekseia Brykina," *Sel'skaia molodezh*, no. 7 (1970): 6–7.

39. See for example V. I. Perevedentsev, *Migratsiia naseleniia i trudovye probleny Sibiri* (Novosibirsk: Nauka, 1966); T. I. Zaslavskaia, ed. *Migratsiia sel'skogo naseleniia* (Moscow: Mysl', 1970); V. I. Staroverov, *Sotsial'no-demograficheskie probleny derevni: Metodologiia, metodika, opyt analiza migratsii sel'skogo naseleniia* (Moscow: Nauka, 1975).

40. S. G. Gaiazova, "Nekotorye voprosy migratsii i estestvennogo dvizheniia sel'skogo naseleniia," in A. Z. Makov, ed., *Migratsiia naseleniia RSFSR* (Moscow: Statistika, 1973), 88.

41. Ibid., 89.

42. Cynthia Buckley, "The Myth of Managed Migration: Migration Control and Market in the Soviet Period," *Slavic Review*, vol. 54, no. 4 (1995): 896–916.

43. Victor Zaslavsky, *The Neo-Stalinist State* (Armonk, NY: M. E. Sharpe, 1981), 144–46, 188–89; Ia. A. Davidovich, A. G. Kosaev, and M. N. Podol'naia, "Privlechenie i ratsional'noe ispol'zovanie inogorodnikh rabochikh," *Sotsiologicheskie issledovaniia*, no. 4 (1981): 123–28; Dietrich Andre Loeber, "Limitchiki: On the Legal Status of Migrant Workers in Large Soviet Cities," *The Soviet and Post-Soviet Review*, vol. 11, nos. 1–3 (1984): 301–08. Quotation on 304.

44. Zaslavsky, *Neo-Stalinist* State, 144–45. For another case of internal migrants widely regarded as aliens, see Leslie Page Moch, *The Pariahs of Yesterday: Breton Migrants in Paris* (Durham: Duke University Press, 2012).

45. Gorbachev, *Na puti k gorodu*, 127.

46. See B. S. Khorev and V. N. Likhded, *Zhitel' sela—rabotnik goroda* (Moscow: Finansy i statistika, 1982), 36–37.

47. Robert C. Stuart and Paul R. Gregory, "A Model of Soviet Rural-Urban Migration," *Economic Development and Cultural Change*, vol. 26, no. 1 (1977): 85–86. Stuart and Gregory assert that "males predominate especially in the younger age ranges." But according to the 1970 census, females outnumbered males in both the RSFSR and the USSR among those residing for less than two years in the place where the census was conducted. See Tsentral'noe statisticheskoe upravlenie pri Sovete Ministrov SSSR, *Itogi Vsesoiuznoi perepisi naseleniia 1970 goda*, vol. 7 (Moscow: Statistika, 1974), 8, and above n. 13.

48. "Bespornaia ochevidnost,'" *Sel'skaia molodezh*, no. 12 (1970): inside cover-4.

49. Mervyn Matthews, *The Passport Society: Controlling Movement in Russia and the USSR* (Boulder: Westview Press, 1993), 33–35: "A passport allowed immediate identification, the establishment of family status, etc., and could make travelling easier."

50. Denisova, *Ischezaiushchaia derevnia Rossii*, 144.

51. Ibid., 123–4.

52. Kommunisticheskaia partiia Sovetskaia Soiuza, *Programma Kommunisticheskoi Partii Sovetskogo Soiuza priniata XXII s"ezdom KPSS* (Moscow: Pravda, 1961), 83, 85.

53. Denisova, *Ischezaiushchaia derevnia Rossii*, 125, 129. This downward trend would continue into the post-Soviet period. By the census year of 2002, 37,000 (24 percent) of the 155,000 villages within the Russian Federation contained 50 or fewer people and 13,000 "emptied out altogether." *The New York Times*, Feburary 5, 2004: A9.

54. Ibid., 142–3.

55. Viktor Konov, "Prodolzhenie sleduet," *Sel'skaia molodezh*, no. 4 (1974): 12–14; An. Makarov, "Vysota," *Sel'skaia molodezh*, no. 3 (1974): 25.

56. *Sel'skaia molodezh*, no. 9 (1970): 2.

57. *Piatachok* (Aleksei Khaniutin, dir., 1987). The film is available online at http://films.academic.ru/film.nsf/9498/Пятачок in six parts. The relevant clip is at Part V (2:30–2:50).

FOUR

Brezhnev's "Little Freedoms"

Tourism, Individuality, and Mobility in the Late Soviet Period

Christian Noack

My chapter deals with two instances of gradual redrawing of the boundaries of the *acceptable* in the late Soviet Union, both in discourse and practice. Both of my cases, *family vacation* and the *freedom of movement* for *motorised tourists* are in one way or the other linked to the emergence of *wild tourism,* the individual and nonorganized form of travel and vacationing in the Soviet Union. I suggest that the history of Soviet tourism provides an ample ground for the study of a "middle ground," in which negotiations between Soviet ideologists and administrators on the one hand and Soviet citizens practicing tourism on the other were possible. I could think only of a few other state-sponsored undertakings that were so readily appropriated by the population like Tourism, with education and "culturedness" probably being the notable exceptions. If this working hypothesis should prove to be viable, then the already firmly established dichotomies in the analysis of late Soviet realities so convincingly criticized by Alexei Yurchak . . . do not make much sense. If I stick to some of them in the following passages, this is largely for heuristic purposes.

Tourism in the USSR developed indeed for much of the twentieth century as a state-sponsored project in the wake of the secular transformations of economy and society. There had been almost no domestic tourism in Russia before 1917, consequently the Bolshevik regime from early on attempted to fashion it according to its own ideas. In the Soviet discourse, vacationing was basically seen as therapeutic. *Otdykh* (recreation), or the treatment in one of the state-financed health resorts, aimed primarily at the restoration of a worker's capacity for labour.[1] Under Stalin, the organization of recreation acquired the form of package tours or vacations organized for workers through the trade unions in their enterprises. Such groups were sufficiently easy to plan, administer, and control; the distribution of vouchers (*putevki*) became part of the gratification system awarding political conformism and good labour performance.[2] This Soviet brand of social tourism is strongly reminiscent of contemporary Italian or German projects, yet it became a mass phenomenon exclusively in Soviet rhetoric during Stalin's times.

The 1960s and 1970s, however, saw not only a significant increase in salaries and free time available to the Soviet citizens, like the five-day working week introduced in 1968. From 1961 onward the Soviet budget allotted significantly more money for the extension of the holiday facilities run by trade unions. The capacities of the so-called "organized" domestic tourism (as opposed to the nonorganized or "wild" individual tourism) doubled between 1965 and 1980. Annual growth rates in terms of accommodation capacities surpassed 10 percent annually in the late 1960s. In terms of social composition, but also in their outlook, the Soviet holiday resorts "democratized." They did even more so because of the number of "unorganized" travellers quickly surpassed that of "organized" travellers. This is true at least during high season and in the most popular destinations, such as on the Black and Baltic Sea shores and in the Caucasus, when up to five times more "unorganized" tourists frequented the southern resorts. I suggest that this quantitative enlargement process was accompanied by substantial redefinition of what tourism and recreation meant in the Soviet discourse. In my opinion, this redefinition increasingly responded to popular demands "from below" which were in some way or another integrated into the "official" definition of Soviet tourism, even if that entailed questioning some of the latter's basic assumptions.

With the emergence of real instead of imagined mass tourism this discourse became increasingly ambiguous, as several of the new ideas contradicted certain stereotypes and habits established in the 1920s and 1930s. Indeed, such Stalinist clichés continued to be reiterated in mass media (print, films, TV) or more specialized travel literature (hand- or guidebooks, dedicated journals).[3] According to these stereotypes, the Soviet Union from its early days opened the health resorts, earlier a privilege of aristocracy and exploiters, for the toiling masses. A "purposeful" style of collective travel and tourism developed which allegedly contrasted the parasitic and passive pastimes of bourgeois vacationing. In the first part of my chapter I discuss how this ostensible ideological rigour was continuously undermined in a public discourse on family vacation which involved both tourists and Soviet tourism managers.

FAMILY VACATION

The infrastructure of organized Soviet tourism was geared at supplying individual members of a labour collective with rest and/or recreation. In practical terms this meant that workers were provided with (or could, in some cases, acquire) vouchers (*putevki*) which entitled them to boarding and lodging in health or recreation facilities, such as sanatoria, rest homes, tourist bases, and the like. In rare cases only, transportation to or between the destinations was inclusive. Soviet holiday facilities were usually built to offer accommodation to several people (usually between six and twelve) in one room. Neither were there quarters for married couples, nor did Soviet holiday facilities usually cater for several generations simultaneously. On the contrary, children were offered vacations with their peers in pioneer camps. In cases that they were weak or ill, they could be treated in one of the many specialized children's sanatoria. Even if a married couple would work in one and the same Soviet enterprise or institution, it was extremely unlikely that they could purchase vouchers for the same destination at the same time. "The vacation was for the good of the producer, not the producer's spouse or children."[4]

In other words, the gradual restitution of the family as the basic instance of socialization under Stalin left little traces in the way Soviet vacationing was organized. Families who wished to spend, for example, the summer vacations could still visit relatives or retire to the dacha, which a majority of Soviet citizens actually did until the very last days of the Soviet Union.[5] Or they could try to travel as unorganized, "wild" tourists.

Early references pro and contra family vacation in the Soviet Union date back to the 1950s and reflect to the above-cited utilitarian early Soviet approach to recreation: vacations had to serve the purpose of recovery and restoration of the individual laborer's abilities. Against this backdrop, toilers needed physical rest, whereas the growing number of white collar workers exposed to intellectual rather than physical stress required a peaceful and quiet recreation. Children were considered to endanger calm and peace, and family visits were reluctantly tolerated in Soviet recreational facilities for very short periods of time only.[6]

I came across a second thread in medical periodicals of the time, however, which advocated joint medical treatments of children with the parents (mothers in the first place)[7] in children's sanatoria. Here the advantage of admitting parents was discussed somewhat differing yet also utilitarian terms. Looking back on his administrative work in a famous Soviet children's resort, Anapa, the chairman of the local Health resort council (*Kurortnyi sovet*), V. V. Avanesov wrote in 1970:

> . . . there is no reason why parents and children should be separated during their recreational vacations at a health resort. Accommodating

> parents and children together facilitates the children's treatment, as nobody takes more care of children than their mothers [sic!]. Moreover, this allows us to cure children from the age of four, at an early stage of their illness. This results in more effective therapies and earlier prophylaxis in case of chronic diseases.[8]

Already by 1970, this seems to have become common wisdom in the USSR, and the number of children's health facilities accommodating family members at least for a time was growing slowly but steadily. But the argument was obviously valid also the other way around. A Moscow-based physician, for example, wrote in 1968 that mothers would recover more quickly if they could be assured that their children would be well looked after. Moreover, a sojourn in the health resorts would be useful for the children as well, as they would often be ill fed in cases when their mothers were absent from home.[9]

In practical terms, such insights were very difficult to implement in the Soviet recreational system. Outside a few specifically equipped sanatoria or rest homes it was perhaps conceivable to put up additional cots for parents in children's facilities, or to help parents with procuring private accommodation at a health resort.[10] None of the sanatoria or rest homes for adults, however, had any facilities for children, from cots to amenities like playgrounds and rooms, or kitchens that could provide children's equivalents to the meticulously regulated time regimes or diets.

Nonetheless, beyond the limits of the utilitarian discourse on recreation, Soviet officials in the 1960s became increasingly responsive to public demands, which resulted inter alia in a revival of empirical social research. The *Komsomolskaia Pravda* published questionnaires and offered its readers the opportunity to express their opinions on *how they wanted to spend their holidays*. In 1966 more than twelve thousand Soviet citizens responded to the query, and the results, not fully published at the time, mirrored clear preferences. Active vacationing with frequent relocation from place to place was preferred by almost three quarters of the respondents, while only one fifth favored travel to one location and spending their holidays there. Incidentally, this was the default mode in the Soviet recreational system. Interestingly, no less than 45 percent of the respondents would have preferred family vacations compared to 42 percent with friends and colleagues (default) and 12 percent with strangers.[11] This preference for family vacation, as well as the difficulties to realize it, were confirmed by other surveys conducted during the 1960s and 1970s.[12]

Indeed, we find a basic acceptance of the concept of family holidays without references to medical needs as early as 1960, thus precisely in the period when the extension of the Soviet vacationing system was negotiated. In this year the chairman of the Soviet trade unions, Grishin, suggested the creation of special rest homes for families in a letter to the Council of Ministers of the USSR.[13] More and more often the issue of family vacations was taken up by Soviet media, frequently with reference to the growing number of unorganized tourists against the backdrop of the deficiencies of the organized sector.[14]

Obviously little changed in practice, as we see as late as 1965 strong resistance from the "practitioners" when the trade unions summoned their responsible ones from the regions to a conference in Moscow. Upon this meeting, among other things, a broad-scale opening of Soviet facilities for family vacations was discussed. Put under pressure from their superiors in Moscow who referred to the obviously growing public demand, some functionaries denied both the necessity and the feasibility of family vacation. Under the applause of his colleagues the chairman of the Yalta council, Rozanov, stated unambiguously:

> I conferred with some of the experienced comrades, and we categorically reject the idea of parents and children vacationing together. Neither for the former, nor for the latter this will be recreation; this is a hideous spawn of fantasy that nobody needed. Children should get what children require, the same applies to adults. . . . A child should be brought up collectively with other children, not among adults. What shall we teach fourteen-year-olds at Yalta beach, when women at the same time complain that topless sun-baths are forbidden? That is where this will lead us. Children should spend their holidays in children's collectives, with clear time regime and under supervision. It is a mere invention that mothers want to spend a whole month with their children; there is no reason to believe this.[15]

Comrade Rozanov could indeed have quoted numerous complaints of vacationers about the presence of children in recreational facilities.[16] Still worse, family vacations would have faced him and most of his colleagues with almost insurmountable practical obstacles, beginning with the architecture of sanatoria and rest homes. Very few had a suitable room size for families, any equipment or personnel to provide children with equivalent of medical care, not to mention healthy boarding or sound cultural entertainment considered to be fundamental in the Soviet concept of recreation. Even more challenging, judging from the discussion, was the necessity to restructure the whole system of voucher distribution. The deputies' insistence on this point was perhaps more than just an attempt to play the ball back into the Central Council's field. As a matter of fact, children and spouses were as a rule not members of one and the same labor collective, and thus as a rule not entitled to vouchers for the same recreational facilities. Another argument was that this restructuring would imply a reduction of the total capacities. In a period when all signs were set for the extension of accommodation, this was a serious counter-argument.[17] The all-Union chairman Kozlov, however, appeared unmoved and informed his employees that the demand for joint vacationing for parents with children was growing, and that it was within their sphere of competence to provide the facilities for it.[18]

By contrast, the much more primitive architecture and equipment of buildings in the tourist sector might have been easier to change and adopt, and indeed the idea of family vacations was actively promoted here: "Mama, papa, i ia- turistskaia semia."[19] Whether large decommissioned army tents, of which most of the tourist bases consisted during the 1960s, were any more suitable for families is debatable, however.[20] With more money channelled in the cheaper tourist and recreation facilities during the extension of the campaign of the 1960s and 1970s, small four- or six- bed wooden cabins emerged on those bases which were considered to be more suitable for families.[21] As the tourist councils were also organizing round trips, the chairmen of Moscow's tourism council, Abukov, also strove to flag as many of them as possible as "family friendly" in 1965. Again, the appropriateness of trains and buses as family accommodations seems fairly debatable in retrospection.[22]

In the tourist sector, however, resistance rooted in a rather robust definition of what "real" tourism was supposed to be in the Soviet: Annoyed by the large number of citizens who obviously regarded tourist facilities as cheaper alternatives to stationary vacations, camp and base directors frequently emphasized the need for physical preparedness that tourist hikes allegedly required, and thus ruled out that the hiking routes were suitable either for elderly tourists or children.[23] Others displayed more willingness to adjust their work according to popular demand. A Krasnodar-based official reminded his colleagues in 1974 that "in case we break up families, they won't like the Borshch' in our rest home, the sugar in our tea will be regarded as insufficiently sweet, and the sea in Gelendzhik as not black enough."[24]

During the following years, both tourist and health resort authorities in Moscow exhorted their subordinates routinely to organize the accommodation of families in their facilities. The health administration promised to double the capacities for families to some fifty thousand places in 1972, which was not too impressive given the total number of around eight hundred thousand beds provided. Soviet journals often featured stories about family vacations.[25] Guidebooks documented the existence of family friendly accommodations, too.[26]

Quite obviously, the Soviet "tourist industry" bowed to popular demand, even if it very basically contradicted both its philosophy and its structure. Indeed, many managers obviously felt like they were caught between a rock and a hard place. But insight grew that Soviet tourists would increasingly ignore rules and regulations anyway and turn up with their whole families, whether furnished with *putevki* or not.[27] Pressured from above, local Soviet recreation managers generally lacked the funds and materials to provide the services expected from them, which more often than not resulted in the vacationers paying the bill.

A case in point is the experience of Vladimir Popov, a journalist with *Pravda*. He had obtained three vouchers for the *pansionat*[28] Anapa and travelled with two children aged twelve and fifteen to the Black Sea in July 1972. Upon arrival at the recreational facility Popov was told that his vouchers had been "annulled." The director of "Anapa," comrade Litvinenko, refused to accommodate the Popovs and a number of other vacationers arriving the same day. Only an intervention by the chairman of the Health resort council, whom the stranded vacationers succeeded in mobilizing, Litvinenko grudgingly accepted the Popovs into the obviously overcrowded *pansionat*. In his complaint to the Health resort council, dated August 1, 1972, Popov detailed some of the conditions during their vacations:

> I had to share my bed with my son for 24 days because three people were accommodated in two-bed rooms and additional convertibles were not available. We were no exception, in all rooms in corpus five guests were accommodated like this. They told us that Moscow had issued 24 vouchers over the limit. Yet they have 100 rooms in a new building! It is also hard to understand, then, why the director encouraged other people to stay on after they had stayed for 24 days, as there was allegedly no room to house guests.[29]

Popov's letter goes on to discuss the inappropriate food in the canteen and finally described how during his sojourn two workmen incredibly slowly welded something on the future playground in front of the corpus. Anapa's overcrowded beaches were another nightmare for Popov, who wondered why the resort did not dispose of a reserved stretch for organized tourists, off limits for their "wild" counterparts. In due consideration of Popov's professional background the local Health resort council hurried to investigate his complaint, just to find his description of the situation largely appropriate. Worse still, an inspection of the same *pansionat* Anapa eight years later turned out that the overall conditions had changed rather to the negative, and that the facility continued to accommodate additional vacationers in buildings not suitable for this purpose—for example, a local school.[30]

The case of the Popovs is by no means singular. Russian archives brim with complaints and follow-up investigations on the inflexibility of the local tourism management. Popov, as a journalist, might have been well aware of those deficits not just from firsthand experience, but also from their broad discussion in the Soviet press. Probably not accidentally, his complaint touched upon almost all of the sore spots in the discussion, from the inconsistencies of vouchers system to the lack of child friendly accommodation and boarding. Against this backdrop I tend to interpret the emergence of the discourse on family tourism and the (however insufficient) implementation of family holiday in the Soviet Union as continued negotiation process, which slowly but surely eroded the ideological basis on which Soviet tourism had originally been built.

FREEDOM OF MOVEMENT

Many Soviet managers were thus fully aware of the incapability of the inherited Soviet social tourism to cope with the developing mass tourism set upon the agenda by the highest echelons of power in Moscow. I tend to interpret the relatively broad acceptance of individual "wild" tourism by the same tourism officials in this light. Accepting it meant also accepting the degree of improvisation that went with it, thus managing "wild tourism" offered opportunities, or at least a pretext, to operate in grey zones like the management of private accommodation and thus to compensate for some of the insufficiencies of the state-run system. This acceptance translated into a paternalistic discourse, according to which individual tourists were treated as second-class travellers excluded from the benefits of social tourism, but all the same deserving the pastoral care of tourism and health resort councils. The latter created, during the 1970s, several bureaus meant to provide paid services to the individual travellers. Soviet tourism managers had to realize, however, that the dynamic growth of individual tourism overstrained local capacities in the most popular destinations. The second part of my chapter will focus on the interplay between those tourism functionaries and the growing number of "unorganized" tourists, and in particular with the increasing individual mobility of motorised travellers.

By definition, tourism and travel are about the movement of people through space. Among the many obstacles for the development of Soviet tourism the lack of transportation capacities was one of the most debilitating. Until the 1960s, travelling through the Soviet Union meant mainly travel by train, more rarely by bus or boat. Only very few privileged citizens owned cars, there were practically no private automobiles until the end of Khrushchev's reign. Flights became available to tourists, too, but only by the end of the 1960s.

The lack of transport was made worse by the fact that the tourism administrations had to negotiate with branch ministries, like those for the railways or the river navigation (*rechflot*), to secure places and preferential tariffs for Soviet tourists. In that they displayed some degree of creativity, for example in the case of the organisation of so called tourist trains. With the bulk of Soviet passenger trains offering sleeping coaches anyway, the tourism councils hired trains to serve both as means of transportation and as accommodation for tourists during the trips, usually from the regions to the major urban centres of the Soviet Union.[31] By contrast, tourism, however, was of secondary importance to the functionaries in such ministries, and there were only limited attempts to fend off of the seasonal peaks in train travel by offering additional trains services to the most popular holiday destinations. The rank and file Soviet tourist, whether organised or not, had to pay the bill for this. As mentioned above, most of the vacation packages that could be acquire through the trade unions—be it a sojourn at a sanatoria or the participation in a tourist hike in Crimea—were sold without tickets to the destinations. Hence vacationers had to queue from the moment tickets went on sale (ten days ahead of the travel date), and the situation was acerbated by the fact that due to the lack of a reasonably well working reservations system, tickets were sold one-way only throughout much of the Soviet period.[32]

In other words, queuing for the return trip started during the actual vacations, and this could be tricky in cases where the destinations had no railways stations or ticket offices. Not to mention the problems of tourists who participating in a hike from place to place. For the tourist administration, too, this system implied many unwanted knock-on effects. As the duration of stay in most vacation facilities was uniform and mass arrivals and departures coincided, many tourist literally stranded in the resorts, putting additional strains on accommodation and boarding facilities.[33] Against this backdrop, local councils employed agents to help vacationers obtain tickets, and looked for alternative transport facilities.[34]

Soviet tourist councils toyed, for example, with the idea of organising hitch-hiking on a massive scale during the mid-1960s: Regional and republican councils issued little booklets to tourists and drivers in which routes and distances on which tourists were taken along could be noted. The "best" drivers were promised awards.[35]

It is against this backdrop that motor tourism, once it began to develop during the 1960s, was seen in a thoroughly positive light by many tourism functionaries, although it allowed for much more individualistic travel than the rank and file Soviet package tour. The illustrated monthly "Turist" published many articles featuring motor tourism as very suitable form to exploit the beauty of the motherland and invited representatives of the road authorities and the militia to provide drivers with helpful advice.[36] Sections for motor tourist sprang up in all tourist councils, and judging from the archival material they were very actively lobbing motor tourism within these structures and beyond.[37] On the one hand this is not so surprising if we take into account that obtaining a car still required being part of the privileged elite in the Soviet Union. On the other hand, there were good reasons for lobbying, as the network of roads and services was thin, to put it mildly.[38] Nor were good maps available, and "Tourist" regularly featured detachable road maps for the most frequently visited republics and regions of the USSR.[39]

This is quite remarkable against the backdrop of the traditionally less tolerant attitudes towards individualism in tourism. If Soviet tourism authorities had earlier advertised individual forms of travel, for example grass-root forms of self-organised travel like *samodiatel'nyi turizm,* they had always insisted on its collective character, its firm integration into the production process, its purpose in the context of a scientific conquest of the Soviet space and so forth. Hence many bureaucratic instruments for control of tourists' movement were implemented and individualistic "misuse" of the freedom to travel within the USSR denounced as "tramping."[40] Late Soviet press coverage continued to emphasise the need for organisation and discipline in motor tourism, but in general accepted the main aim was now the individual tourist experience. There was nothing wrong, then, in travelling the USSR with private cars.

The tourism authorities themselves pledged to serve the new clientele of automobile tourist with new forms of accommodations, camping sites and motels.[41] Although particularly camping sites would have been inexpensive to set up, it turned out to be astonishingly difficult to provide for them in the popular destinations. Their number remained ridiculously low, for example on the Black and Baltic seashores, and more often than not it appears that the local authorities redefined wild camping sites into official ones.[42] One of the reasons might have been the unwillingness of local municipalities to provide suitable lots of land, as this was their main lever in negotiating return services, for example by enterprises setting up recreation facilities.[43]

Be that as it may, a growing number of car owners and drivers in the Soviet Union used their cars for leisure trips, and they did so in particular during their summer vacations. Cars allowed for long distance trips, say from the industrial areas of Central Russia to the Black Sea and the Caucasus, but it also extended the scope of short weekend trips, earlier limited to the suburban railway system, to a diameter of 200 to 250 km around the urban centres.[44] This meant that many car owners, frequently with their families, travelled to the popular destinations on their own. Even if the latter lacked the most basic facilities to accommodate them, beginning from parking lots. This should not come as a surprise, as the central parts of many Soviet spas were off limits for motor traffic since the times there had been no private traffic. The basic aim was the preservation of tranquillity around the medical facilities.[45]

Willingly or unwillingly, many car drivers joined the stream of so-called "wild tourists" in the quest for a more or less improvised holiday accommodation. They stopped somewhere in the hinterland of the spas or coastal resorts, to put up their tents or simply to sleep in their cars. As a result, all kinds of improvised camping sites sprang up.[46] Anapa, for example, counted three official parking lots in 1968, which allegedly catered for some 60.000 motor tourists during the 1968 season, while there were no less than 58 improvised sites (*gorodki*), partly on the territories of pioneer camps, counted in the same year. On the eastern shores of the Black Sea the influx of summer vacationers swelled with the arrival of weekenders from southern Russian and Ukrainian towns. This caused additional strains in the resorts beyond "wild camping," a these tourists poured on the overcrowded beaches and had to be supplied with food and water.[47] Similar tendencies could be observed along the Baltic coast, particular in the vicinities of Riga.[48]

Strains for the resorts were considerable. To take the example of Anapa again, this had off season been a small town with some 50.000 inhabitants. Up to 150.000 additional visitors frequented the town on weekends during high season. 75 cafes, restaurants and canteens run during the high season offered altogether 5,700 places, a ridiculous number given the average Soviet citizen's habit of lunching and dining in factory run canteens. The local bread baking factory was unable to meet the demand and some 20 tons of bread had to be brought from Novorossiisk on a daily basis. Among the deficit articles in local shops a 1969 report listed fruits, potatoes, oil, pasta, tea, confectionary, tobacco, matches, shoes and swimwear.[49]

As a rule, infrastructure—the supply with water, food, electricity and communication—in resort towns was either rudimentary or non-existent. Anapa's water supply could cover only the needs for one third of the organised tourists during high season, to the result that water was available only in limited quantities in some parts of the town at a time. The building of a water pipeline over some forty kilometers from the Kuban river did not materialise before the mid-1970s, and the health resort did not dispose of a working sewage system during the whole 1960s.[50]

For the tourists themselves this meant extraordinarily primitive living conditions, which included either endless queuing for food and drinks or self-catering, and sleeping in their cars or in parks with limited if any access to public conveniences like toilets or douches. The situation was not much different if they chose to stay on one of the parking space managed by the municipality (from 1975 the Health resort council). These were as a rule improvised facilities, without trees or shade, located far from the town centre and providing little or no amenities at all. Water supply was breaking down regularly, and waste was collected only accidentally. There was very little incentive indeed to use them and to pay the tariffs of 30 kopecks per night.[51] The few public toilets in Anapa were considered of being "in an unsatisfactory sanitary condition" by the local authorities themselves, and public baths and douches were practically absent, even on the beaches.[52] Against this backdrop it is not entirely surprising that epidemics flared up regularly, and viral or bacterial infections hit organised and unorganised tourists without much of a difference.[53]

With the rising numbers of motor tourists, municipalities and local tourism and health resort councils faced a dilemma: If they blocked the popular destinations for motor tourists, they were contradicting the established discourse on tourism, which had, from the early days juxtaposed the "inclusive" character of Soviet tourism and the allegedly exclusively "bourgeois" privilege on travel and recreation in the West. Ironically, under the conditions of "developed socialism," restricting car owners would have meant annoying a by Soviet standards influential and well-to-do clientele. In the case of Anapa, the local militia above all pressed for restrictions on motor traffic. The militia likewise insisted on the necessity for all unorganised visitors to register upon arrival in their holiday destinations, including a registration of their cars in 1965.[54] Pointing at the allegedly high number of road accidents, the *nachalnik militsii* demanded in 1967 to ban or at least to limit the circulation and the parking of private cars and motorcycles. Anapa's town council indeed issued a ban for private parking within the city centre in February 1967 and extended it to the zone adjacent to the beaches in April the same year. Wild camping on the beach was also interdicted.[55] In other words, cars were deviated from the centre of the resort, and this practice was continued well into the 1970s.[56]

However, once the local authorities basically accepted the right of Soviet citizens to motorised tourism, they also recognised that bans alone would be of limited effectiveness. Whether or not motor tourists were indeed seen as affluent "customers," the local Health resort council and the municipality decided to offer improve services to this group of tourists from the mid 1960s. In financial terms, putting up a few barracks or a toilet and washroom would not have been extremely costly, yet clearing large, non built-upon lots proved to be much more difficult within Anapa. The main reason was that both municipality and Health resort council were interested in allotting such building spaces to resourceful 'developers,' i.e. Soviet enterprises and institutions who could in return be charged for the maintenance and extension of local infrastructure. In Anapa, for example, the lion's share in the cost for building water supplies and canalisation jointly came from the trade unions (through the Health resort and tourist councils) and the enterprises running facilities there.[57]

If it was difficult to build camping grounds or other accommodations for motor tourists in town, other problems arose when they were located to further afield: In this case, water supplies and sewage systems would have to be built, and waste collection and regular public transport would have to be organised at significantly higher costs.[58] Hence the building of such sites occurred on the plans by the mid-1960s, with a view on the introduction of the five day work week in 1968. In Anapa, however, they never received high priority. Much remained improvisation, like the mentioned re-dedication of the ring road's verges as encampments or the temporary installation of a motor camping on the territory of the town's only tourism facility, the tourist base. The creation of more substantial camping sites in the vicinities of Anapa dragged on until the late 1970s.[59]

Indeed, local authorities lingered between both options—restriction or accommodation of motor tourism. Yet my impression is that they were quite hesitant to resort simply to the application of "commando-administrative measures." This became very obvious when large scale epidemics, including cholera, ravaged the Soviet south, for example in 1970. Central and local authorities firstly tried to pass over the spread of disease in silence. Only when rumours began to spread and people showed first panic reactions, a number of Crimean newspapers began to address the issue openly, quoting experts aiming to calm down the vacationers.[60] Due to these politics of disinformation, the actual number of vacationers, organised and non-organised, seemed not to have decreased significantly in 1970 on the Crimean peninsula. On Russia's Caucasian coast, on the contrary, quite a number of facilities, like a motor tourist base in Dzhubga, were closed for much of August and September. The numbers of organised tourists slumped here in 1970s, and the authorities noted a lower number of unorganised visiting the following year.[61]

The spread of epidemics resulted in a renewed discussion of whether or not the influx of wild tourist to the resorts could and should be capped. A number of Black Sea resorts decreed such a cap. At the same time it was obvious that implementation depended much on the municipalities' ability to enforce adherence to the registration system (*propiska*), which in practice was widely ignored by private landlords who had been allowed to rent out room to non-organised tourists since the mid-1960s.[62] However, a general discussion of representatives from local and regional health councils which was held in Moscow at the height of epidemic, on 7 September 1970, showed that simply curtailing the influx of motor tourists was no longer acceptable even for beleaguered tourism managers: With reference to the Soviet constitution and its 'right to rest,' the plenum criticised a decree authored by the USSR's Council of Ministers which foresaw the "limitation of access to the health resorts." While the participants of the plenum acknowledged that channelling of the seasonal migrations of Soviet tourists was desirable, they rejected any open ban on unorganised tourism. Interestingly, the attending head of the trade unions, Poltoranov, and the chairmen of the central council for health resorts, Kozolov, bowed to these protests and promised to negotiate a less draconic formulation with the Council of Ministers.[63]

CONCLUSION

Using examples from the fields of family vacation and motor tourism, I discussed shifting notions of what was regarded as acceptable tourist conduct in the USSR. I interpret these shifts as results of ongoing processes of negotiations between the population and regime during the late Soviet period. Such negotiations were 'conducted' through specific Soviet channels of communication, like written complaints or letters to the press, later also opinion surveys, to which the regime, in its attempt to placate the population, paid increasing attention.

At the same time, I hope to demonstrate that the "bargaining position" of Soviet tourists differed in both instances. In the case of family vacations, the more or less tacit re-evaluation of the family as a primary agent of socialisation under Stalin had not been "implemented" in many other fields of social policies, form housing to vacationing. It was left to Stalin's successors to improve the situation, which Khrushchev did both with his housing programme and his decision to make "organised" vacations accessible to the broader population. The increasing acceptance of family holidays may be seen as a 'collateral damage' in this process. Sociological surveys and quest of 'wild' tourists to travel as families provide ample evidence for the growing demand, which was accepted increasing by the ideologues and rejected on practical grounds by the managers of organised Soviet tourism. As a matter of fact, Soviet vacationing remained in practice geared towards the individual worker's holidays on the one hand, and the peer group in from of the collective or age group, in case of children, on the other.

Individual auto-mobilisation and motor tourism, for their part, emerged as a societal phenomenon only after the regime gave up its blockade in the early 1960s and private cars became a more common sight. Cars provided citizens with hitherto unknown scope of individual mobility, even if the latter was still severely limited by the lack of infrastructure. With renewed vigour, motor tourism confronted the Soviet tourism managers with an old dilemma, that of desired mobilisation versus necessary control from above. This dilemma had become evident as early as the 1920s, when Soviet tourist functionaries had tried to mobilise workers for tourism in the first place, and had been worried about too much independence of the travellers, on the other. This was amply illustrated in the discourses that evolved around the allegedly "proletarian" model of *samodiatel'nyi* or self-organised grass-root tourism, whose collective character and full integration into the Soviet project of conquering space has always been emphasised.

Against this backdrop, the integration of family vacations and motor tourism into the tourist agenda created contradictions and ambiguities that opened up spaces for deviant interpretations. Indeed, references to and individual re-interpretations of the official Soviet discourse in the long run influenced, modify and diversified the official diction as far as tourism as particular Soviet achievement was concerned. Beyond that, such re-negotiations could have tangible repercussions on the current practices in vacationing, too. In the case of family vacations, the expectancy of citizens travelling as families changed and put tourism managers under considerable strain. Within the limits of the Soviet bureaucratic planning system solutions were slow to realise. At the end of the day, travelling families had comparatively little leverage other than to insist, through their sheer physical presence, on an adjustment of the practice to the promises of the public discourse. Like in the sphere of consumption, many of these promises were not redeemed even if the regime diverted more and more investment into the production of food and commodities, and the ultimate outcome was disappointing.

Compared to the travelling families, motorised tourists where much more independent, hence agency lay much more with the citizens / tourists themselves. Although frequently straining the capacities to the limits and thus a nuisance to municipalities and local tourism managers, Soviet authorities were obviously very reluctant to ban or marginalise automobile tourism. Again they opted rather for an accommodation of popular demand. The case of Anapa, however, clearly demonstrates the limits of Soviet tourist infrastructure to cope with the dynamic development of individual and motorised tourism.

In both cases I tend to interpret the developments in Soviet tourism as a part of a larger negotiation process in the late Soviet Union which resulted in significant shifts in the perceptions of what was seen as public and private. As a result of such negotiations, agendas like the right to an individual family life or the right to individual mobility were not just tacitly accepted, as the classical formula of Brezhnev's "little deal" would have had it. On the contrary, they were increasingly incorporated into the official definition of what "Soviet tourism" meant thus became "in principle" enforceable in dealings with Soviet institutions.

NOTES

1. "The tasks of the health resorts is not the yielding returns, it is exclusively the repair of the toilers' health." Deputy Mogilevich at the Fifth Congress of the Soviet Health Administration, 1924. Quoted in D. Gribanov, "'Rol' vserussiiskikh zdravotdelov v stanovlenii i razvitii kurortnogo dela v SSSR (1917–1925)," *Voprosy kurortologii, fizioterapii i lechebnoi fizicheskoi kul'tury* [hereafter *Voprosy kurortologii*] 6 (1962): 553–4, quote 554.

2. Igor Orlov, Elena Iurchikova, *Massovyi turizm v stalinskoi povsednevnosti*, Moscow: 2010 provide a detailed descriptive summary of primary sources preserved in Russian archives.

3. I have discussed this in some depth elsewhere, cf. Christian Noack, "A Mighty Weapon in the Class War: Proletarian Values, Tourism and Mass Mobilisation in Stalin's Time", *Journal of Modern European History* 10,2 (2012) 233-256; Christian Noack, "Building Tourism in One Country?: The Sovietization of Vacationing, 1917-41", in Eric G. Zuelov (ed.) *Touring Beyond the Nation : A Transnational Approach to European Tourism History* (Farnham: Ashgate, 2011) 171-195.

4. Diane P. Koenker, "Whose Right to Rest? Contesting the Family Vacation in the Postwar Soviet Union," Comparative Studies in Society and History 51,2 (2009) 401-425, quote 414.

5. In 1989, 51.8 percent of Soviet citizens spent their holidays at home, while only 10.4 percent wished to do so. 28.3 percent visited relatives or friends (12.1 percent wished to). In all categories referring to organized tourism, the number of people actually embarking on these forms of recreation was much lower than the number of those who would actually have wished to do so. *Okhrana zdorov'ia v SSSR* (Moscow 1990), quoted in Monika Henningsen, *Der Freizeit- und Fremdenverkehr in der (ehemali-*

gen) Sowjetunion unter besonderer Berücksichtigung des Baltischen Raumes , (Frankfurt: Peter Lang, 1994) 85-87.

6. Koenker, "Whose Right to Rest?", 415.

7. Interestingly, the terminology was quite unstable in those early days and lingered between "mat' idit'ia" (Mother and child, collective singular), "mat' irebënok" (Mother and [one] child, singular) or, less frequently, "roditeli s det'mi" (Parents with children).

8. Archivnyi otdel administratsii goroda-kurortaAnapa (AOAGKA) f. 300, d. 190, ll. 57-58 (1967, quote); d. 197, l. 82 (1972).

9. N.G. Sarkisova, "Iz opyta raboty sanatoriev dlia materei s det'mi", *Voprosy kurortologii* 3 (1968) 212-215. The author insisted on separate accommodation and boarding within the facilities, though.

10. GARF f. R 9493, op. d. 1664, l. 35-36 (1972) deals with parents complaints about this practice. No less than 5,000 private beds were provided for patients of the health resort for example in Anapa in 1975, AOAGKA f. 300 d. 305, l. 99 (1975).

11. B.A. Grushin, *Chetyre zhizni Rossii v zerkale obshestvennogo mneniia. Epokha Brezhneva chast' 1,* (Moscow: Progress-Traditsiia, 2003) 136-176.

12. In extracts for example in V.I. Azar, Ėkonimica I organizatsiia turizma (metodologicheskie voprosy), (Moscow: Ėkomonika, 1972): V.I. Azar, Otdykh trudiashchikhsia SSSR (Moscow: Statistika, 1972).

13. Gosudarstvennyi arkhiv Rossiiskoi federatsii (GARF), f. R 9493, op. 8, d. 4, l. 14, quoted in Koenker: "Whose Right to Rest?" 420.

14. See for example Literaturnaia gazeta, 28.6.1972, 12; Literaturnaia gazeta, 28.12.1977, 13; Rabotnitsa 10/1985, 22; Bernd Knabe, "Der Urlaub des Sowjetbürgers," *Osteuropa* 29 (1979), 300-310, 371-382, particularly 373-374.

15. GARF f. R 9493, op. 8, d. 698, ll. 108-109.For similar arguments see Koenker: "Whose Right to Rest?" 418, note 81.

16. Gosudarstvennyi arkhiv Krasnodarskogo kraia (GAKK) f. R 1472, d. 420, l. 156-157.

17. GARF f. R 9493, op. 8, d. 698, l. 20-42, 107-108.

18. Ibid. l. 198-199. For a similar discussion on the regional level see GAKK f. R 1427, l. 156-157, 171 (1965).

19. Poster, Russian State Library Collection. See also: "Rezul'tat—zdorov'e", *Turist* 1 (1978) 16.

20. GAKK f. R 1624 op.1, d. 314, l. 19. See also a discussion on this issue in Moscow in April 1963, GARF f. R 9493 op. 8, d. 428, l. 111.

21. GARF f. R 9520, op. 1 d. 1503, l.6 (1971).

22. GARF f. R 9520, op. 1 d. 750, l. 21-22 (1965)

23. GARF f. R. 5451 op. 24, d. 2252, ll. 201-201, d. 2628, l. 196; GAKK f. R 1472, op. 1, d. 420, ll. 156-157.

24. GARF f. R 9493, op. 8. d. 1981, l. 197.

25. AOAGKA f. 300, d. 405 (1978). "Puteshestvuet zem'ia: Zhenja i maksim" *Turist* 1 (1978) 16; See also photo-feature "Vykhodnoi den' Aleshi Trubnikova" *Turist* 4 (1966) 24-25 about a three year old fellow-traveller in a backpack.

26. The manual *Turistskie marshruty* from 1967, see Koenker, "Whose Right to Rest?", p. 422, note103.

27. An inspection of the motor tourist base "Vysokii bereg" in Anapa in 1970 established that many families with children sojourned there, yet only four of them had vouchers for children as well. See also Koenker, "Whose Right to Rest", 422.

28. In the Soviet recreational system a *pansionat* was a sanatoria without a proper medical department.

29. AOAGKA f. 300, d. 190, l. 57-58.

30. AOAGKA f. 300, d. 575, l. 269-274; d. 735, l. 97; d. 745, l. 120; d. 791, l. 77.

31. GAKK, f. R 1624, op. 1, d. 184, ll. 15; d. 186, l. 21. These tourist trains were still run during the 1970s, see GAKK f. R 1624, op. 1, d. 549, ll. 84-85; op. 2, d. 12, l. 2;

"Puteshestvuite na poezdakh", *Turist* 2 (1968) 10-12; "V puti—romantik. Reportazh iz turistskogo poezda", *Turist* 10 (1976) 10-11.

32. *Turist*11 (1968) 24-25; "Obyknovennyi passazhirskii poezd", *Literaturnaia gazeta*15 (1970) 12-13; "Krugly stol LG: passazhir i poezd", Literaturnaia gazeta 15 (1978) 10.

33. AOAGKA f. 300, d. 399, l. 9 (1976). Cf. Popov's complaint quoted in part one.

34. AOAGKA f. 190, d. 163, l. 333-335 (1967); f. 300, d. 21, l. 118, 131 (1966); d. 44, l. 133 (1967), d. 60, l. 147-148 (1968); d. 80, l. 84 (1969); d. 186, l. 52 (1970); d. 405, l. 66 (1977); d. 455, l. 122 (1978). Similar problems occurred with flight tickets, see AOAGKA f. 300, d. 60 (1968).

35. GARF f. R 9520, d. 1051, l. 1-166 (1966). See also "Avtomobil v karmane: chto takoe avtostop?" *Turist* 5 (1966) 18.

36. "Vesennyj dialog", *Turist* 4 (1966) 26; cf. cartoons like "Bylo l,' ne bylo l'", *Turist* 9 (1966) 19.

37. Sections for motor tourism

38. V. Cherkassov, " Korolevy benzokolonok", *Pravda* 5 August 1979;

39. *Turist* 4 (1966) featured a map with all filling stations in the European part of the USSR. For the Baltic republics see the maps "Latvia", *Turist* 9 (1968) 18-19; "Litva", *Turist* 10 (1968) 20-21; "Estoniia", *Turist 11* (1968) 22-23.

40. Detailed discussion in Noack, "A Mighty Weapon . . . " 238-242.

41. L. Prilutskii "Kempingy, bazy, komfort" *Turist* 2 (1966)

42. In Anapa, for example, the green verge of the circular road was considered as a site for a future camping for motor tourists. AOAGKA f. 190, d. 214, l. 24 (1969).

43. GARF f. R 5451, op. 68, d. 499, l. 76 (1973); AOAGKA f. 300, d. 109, no pagination (1970).

44. Lewis Siegelbaum, Cars for Comrades. The Life of the Soviet Automobile (Ithaca: Cornell University Press, 2008) 235-251.

45. AOAGKA f. 300, d. 60, l. 28 (1968)

46. Cf. Christian Noack, "Coping with the Tourist: Planned and "Wild" Mass Tourism on the Soviet Black Sea Coast", Anne Gorsuch, Diane Koenker (eds.) *Turizm. The Russian and East European Tourist under Capitalism and Socialism* (Ithaca: Cornell, 2006) 281-304, here 294-295, 302.

47. During the 1970 season on average 90.000 unorganised visitors per month came to Anapa, of which 24.000 originated from the Kuban district. AOAGKA f. 300, d. 109, l. 14 (1970). The militia complained about "several hundred additional vehicles over the weekends", AOAGKA f. 300, d. 80, l. 63 (1969).

48. Christian Noack, "'Probably you have heard about all this. . . '" Baltic Seaside Resorts as Soviet Tourist Destinations", *Nordost-Archiv* 20 (2011): 199-222.

49. AOAGKA f. 300, d. 60, l. 14-15 (1968); d. 80, l. 61 (1969); d. 143, l. 9-10 (1971); d. 232, l. 51 (1973).

50. AOAGKA f. 190, d. 164, l. 432 (1968); f. 300, d. 4, l. 34 (1964); d. 60, l. 32, 86, 143-144 (1968); d. 80, l. 64 (1969); d. 109 without pagination (1970); d. 197, l.39 (1972); d. 164, l. 6 (1975).

51. AOAGKA f. 190, d. 165, l. 161 (1968); f. 300, d. 60, l. 31-32 (1968).

52. AOAGKA f. 300, d. 60, l. 32 (1968).

53. For cases of limited epidemics in several health facilities and localities see AOAGKA f. 300, d. 80, l. 77 (1969); d. 197, l.91 (1972). Due to the sometime primitive equipment and unprofessional supervision pioneer camps seem to have been hit quite frequently, AOAGKA f. 300, d. 254, l. 10 (1973). All the Health resorts council's staff was vaccinated against cholera as a preventive measure in 1975. AOAGKA f. 300, d. 310a, l. 167 (1975).

54. AOAGKA f. 190, d. 131, l. 61-63 (1965).

55. AOAGKA f. 190, d. 163, l. 143, 362, 362 (1967): f. 300, d. 38, l. 39 (1967).

56. AOAGKA f. 300, d. 271, l 40-41 (1974).

57. AOAGKA f. 190, d. 131, l. 229 (1965); f. 300, d. 164, l. 6-11 (1971-75).

58. AOAGKA f. 300, d. 109, without pagination (1970).

59. AOAGKA f. 190, d. 163, l. 352, 361-362 (1967); d. 214, l. 23-25 (1969); f. 300, d. 60, l. 34 (1968); d. 109, l. 14 (1970); d. 503, l. 7 (1978).

60. "Idet remont uskorennyi", *Kurortnaia gazeta*(Yalta) 7 August 1970; "Ovoshchi i frukty dolzhny byt' chistimi", *Krymskaia Pravda* 10 September 1970; "Infektsii—nadezhnyi zaslon", *Kurortnaia gazeta* 25 August 1970; "Reidi sanitarnykh patrulei", *Kurortnaia gazeta* 8 September 1970;"Vibrion v zapade", *Kurortnaia gazeta* 9 September 1970. I am indebted to Aleksei Popov (Simferopol') who has made these materials available to me.

61. GARF f. R 9493, op. 8, d. 1527, l. 30 (1971); f. R 9520, op.1, d. 1503, l. 247 (1971); GAKK f. R 1624, d. 583, l. 1-20.

62. GARF f. R 9493, op. 8, d. 1527, l. 28-30 (1971). For private rooms see Christian Noack, "Coping with the Tourist", 295.

63. GARF f. R 9493, op. 8, d. 1351, l. 27, 30 (1970).

FIVE

Everything Was Over before It Was No More

Decaying Civilization in Late Stagnation Cinema[1]

Andrey Shcherbenok

The impetus behind this article is the striking contradiction between the reported contemporaneous perception of the stagnation sociopolitical world as static, stable, and potentially everlasting[2] and the impression of that world conveyed by many films of that era, especially by those that acquired cult status among late-Soviet intelligentsia. In Stagnation-era films[3] set in their historical present we regularly encounter a decaying civilization that is undergoing a profound crisis with uncertain outcomes. If anything, the USSR in these films does not appear rock-solid and permanent. To paraphrase John Barth, Stagnation cinema can be called "the cinema of exhaustion,"[4] except that what is exhausted is not so much the cinematic medium itself as the social reality it inhabits and represents.

One can start with the medium, though, as it does not remain unaffected by the aura of decay. For one thing, Stagnation films have a very particular "look": one can usually recognize a film of the period from a random still frame, even when the shot has no identifiably Soviet details. This is not true of a random shot from a Thaw film, which can be easily mistaken for European New Wave, or a Stalinist film, which often resembles Hollywood. One thing that allows for immediate recognition of a Stagnation film is the color scheme, an unforgettable greenish palette that one does not find in Stalinist or Thaw color films. On the technical level, this may result from the characteristics of late Soviet color film stock produced by the Svema factory in Shostka. However, even if unintentional on the part of directors and cameramen, this color scheme become a signature mark of Stagnation cinema that cannot but influence the perception of these films' depicted, "diegetic" world. With these colors, even a sunny summer day in the countryside appears rather drab, to say nothing of the seasons and settings that Stagnation cinema favors more.

The choice of the weather is another peculiarity of Stagnation cinema. In striking contrast to, in particular, Stalinist cinema, in which it is almost always summer, Stagnation cinema prefers late fall and wet, dirty winter. Even when the fall is early—as in *Vacation in September* (Vitaly Melnikov, 1979)—it is going to rain miserably through the day when the main action takes place.

Another contributor to the drab appearance of the Stagnation cinema's diegetic world is the choice of settings. Stagnation films happen to be very realistic in terms of showing standard apartments, ordinary means of transportation, and cheap mass-market decorations. Such ordinary settings definitely look grim for today's viewer—this viewer, after all, has been taught by Hollywood and post-Soviet Russian cinema to perceive glamorized, brighter-than-life cinematic reality as the unmarked cinematic norm. However, they should also have looked grim to contemporaneous viewers who were aware of Hollywood and European cinema and had seen a lot of Stalinist films which tended to choose (or build) much better looking streets and houses for their settings.

Not only are Stagnation cinema's settings ordinary, they are peculiarly dilapidated. In this, Stagnation films contrast most strongly with Thaw films that were made just a decade or two earlier. *Khruschevki*[5] in Thaw films may be small and crowded, but they are—and look—brand new. The same is true of the streets—in the 1960s, even when we see a town under construction, some kind of Radiozavodsk in the middle of the taiga,[6] we, of course, do not see tidy streets with lawns and flowers, as we would have in a Stalinist film,[7] but at least the freshly built streets have brand new pavement. In other words, Khruschev's construction boom is very much shown as such, and the older Stalinist buildings in Thaw films do not display many signs of wear, either.

In Stagnation films it is all different. Although more new square meters per year were built in late Stagnation period than under Khruschev, judging by films alone you would never guess it. Of course, *The Irony of Fate* (Eldar Ryazanov, 1975) shows you freshly built residential areas because it needs them for the plot, but as you zoom in to these apartment blocks in many other films their newness evaporates. *Brezhnevky* in Stagnation films mostly look as if they have already survived the prolonged post-Soviet infrastructural underfunding. Even when a family in a film moves into a new apartment, as in the aforementioned *Vacation in September* or *The Old New Year* (Ardashnikov, Efremov, 1980) (here the title is, of course, quite telling), it does not look new. In Stagnation cinema buildings are dilapidated inside and outside, the asphalt is cracked, and the busses are dirty and rusty. Even the *Zhiguli* cars, which were being mass-produced at the time, manage to look remarkably worn out.

This is not to say that there is no goodlooking or even glamorous housing in Stagnation cinema; there definitely is. But when it does appear, it is not as a detail of the background but as an important theme. Pristine looking urban environment does not surround characters—it is being actively created through the effort that drives the story. Yuliy Raisman's 1984 film *The Time of Desires* is a clear case in point. The film's heroine applies a lot of energy to move to a luxurious apartment in the "quiet center" of Moscow, forcing her husband to abandon his steady lifestyle. In the end of the film her husband suddenly dies as she is shopping for a new chandelier—a clear retribution for her excessive materialism. The apartment that the heroine acquires is neat and freshly renovated, but it is located in a classical Stalinist building—paradoxically, the desire to live in a nondilapidated environment is directed to the past, not to the future.

The characters in Stagnation films, just as the walls that surround them, all have a history, which tells. They are hopelessly stuck in problems that emerged in the past but cannot be resolved in the present. A person experiencing a midlife crisis is this cinema's paradigmatic protagonist. A male hero is often stuck in one or several relationships that he can neither develop nor abandon; his work has stopped satisfying him, but he cannot think of anything better to do. The same is true of female heroines, who either suffer because they do not have a family, as in *A Lonely Woman Is Looking for a Relationship* (Vyacheslav Krishtofovich, 1986) or, if they do, they realize that this is not what they really want in life, as in *The Wife Left* (Dinara Asanova, 1979). The urge to change something combined with an inability to act leads to hysterical, erratic behavior, the best examples of which are Yankovsky's character in *Dream Flights* (Roman Balayan, 1982) and Basilashvilli's character in *The Autumn Marathon* (Georgy Danelia, 1979).

If the absence of a resolution connotes permanence, than this cinema *is* about "foreverness"—and, indeed, the circular composition in melodramas like *The Winter Cherry* (Igor Maslennikov, 1985) does suggest some kind of a repetition compulsion, as does the failed suicide of Oleg Dal's character in *Vacation in September*. Nevertheless, we do not normally think of hysteria as something potentially everlasting, even if it is incurable—the temporality of hysteria is that of exhaustion, not stability. In the case of any particular character exhaustion might lead to resignation and hence the maintenance of the status quo. However, when such an individual situation is universalized and repeated from one film to another, it becomes a social symptom; late Soviet society at large does not seem to be able to overcome the crisis, to which the collapsing environment conveys intersubjective historical directionality.

The inability to resolve vexing existential dilemmas is explicitly connected to the crisis of the late Soviet value system and, by extension, the discourses that could uphold it. Such crisis is nothing new for a Soviet screen, but it takes different forms in different epochs. In Stalinist cinema of the 1930s the subject can encounter the limit of the ideological field and experience the impossibility of ideological totality.[8] For example, the subject can stumble upon the contradictions in the Party line and find herself unable to make sense of the Party's policy. In Stalinist cinema, however, such encounters do not undermine the ideological discourse but are used to reinterpellate the subject into the antinomic Stalinist ideology and help her to actively engage antagonistic social reality.[9]

Thaw cinema, which is marked by what Aleksandr Prokhorov terms "inherited discourse," is characterized by a paradoxical situation where the (inherited) Stalinist value system is still there but the official discourse that would uphold it is no longer functional.[10] An early example of this situation is Mikhail Shveitser's *Another's Kinsfolk* (1955) where the protagonist discovers that his values of collective solidarity and common good do not appeal to his young wife's materialistic and egotistic relatives in the village. In a striking reversion of the Stalinist collectivization narrative, the hero is unable to authoritatively defend his position and escapes with his wife to the city. However, the city in Thaw cinema is not a bastion of true socialist beliefs, either. Marlen Khutsiev's *I Am Twenty* (1964) has a highly symptomatic scene where a young scoundrel played by Andrey Tarkovsky mocks the toast for the popular suffering during the Great Patriotic War. What is symptomatic is not the mockery itself but the fact that no one can find authoritative words to counter it—instead, one girl slaps Tarkovsky's character, producing an inarticulate groan. This episode perfectly exemplifies the combination of a continuing belief in Soviet ideological tenets and the perceived inability to justify them discursively.

What, then, happens to Soviet values during Stagnation? Alexei Yurchak writes about the ritualization of the "authoritative discourse"—the obligatory political discourse of the Party leaders, *Pravda* front-page articles, and rank-and-file activists. What is important for Yurchak's argument is that the automatization of this discourse does not undermine the belief in socialism. As the authoritative discourse loses its constative meaning and becomes performative, it functions to create and sustain more or less heterotopic social spaces, from the Komsomol cell in a workplace to all kinds of clubs, studios, and informal venues where people can do what they call "meaningful work." This "meaningful work," although displaced in relation to the "authoritative discourse," may very well display genuinely communist values and aspirations.[11]

One striking difference between the Thaw and the Stagnation in Prokhorov's and Yurchak's accounts, respectively, is different perception of the shared disfunctionality of the authoritative discourse. In the Thaw, the lack of the constative meaning in this discourse was perceived as a sign of crisis and led to (ultimately futile) attempts to reform it, as in the famous "return to Lenin" movement. In the Stagnation era the lack of constative meaning becomes neutral. People during the Thaw were deeply disturbed by their inability to find appropriate expression to their socialist beliefs; people during Stagnation, apparently, had little problem preserving their socialist values without the assistance of the authoritative discourse.

There is, indeed, a great deal of this neutral, ritualized, performative authoritative discourse in Stagnation cinema. It fills the background of the diegetic world, from street slogans to sound bites from the radio and the TV. It works to form a realistic background to action precisely due to its lack of meaning, just as redundant descriptions in *Madame Bovary* analyzed by Roland Barthes produce the "reality effect" because they fall out of the structure of meaning.[12]

Nevertheless, there is a strong sense that the socialist value system was far from being as impervious to the semiotic decomposition of the authoritative discourse as Yurchak's account might suggest. In the (rare) cases when the authoritative discourse comes to the foreground and is given a constative meaning, as in the worlds of an elderly schoolteacher from Gleb Panfilov's *The Theme* (1979, released 1986), it not only misses the concrete living reality of the characters but works to additionally underscore the deep ideological crisis they are undergoing. Unlike in Mikhail Kalatozov's *The Cranes Are Flying* (1957) where it was clear that Boris is right to volunteer to the front, even though his father mocks the grand words that normally accompany this decision in the official parlance, nothing is clear any more in *The Theme*, in or beyond discursive expression.

Unlike what the model of the performative creation of meaningful spaces would suggest, the "nonauthoritative" colloquial discourse of cinematic characters does not strike one as self-sufficient and freely developing on its own terms. In all the Stagnation films I mentioned above we encounter the symbolic lack that is very much perceived as such and effectively blocks the possibility of "meaningful work" or any other meaningful activity for that matter. One scene in *Dream Flights* where Oleg Yankovsky's character, Sergey, is trying to get a leave of absence from his boss, is particularly emblematic in this respect. Sergey says that he needs to get off work to meet his old mother at the railway station. What is most important in our perspective is that Sergey does not use the authoritative discourse; instead, he speaks like a "normal person" and appeals to very meaningful socialist values—compassion, friendship, respect for the elders—which, presumably, remained intact through the Stagnation. In reality, Sergey only wants to see his young mistress, so all his sincere appeals are just as fake and devoid of constative meaning as the radio broadcast we hear at the background.

Since Sergey does not believe what he proclaims with such an air of sincerity, his discourse partially resembles *stiob*, a kind of ironic reenactment of the official discourse. It is different from *stiob*, however, in that what is being reenacted is not the formulaic authoritative discourse of the Party but rather its "second level," the "meaningful" socialist values. Sergey does not "mock" a speech about socialist solidarity or the unity of the public and the private; instead, he appeals to the (socialist) humanity of his boss, who, unlike a capitalist boss, is expected to care about his employee's personal life and problems outside of work. These "genuinely socialist" values of friendship and compassion are located precisely on the level of "meaningful interaction" that should not be affected by the ritualization of the authoritative discourse. Yet in the film they *are*. Moreover, since Sergey is extremely sympathetic and provides an undisputable center of spectatorial identification throughout the film, there is no alternative, better ideological standpoint that film would position as a possible way out of the existential deadlock. The social world in *Dream Flights*, just as in many other cult Stagnation films, is portrayed as decaying at an alarming rate.

Here, of course, one has to admit that this is all "just cinema" which does not have to accurately portray the state of consciousness of its real historical audience. One can also observe that the age of these films' central characters, as well as the age of the viewers who most admired them, is older than that of "the last Soviet generation," analyzed by Yurchak, and this last generation might have been more impervious to the sense of crisis than people ten years their seniors. Nevertheless, the cult status of the prolific cinematic tradition of doom and despondency in precisely the intelligentsia milieu that admittedly perceived the Stagnation world as everlasting raises a lot of interesting questions about the nature of political beliefs, social values, and the workings of ideology that need further theoretically informed consideration.

NOTES

1. This chapter has been previously published in *Novoe Literaturnoe Obozrenie*, 2013, No. 123 as "Tsivilizatsionnyi krizis v kino pozdnego zastoia."

2. This perception was analyzed in Alexei Yurchak, *Everything Was Forever Until It Was No More: The Last Soviet Generation* (Princeton and Oxford: Princeton University Press, 2005).

3. Here and below I will use the phrase "Stagnation cinema" but will mostly write about late Stagnation cinema (the late 1970s and the first half of the 1980s). While there are earlier examples of the phenomena I am going to describe, the aspects of the Stagnation cinema that interest me here only became fully manifest in the second half of the era.

4. John Bart, "The Literature of Exhaustion" in his *Friday Book: Essays and Other Non-Fiction* (London: The Johns Hopkins University Press, 1984), 62–76.

5. A colloquial word for Khrushchev-era residential apartment buildings contrasted with *Stalinki* on one end and *Brezhnevky* on the other.

6. *Two Sundays* (Vladimir Shredel, 1963).

7. A Stalinist film could show you dirt and barracks of a building site, as in *Komsomolsk* (Sergei Gerasimov, 1938), but it makes sure to show you the brand new city that emerges out of it in the end.

8. On the (im)possibility of ideological totality, see Ernesto Laclau and Chantal Mouffe, *Hegemony and Socialist Strategy* (London and New York: Verso, 1985), and Slavoj Žižek, "The Spectre of Ideology," in *Mapping Ideology*, ed. Slavoj Žižek (London and New York: Verso, 1994), 1–33.

9. For an example, see my analysis of Fridrikh Ermler's *The Peasants* (1935) in "The Enemy, the Communist, and Ideological Closure in Soviet Cinema on the Eve of the Great Terror," *Kritika: Explorations in Russian and Eurasian History* 10, 4 (Fall 2009): 753–77.

10. Aleksandr Prokhorov, *Unasledovannyi diskurs: paradigm stalinskoi kultury v literature i kinematografe ottepeli* (St. Petersburg: Akademicheskii proekt, 2008).

11. Yurchak, *Everything Was Forever*.

12. Roland Barthes, *The Rustle of Language* (Berkeley and Los Angeles: University of California Press, 1989).

Part 2

The Soviet Union and the West

Exchange, Imagination, and Competition

SIX

Stagnation or Not?

The Brezhnev Leadership and East-West Interaction

Sari Autio-Sarasmo

The era of Leonid Brezhnev's leadership (1964–1982) is often defined as an era of "stagnation" where the term was connected to the economic downturn and its ramifications. This definition is inherently connected with the final years of the Brezhnev leadership (1973–1982). According to Philip Hanson, the Soviet economy had already started to slow down in the mid-1970s, which was acutely felt in the Soviet managerial and professional middle class. According to their everyday experiences, the economy was stagnating or falling, which turned the economic optimism of the 1950s and 1960s into economic pessimism in the 1970s.[1] On a macro-level, the feeling of stagnation was strengthened when the Soviet Union compared its performance in economy, science, and military capacity to the other superpower, the United States.[2] The experienced "stagnation" was not only based on the impression of the economy slowing down. The atmosphere was fortified also by several other factors, such as changes in the international politics of the Cold War and a change in intrabloc relations. The Brezhnev period, especially the occupation of Czechoslovakia in 1968, has been seen as an end of the era of "cosmic utopianism" that had emerged in the Soviet Union and the whole socialist bloc during the Khrushchev era.[3] From this point of view, after a dynamic start, the Brezhnev leadership faced the clashing of modernization aims and the realities of a planned economy, which drove the Soviet Union into the slippery slope of economic recession. The question remains: is this the whole picture of the era?

During the Khrushchev era, economic modernization became one of the main aims of the Soviet leadership. Although the aim of modernizing the Soviet economy remained the same under Brezhnev's leadership, the pace slowed down, and the system seemed to transform into a bureaucratic and corrupted one.[4] Reconsidering the Brezhnev era from the point of view of stagnation,[5] it is important to take into account the factors influencing the activities of the era: the circumstances, the long-term processes of continuation, and the wider context.[6] The starting point for this analysis is that during the Brezhnev era, these three factors were intertwined and connected to the long-term modernization process of the Soviet Union, and the wider context, the Cold War. The approach, emphasizing the interaction and cooperation instead of conflict and confrontation, has focused more thoroughly on the role of the East in the Cold War change. This has transformed the view of the role of the Soviet Union and the Soviet bloc in the change that took place during the Cold War. Thus, it is reasonable to ask how does the new approach change our understanding of the stagnated Brezhnev era? In this chapter, the approach of multilevel interaction[7] is applied in the analysis of the East-West interaction in the field of scientific-technical cooperation. The aim is to find out whether the picture of the Brezhnev era is about to change.

The approach of multilevel interaction targets the intermediate (individual states, organizations) and microlevel interaction (enterprises, individuals) instead of a macrolevel analysis focusing on superpower politics. Soviet activities in the East-West interaction become evident only when the focus is on microlevel interaction. Through the investigation of "behind the scenes activities" and microlevel cooperation, the "invisible actors" become visible and the field of activities looks quite different compared to the view given by studies focusing on macrolevel politics. At a time when the superpower competition was the hot spot in world politics, microlevel East-West interaction flourished in Europe.[8] In the 1950s, the Soviet Union started to knit a network of bilateral cooperation partnerships with selected Western European states, not only because of the geographical proximity, but also because of mutual advantages for both sides of the Iron Curtain. Soviet interaction with the West was especially active during the Brezhnev leadership—does this intermediate and microlevel activity challenge the label of stagnation to the Brezhnev era? In order to grasp the practical level of East-West interaction, we shall focus on the Soviet scientific-technical cooperation with Finland and West Germany.

THE LONG-TERM PROCESS OF SOVIET MODERNISATION AND THE COLD WAR

East-West interaction was strongly connected to the Soviet Union's long-term aim to modernize its economy. During the Brezhnev leadership, modernization goals were based on the Western model adopted by Khrushchev in mid-1950s. The main aim in modernization was to transform extensive economic growth into an intensive one, based on technological progress and especially on the exploitation of automation in industrial production. In order to meet the modernization plan, the Soviet Union needed Western technology and know-how.[9] The main stimulus for the Soviet Union to establish new contacts with technologically advanced states and to interact with the West was to transfer technology and related knowledge to the Soviet Union.[10] This new collaborative approach toward the West was inaugurated during the leadership of Nikita Khrushchev (1956–1964), and it was continued by Khrushchev's successor Leonid Brezhnev (1964–1982).

The context of the Cold War dictated the circumstances where the Soviet Union had to seek possibilities to fulfill the modernization plan. Technology and especially post-World War Two technological innovations had become sensitive issues of superpower politics. In order to forestall the economic development of the Soviet Union and to restrain the expansion of the socialist bloc, the United States raised a multilateral high-technology embargo (CoCom), which was implemented by NATO members in 1949.[11] The CoCom's aim was to control all trade in technology during the Cold War. In this situation, in order to obtain the technology and related knowledge it needed to meet its modernization plan, the Soviet Union had to seek alternative ways to transfer technology.[12]

Realizing that the existing system of technology transfer was not effective and did not boost the domestic R&D, the Soviet Union started to build up the system of scientific-technical cooperation with the West. The Central Committee of the Communist Party decided that the system of technology transfer had to be reorganized. In 1958 the new State Committee of Science and Technology (GKNT) was established to coordinate the technology transfer and take care of the diffusion of new technologies to the Soviet research institutes, design bureaus, and production facilities.[13] The GKNT became the main organization in the East-West interaction on the Soviet side, and it remained the main actor until the end of the Cold War. The GKNT was especially active during the era of détente in the 1970s, and the activities continued during the "cold" 1980s almost in the same level. According to the CIA, in the 1980s the GKNT was not only coordinating legal actions, but also supporting illegal efforts to acquire foreign technology to the Soviet Union.[14]

During the Khrushchev era, the Soviet Union created a system of scientific-technical cooperation that enabled officially approved non-commercial connections with Western partners. The system of scientific-technical cooperation first started within the Eastern bloc, but the main focus was on the West. The scientific-technical cooperation with the West was organized through the GKNT establishment of the new transfer system needed a testing site. Creating a new kind of bilateral relationships with neighboring Finland was an easy task for the Soviets, since these two states shared a long history of trade.[15] Based on already active trade relations, an international Soviet-Finnish agreement on scientific-technical cooperation was signed in 1955.[16]

The agreement with Finland was the very first agreement with a capitalist state, and it served as a model for other Soviet bilateral agreements with Western states in the future.[17] Although Finland was the first Western partner in scientific-technical cooperation, the main target for the Soviet Union was West Germany. The technologically advanced West Germany had sold the technology and related knowledge needed in the Soviet Union in the 1950s.[18] The establishment of bilateral cooperation between the Soviet Union and West Germany, however, proved to be a complicated process. West Germany was a member of NATO and CoCom[19] and thus the cooperation was more restricted than with neutral Finland. In spite of the political tensions, West Germany and the Soviet Union had a mutual interest in cooperation, which led to more intense interaction. A more systematic exchange started in the late 1950s, but the most active cooperation took place during the Brezhnev era.[20]

Brezhnev's Strategy of East-West Interaction: Transformation of Scientific-Technical Cooperation Into a Technology Trade

From the point of view of stagnation, the most interesting phenomenon in the East-West interaction was the transformation of the scientific-technical cooperation into an exchange of technology. This process proved that the Soviet policy was active and target-oriented and also that Soviet actors were able to adapt their aims and goals to the changing situation. The transformation was possible because of the flexible system of scientific-technical cooperation. Its key objective, "to exploit faster the achievements of science and technology and the new methods of production,"[21] offered a versatile tool for the Soviets to enhance their modernization goals. Although full speed was achieved in the 1970s, firm foundations for the future had already been laid in the Khrushchev era.

In the beginning, cooperation consisted of reciprocal visits to basic industrial production units, participation in technology fairs, and meetings with specialists. Organized by the GKNT, these visits to factories and production units were rather harmless and possible to manage without too complicated official arrangements.[22] Although cooperation was relatively low-level, the transfer of knowledge and expertise took place and set the stage for further development in all scientific-technical partner states, especially in Finland and West Germany. The nature of the scientific-technical cooperation started to change during the 1960s, when it became clear that the Soviet bloc was not able to attain the technological level that was needed to modernize the economy.[23] During the early years of Brezhnev's leadership, scientific-technical cooperation took another course, and visits were directed increasingly to research institutes and high-technology enterprises, focusing rather on transfer of specific knowledge and technology. The trips became much better prepared, and Soviet specialists were assigned clear programs for their visits.[24] The plans were based on thorough and careful analysis of the partner's technological development and advantages. The Soviet embassies closely followed the economic development and situation in their station countries paying attention to Soviet interests.[25] In the late 1950s, the information was based on reports submitted by Soviet specialists following their visits to Western technology advisors in Soviet embassies in Western countries and collected information about the latest technological developments and sent their to findings to the GKNT.[26]

Based on the information obtained, the GKNT chose partners for bilateral collaboration. This change of course was strongly supported in the official decisions and speeches. A decree was issued in 1968 entitled "raising the efficiency of the work of scientific organizations and accelerating the utilization of the achievements of science and technology into the national economy"[27] that fit well with the key objective of scientific-technical cooperation. In his official speeches, Brezhnev strongly emphasized the role of science and technology in the development of the economic system.[28] In the same way as it did under the leadership of Khrushchev, official rhetoric in the Brezhnev era justified East-West interaction by linking it to economic modernization. Technology transfer was connected to the postwar scientific-technical revolution in the West and the imperative that the Soviet Union take part in these developments. Later, this argument was widely used by the smaller East European states to justify connections to the West.[29]

How was this kind of interaction possible in the circumstances of the divided world in the Cold War era? First of all, the scientific-technical cooperation was official and open based on intergovernmental agreements, and thus there were no evasive elements of activity. A more practical reason for the wider space to maneuver was the fact that the East-West interaction in the field of scientific-technical cooperation was not visible on the macrolevel and thus was not an issue in conflict-oriented superpower discussions. The interaction took place "behind the scenes" and consisted of practical cooperation on the lower level, of which the Soviet-Finnish cooperation was a good example. The Soviet Union had a long history of cooperation with Finland and thus in the beginning there was nothing alarming in the development of Soviet-Finnish scientific-technical exchanges. When superpower politics became more tense, the

United States paid more attention to collaboration with the Soviet Union. In 1979, the United States analyzed the cooperation as "suspicious"[30] and later in the 1980s, took a more decisive role in the CoCom toward the East-West technology transfer. The interest of West European CoCom partners, such as the United Kingdom, France, and West Germany, cooperation with the Soviet Union was strong since the 1950s. However, the United States opposed this cooperation, especially in the field of technology. In spite of the negative attitude, there was no way for the United States to intervene in the development. All restrictive CoCom decisions had to be unanimous, and other partners did not share the strategic fear of the United States.[31]

For the Western partners of the Soviet Union, admissibility and especially the invisibility of the cooperation made the interaction easier. When cooperation took place on the enterprise level, there was more room to maneuver and to collaborate departing from one's own needs. In Finland, the cooperation was handled on the state level by the Soviet-Finnish commission on scientific-technical cooperation, which defined official activities. For example, the commission would officially discuss East-West trade during its Soviet-Finnish seminars.[32] Yet, the realization of the official recommendations took place on the practical level. The practical cooperation that took place on the microlevel between Finnish universities, research institutes, and enterprises was free from state-level intermediaries.[33] In West Germany, the GKNT established direct connections with West German enterprises through the Soviet embassy in Bonn.[34] This helped to establish cooperation directly at the grassroots level with the chosen enterprises that produced the needed technology, and also to bypass politically problematic state-level negotiations. This was important especially in the 1960s and 1970s, when the cooperation was increasing and getting more trade-oriented both in Finland and in West Germany. This proved to be an advantage for the Soviet Union's aims to develop the cooperation more in the direction of technology trade.

THE BREZHNEV LEADERSHIP REDEFINES THE GOALS FOR EAST-WEST INTERACTION

When Brezhnev took the leadership, most of the Khrushchev reforms were cancelled, but the system of scientific-technical cooperation was advanced. It proved to be a very useful tool to develop East-West interaction further in the 1970s, during the era of détente in the superpower relations.[35] In addition to increased macrolevel political activities, the Soviet Union increased interaction "behind the scenes" by furthering bilateral cooperation with the western European states. On the microlevel, practical scientific-technical cooperation was more active and target-oriented than ever—not only in quantitative but also in qualitative terms.

The occupation of Czechoslovakia became one of the watersheds during the Brezhnev era, changing the atmosphere in the Soviet bloc and serving as a turn toward stagnation. In the wider Cold War context, the occupation had relatively small effect on high politics[36] but even less effect on East-West scientific-technical cooperation. After the Soviet invasion of Czechoslovakia in 1968, the responses of Soviet partners in scientific-technical cooperation were thoroughly monitored by the Soviet embassies in the West, and the information was analyzed by the GKNT. According to several secret GKNT reports, no serious consequences of the events of 1968 were evident.[37] The cooperation had developed satisfactorily with Finland during the latter part of 1968, which helped the Soviet side to continue and even strengthen the cooperation in 1969.[38] According to the report monitoring West Germany, the occupation had stirred some negative political attitudes, but, ultimately, scientific-technical cooperation had intensified in 1969.[39] This proved to be a different outcome than what was expected at the time. Stanford Research Institute organized a meeting "dedicated to a free exchange of views among participants on problems and opportunities involving East-West trade" in Vienna in November 1968, where the aim was to discuss "off-the-record" about the problems of East-West trade. In the meeting, events in Czechoslovakia and Soviet occupation were also discussed, and it was expected that the normalization of trade would take at least a couple of years.[40] While this was the case on the macrolevel in scientific-technical cooperation, the pace was faster.

A further development of the scientific-technical cooperation was of importance to the Soviet Union. In the changing situation, the Soviet leadership had to redefine its goals. In 1969, an extensive analysis was conducted of the prospects of the Soviet technological development and the scientific-technical cooperation. A deepening cooperation with Western specialists and enterprises was seen as one of the main factors in the process. The scientific-technical cooperation began to enter into the system of foreign licenses. These were important for the Soviet Union, not only because of the revenue from selling domestic licenses, but also as the way to develop the domestic technological basis by purchasing foreign licenses. The poor quality of Soviet technology was recognized, and the international licensing was seen as one solution to solve the problem.[41] These plans and concerns were connected to developments in the Soviet R&D.

In addition to international licensing, straightforward and semilegal copying became part of the technological modernization process. This, however, proved to be a problematic strategy. After the decision to give up domestic R&D in computer science in favor of copying the IBM 360 series in 1969, the Soviet Union needed cooperation with Western partners in the field of computer science more than ever. The Soviet Union had already copied IBM computers and created the "Ryad" computers. The Soviet Union was able to get technology through illegal trade and spying but the problem was the knowledge needed to use the technology, such as programming and software. Thus, the main challenge for the GKNT was to gain access to programming information and to educate Soviet computer specialists with original IBM devices.[42] This was possible through scientific-technical cooperation. A specific Soviet-Finnish working group in the field of computer science was established in early 1970, and cooperation was boosted during the next two decades.[43]

A new strategy for technology transfer was necessary because the need of foreign technology had increased, due to the decisions to diminish domestic R&D and to focus on raw material-based industry—as well as to prioritize the military-industrial complex.[44] Because of the CoCom and strengthened restrictions in the technology trade in the 1980s, the Soviet Union had to focus on already existing cooperation and to push it into the direction of technology trade. The Soviet leadership had to redefine their approach to bilateral cooperation and economic modernization. This change of approach is clearly visible in the case of Finland. The enterprise Nokia[45] had created a beneficial trade connection with the Soviet Union in 1957 through the commission of Scientific-Technical Cooperation.[46] By the 1970s, Nokia already had direct trade relations with the main Soviet ministries. The development of Finnish technological know-how was visible in the trade connections. In the 1980s, Soviet trade with Nokia had expanded into the field of automatic telephone exchanges, robotics, automation, computer technology and wireless communication systems. The cooperation proved to be beneficial for both trade partners. Through the Soviet trade, Nokia managed to generate a remarkable level of growth and to avoid economic meltdown during the economic recession in Finland in the 1980s.[47] For the Soviet Union, collaboration with Nokia offered a possibility to access technology that was unavailable in the open market. The lower level practical cooperation, however, was connected to the circumstances created by the wider context in the mid-1980s. In order to acquire components from the United States, both Nokia and Finland had to make secret agreements with the United States in order to continue trade with the Soviet Union.[48]

Cooperation with West Germany was the main target for the Soviet Union. A trade agreement between the Soviet Union and West Germany was concluded in 1958, and soon after that, scientific-technical cooperation was activated. In the 1960s, cooperation was based on Soviet experts' visits to West German enterprises and production units, but already in the 1970s, connections in high technology trade were established through the scientific-technical cooperation. Through Willy Brandt's new *Ostpolitik* and after concluding the Moscow treaty in 1970,[49] , cooperation and trade reached a new level, with active discussions between the Soviet partners and West German enterprises.[50] In 1971, the GKNT reached an important goal in the cooperation with Siemens, when it concluded an agreement on scientific-technical cooperation with the enterprise.[51] The agreement did not differ from the intergovernmental agreements on scientific-technical cooperation, although it was established between the Soviet state committee and a West German enterprise. The agreement not only dealt with technology transfer, but included wide scientific cooperation in the field of computer science. The agreement with Siemens was an important step for the Soviet Union and the GKNT. According to the official reports, the contract enabled a more active collaboration and raised the bilateral East-West cooperation to a new level.[52]

While Soviet work with Nokia opened more intensive cooperation on both ends, the GKNT-Siemens agreement initiated a completely new level of collaboration between the Soviet Union and West Germany. Siemens launched the export of computers and components to the Soviet Union and to the other CMEA countries.[53] In 1972, Soviet Union and West Germany established a joint commission was established on economic, technical, and scientific cooperation. In the same year, a general agreement on trade was concluded, which signified the normalization of trade relations between West Germany and the Soviet Union.[54] West German exports to the Soviet Union almost doubled from 1970 to 1972, and by the mid-1970s, West Germany had become the largest Western exporter of machines and instruments to the Soviet Union.[55] This development is evident also in the secret GKNT plan for the years 1973–1975 that envisaged wide-ranging and increasing cooperation with West German enterprises.[56] In West Germany, Siemens was not the only enterprise that interested the Soviet Union. The GKNT had active cooperation with BASF, Telefunken, and Daimler-Benz, to mention only a few. Besides Finland and West Germany, the Soviet leadership actively sought cooperation with Western states. During the 1960s and 1970s, the Soviet Union signed numerous bilateral agreements on scientific, technical, and cultural cooperation with Western governments.[57] In 1975, the GKNT signed an agreement on scientific-technical cooperation with the Swedish enterprise Sandviken. The aim of the agreement was mutual benefit, and the practical side of the cooperation was not only the transfer of technology (e.g. rock drilling products) but also joint research and R&D.[58]

"Behind the Scenes" Cooperation Intensifies the Process of East-West Interaction

During the Cold War, personal contacts became extremely important in East-West interaction. The scientific-technical cooperation between the Soviet Union and West European states aptly illustrates the role of individuals in this interaction. The agreements and practical cooperation were personified in the work of the people involved in activities. They were often invisible in the political arena, but influential actors behind the scenes. Of course in Finland and West Germany, the governmental leaders, such as the president of Finland Urho Kekkonen and the West German Chancellor Willy Brandt, were key figures in the Soviet cooperation and, in the end, also the guarantors of the interaction.

This being said, the main activities took place behind the scenes and between invisible actors. When analyzing the Soviet part in the East-West interaction, the deputy director of the GKNT, Dzhermen Gvishiani,[59] is undoubtedly one of those influential actors. Gvishiani was the son-in-law of the Soviet Premier Aleksey Kosygin, but also a scientist himself, and a member of the Soviet Academy of Science. During the 1970s, he participated in almost all East-West agreements as a representative of the GKNT, not only in scientific-technical cooperation,[60] but also in other international agreements, such as the establishment of the Institute for Applied Systems Analysis (IIASA). Negotiations that led to the establishment of this "US–Soviet-led think tank" in Vienna in 1972 had a long history, starting in the mid-1960s. The IIASA as such is a good example of macrolevel East-West interaction during the détente era, but it is an even better example of the "dynamic" image of Soviet science during the early Brezhnev era. Although the endeavor was based on a U.S. initiative, the participation of the Soviet Union in the IIASA was seen as indispensable because of the high quality of system analysis in the country.[61] In the Soviet Union, especially in the late 1960s and early 1970s, there were several projects aiming at the creation of large networks of automated management systems (*avtomatizirovannye sistemy upravlenniya*, ASU).[62]

Personal contacts were important also for the Finnish participants in the East-West interaction. Both Nokia and the Soviet government highly valued their trade in technology. The more advanced the technology, the more important the role of personal contacts became. Although a private enterprise firm in neutral Finland, Nokia had to follow the foreign policy of its home country. Finland, although not a member of CoCom, was following the CoCom lists[63] because the Finnish industry depended on Western and especially American components.[64] Accordingly, alongside intensifying cooperation with the Soviet Union, the role of the United States was strengthened. Being the main supplier of the components used by the enterprise, the United States had its say in the cooperation. In this situation, the solution was mediated through the personal connections of the cooperative partners. Nokia's CEO made a personal agreement with the Pentagon to provide information about technological progress in the Soviet Union.[65] After the contract was made, Nokia was able to continue to trade with the Soviet Union as it had done before. In the Soviet Union, all major contracts with Nokia were based on personal contacts, and because of these personal connections, Finland was able to continue to trade in both directions. In West Germany, individuals became equally important in cooperation. Personal contacts between the heads of states,

Willy Brandt from West Germany and Leonid Brezhnev from the Soviet Union, furthered the East-West interaction remarkably. The invisible actors behind the scenes existed also in West Germany; the most notable of these was Otto Wolf von Amerongen, who participated in most of the negotiations between the Soviets and West Germans during the Cold War era.[66]

Behind-the-scenes interaction combined with personal contacts created favorable conditions for East-West interaction especially in Europe. The Soviet Union was willing to seek contacts, and it was an attractive partner. In the 1960s and 1970s, the Soviet Union was not seen as a recipient of the Western know-how, but a worthy companion for reciprocal cooperation. In these circumstances, the Soviet leadership was able to redefine their approach to the long-term aim, that is, the Soviet economic modernization, in the wider Cold War context. The scientific-technical cooperation with Western partners gave a tool for the Brezhnev leadership to continue the long-term project of economic modernization. In line with the transformation of scientific-technical cooperation into a technology trade, the process of East-West interaction started to take shape. The main factor that furthered the emergence of the process of East-West interaction was the Soviet scientific-technical agreements with the Western states. Based on the network of bilateral agreements, the Soviet Union was able to develop further practical microlevel cooperation with Western partners in spite of the end of détente and tightening of the CoCom restrictions after the Soviet invasion in Afghanistan in 1980.

In the East-West interaction, it is possible to recognize a process that was based on a peculiar demand-and-supply system and dictated by push-and-pull factors[67] on both sides of the Iron Curtain. This process was strongly connected to the circumstances created by the wider context of the Cold War. The West met the demand from the East by transferring the sought-after knowledge, which was realized in the broader framework of the push-and-pull factors. Being eager to create demand, the Soviet Union proactively influenced the East-West interaction through bilateral cooperation focusing on related industries and know-how in the West. This process was especially active during the Brezhnev leadership, which continued the long-term modernization process adopted by Khrushchev in the mid-1950s.

In the West, the major actors in the process were those sought to interact with the Eastern bloc for economic benefit: the Eastern bloc was viewed as an attractive trade partner, and in some cases the reciprocity of the cooperation was seen as an incentive. When the economic benefit was a pushing factor for the cooperation, a juxtaposition created by the Cold War division established a strong restraining or pulling factor for the cooperation: any interaction with the Eastern bloc became ideologically charged. This attitude maintained the idea of a technological gap between West and East, and that the transfer of technology created a strategic threat. In the East, the West was seen as a model for economic modernization and a resource to aid it. This was the major push factor for interaction and cooperation with the West. The restraining factor was the same as in the West: the ideologically embedded idea of the enemy. The process of East-West interaction proved to witness its most active and productive phase during the late period of Brezhnev leadership, such as the deepest years of stagnation.

CONCLUSION

As we reconsider the stagnation narrative during the Brezhnev era in East-West interaction, it is essential to keep in mind the multilevel and complex nature of the Soviet society. The wider context of the Cold War created circumstances that made the processes even more complicated. In this chapter, East-West interaction during the Brezhnev leadership has been analyzed in connection to the long-term economic modernization aims and the wider context of the Cold War that set the frames for the circumstances. When defined as economic recession and pessimism, stagnation was clearly present in the Soviet society of the 1970s.[68] However, when defining stagnation as inactivity, the outcome is a different one. Based on the analysis of multilevel interaction, the Soviet Union's activity in the East-West interaction was at its highest during the last years of Brezhnev leadership. East-West interaction in the field of technology transfer and scientific-technical cooperation reached its peak in the years that are traditionally defined as the years of deepest stagnation. During those years, the Soviet Union redefined the long-term modernization strategy by target-oriented pushing the scientific-technical cooperation into the direction of technology trade. The change in cooperative strategies shows that the chosen policies were contested and renewed according to the needs of the Soviet economy and developments in the wider context of the Cold War. The intensified cooperation remarkably accelerated the pace of development of East-West interaction.

Thus, labelling the years 1973–1982 as the years of stagnation is perhaps too one-sided. The fact that the late years of Brezhnev leadership were the most active years of East-West interaction challenges the existing characterisations of the Brezhnev era—i.e., 1964–1973 as the "good years" and 1973–1982 as the years of stagnation. The target-oriented policy, seeking new ways to enhance the economic modernization through cooperation with the West, was implemented in the latter part of the Brezhnev era—i.e., during the deepest years of stagnation. However, the primary objective of the East-West interaction, modernization of the Soviet economy, did not become realized as had been anticipated. In spite of the effective system of technology transfer, active bilateral cooperation, and East-West interaction, the impact of transferred technology on Soviet economic performance was modest.[69] There were some domestic innovations and some cases of successful reverse engineering based on transferred technology, but no important technological breakthroughs emerged. The main aim—intensive economic growth—was not realized, and remained extensive until the very end of the Soviet Union.

The failure of economic modernization based on technology transfer was not (only) caused by the faulty decisions made during the Brezhnev era (influence of stagnate attitude), but also by the inflexible system of the planned economy. Several attempts to strengthen the administrative basis of the assimilation of transferred knowledge to Soviet systems were made during the Brezhnev leadership. The main weakness was that the domestic R&D capabilities were unable to assist in the adaptation and exploitation of new technologies and the inability of the system to generate innovations.[70] At the same time, the Soviet leadership made decisions that strengthened the dependence of the Soviet industry and economy on the imported technology. Due to the dependence on foreign technology and the incapability to diffuse transferred knowledge into the Soviet system, the domestic R&D remained underdeveloped. Decisions made—or rather reforms that remained unrealized—during the Brezhnev era set the basis for a raw material-based economy. By paying for the technology transfer with raw materials and energy, the Soviet Union reinforced the raw material-based economy and became more dependent on technology trade. This created a vicious circle that still exists in contemporary Russia. By failing to modernize the Soviet economy, the Brezhnev leadership created a continuation of the long-term modernization process on the basis that does not support domestic innovations but technology and knowledge transfers. Thus, it is possible to say that during the Brezhnev era, a complex system of interaction, activity, and stagnation existed in the Soviet Union.

NOTES

1. Peter Hanson, *The Rise and Fall of the Soviet Economy. An Economic History of the USSR from 1945* (Longman: 2003) p. 128–129.
2. Moshe Lewin, *The Soviet Century*. (London: Verson, 2005) 478; Hanson *Rise and Fall*, 129.
3. This topic is widely studied in the Cold War as well as Soviet historiography. From the point of view of technology transfer, see e.g. Autio-Sarasmo, S. (2011b) 'Khrushchev and the challenge of technological progress' in *Khrushchev in the Kremlin. Policy and Government in the Soviet Union, 1953–1964*. Smith, J. and Ilic, M. Routledge (eds.), Abingdon 2011, 143–144.
4. See Introduction in this volume.
5. In this paper, 'stagnation' is understood as inactivity to challenge regression.
6. See e.g. Lewin, 341.
7. On the concept of multileveled interaction, see Autio-Sarasmo, S. and Miklóssy, K., 'Introduction: Cold War from new perspective' in *Reassessing Cold War Europe*. (Eds.) Autio-Sarasmo, S. and Miklóssy, K. Routledge, Abingdon 2011.

8. Autio-Sarasmo and Miklossy (2011), 2–8; Europe has been the focus of Cold War studies also in the history of international relations and diplomacy. See e.g. *The Crisis of Détente in Europe: from Helsinki to Gorbachev 1975–1985*. Eb. By Leopoldo Nuti. Routledge Cold War History series, Abingdon 2009; *Europe and the End of the Cold War, A Reappraisal*. Frédéric Bozo at al. (Eds.), Routledge, Cold War History series, Abingdon 2008; *Helsinki 1975 and the Transformation of Europe*. Oliver Bange and Gottfried Niedhart (Eds.), Berghahn Books, 2008; *Origins of the European Security System*, Andreas Wenger et al. (Eds.), Routledge, CSS Studies in Security and International Relations, Abingdon 2007; *European Integration and the Cold War: Ostpolitik, 1965–1973*. Ludlow, N. Piers (Ed.), Routledge, Cold War History series, Abingdon 2007.

9. Autio-Sarasmo, (2011 b), 134–135.

10. Russian State Archive of Contemporary History (RGANI) fond. 5, opis' 61, delo 55a, list 1–220.

11. This topic has been studied widely and there exist myriads of interpretations about the nature of the embargo. See e.g. Hanson, P., *Trade and Technology in Soviet-Western Relations*, London: Macmillan, 1981; Jackson, I., *The Economic Cold War. America, Britain and East–West Trade, 1948–1963*, New York: Palgrave, 2001; Jensen-Eriksen, N., "CoCom and neutrality: Western export control policies, Finland and the Cold War, 1949–1958" in *Reassessing Cold War Europe*. Autio-Sarasmo, S. and Miklóssy, K. Routledge (eds.), Abingdon 2011.

12. Spying and illegal acquisition of technology and knowledge was active behind the scenes, but remain beyond the scope of this study.

13. RGANI f. 5, op. 40, d. 52, ll. 13–19; RGANI f. 5, op. 40, d. 121, l. 29–30; About the establishment of the GKNT in more detail, see Autio-Sarasmo, S. (2011a) 'Knowledge through the Iron Curtain: Soviet scientific-technical cooperation with Finland and West Germany' in *Reassessing Cold War Europe*. (Eds.) Autio-Sarasmo, S. and Miklóssy, K. Routledge, Abingdon 2011, 68–70.

14. The technology Acquisition Efforts of the Soviet Intelligence Services (u). Interagency Intelligence Memorandum, June 1982. NI IIM 82–10006. In http://www.foia.cia.gov/document/0000261337 (accessed August 14, 2015).

15. See e.g. Androsova, T., 'Economic interest in Soviet post-war policy in Finland' in *Reassessing Cold War Europe*. (Eds.) Autio-Sarasmo, S. and Miklóssy, K. Routledge, Abingdon 2011, 33.

16. Asetus tieteellis-teknillisestä yhteistoiminnasta Suomen tasavallan ja SNTL:n välillä, 16.8. 1955. (Decree on scientific-technical cooperation between Finland and the Soviet Union). http://www.finlex.fi/fi/sopimukset/sopsteksti/1955/19550030 (accessed August 14, 2015).

17. Romanov, A., 'Suomen ja Neuvostoliiton välisen tieteellis-teknisen yhteistyön tuloksia' in tuloksia' in *Suomen ja Neuvostoliiton välinen tieteellis-tekninen yhteistoiminta 30 vuotta*, Helsinki 1985, 8.

18. As early as in 1960, West Germany was prioritized over the United States in what came to cooperation in technology transfer; Russian State Archive of the Economy (RGAE) f. 9480, op. 7, d. 805, l. 9; RGAE, f. 9480, op. 7, d. 805, l. 39–41.

19. See e.g. Hughes, R. G., *Britain, Germany and the Cold War. The Search for a European Détente 1949–1967*. Routledge, Abingdon 2007, 90, 126, 132; Rudolph, K., *Wirtshaftsdiplomatie im Kalten Krieg. Die Ostpolitik der Westdeutschen Großindustrie 1945–1991*, Frankfurt, Campus, 2004, 172–176, 188.

20. v. Amerongen, O. W., *Der Weg nach Osten. Vierzig Jahre Brückenbau für die deutsche Wirtshaft*. München, Droemer Knaur, 1992, 83, 137; See also Rudolph (2004), 118, 121, 158–159; About the draft contract of cultural and scientific-technical cooperation between West Germany and the Soviet Union in 1959. See Archive of the Russian Academy of Sciences (ARAN) f. 579, op. 13, d.147, l. 1–15.

21. Kaje M. and Niitamo, O., 'Scientific and Technical Cooperation between a Small Capitalist Country and Big Socialist Country' in *Finnish-Soviet Economic Relations*. Möttölä, Bykov and Korolev (Eds.) London: Macmillan Press 1983, 143–144.

22. Autio-Sarasmo (2011b), 140–141.

23. See e.g. Wilczynski, J., *Technology in COMECON. Acceleration of Technological Progress through Economic Planning and the Market*, London: Macmillan, 1974, 145, 296–297. There were problems in the CMEA cooperation as well, Hanson (2003), 156.

24. Autio-Sarasmo (2011a), 70.

25. Archive of Foreign Policy of the Russian Federation (AVP RF) monitoring on Finland fond135, op. 59, por. 13, p. 127, l. 77–88.

26. RGANI, f. 5, op. 61, d. 59, ll. 45–55.

27. Cooper, J. 'Research, development and innovation in the Soviet Union' in *Economic development in The Soviet Union and Eastern Europe*, Volume 1. Reforms, technology and Income Distribution. (Ed. by Zbigniew M. Fallenbuchl. Praeger Pubvlushers, New York, 1975.

28. Cooper, 170. Cooper refers to Brezhnev's speech in 24th party congress in 1971.

29. Autio-Sarasmo (2011b), 135–136; On the case of Czechoslovakia, see e.g. Nisonen-Trnka, R., *Science with a Human Face: the Activity of the Czechoslovak Scientists František Šorm and Otto Wichterle during the Cold War*, 99–106. Acta Universitatis Tamperensis 1729. Tampereen yliopistopaino 2012.

30. *Soviet acquisition of Western technology*. April 1983 (Library of Congress); *Technology and East-West trade*. Report, Office of the Technology Assessment, Congress of the United States, November 1979.

31. Autio-Sarasmo, S., 'Soviet economic modernisation and transferring technology from the West' in *Modernisation in Russia since 1900*. Markku Kangaspuro and Jeremy Smith (Eds.) Studia Fennica Historica, SKS, Helsinki 2006, 115; *Technology and East-West trade*.

32. A good example is the seminar "New forms of economic cooperation between East and West" held 2.-4.7.1975 in Helsinki. The outcome and discussion were widely monitored in several reports written in the seminar. AVP RF f. 135, op. 57, por. 13, p. 120, l. 25–30.

33. *Suomen ja Neuvostoliiton välisen tiedeyhteistyön kanavat*. Olli Perheentupa (Ed.). Suomen ja Neuvostoliiton välisen tieteellis-teknisen yhteistoimintakomitean julkaisusarja 11. Helsinki 1981, 1–2.

34. Russian State Archive on Economy (RGAE), f. 9480, op. 7, d. 805, ll. 7–8, 12.

35. See e.g. Gaddis, L., *Cold War. A new history*. The Penguin Press, London 2005.

36. See e.g. A. Wilkens, 'New Ostpolitik and European integration in the policies in the Brandt era', in P. Ludlow (ed.), *European Integration and the Cold War. Ostpolitik-Westpolitik, 1965–1973*. Routledge, Cold War History series, 2007, 72.

37. RGANI, f. 5, op. 61, d. 59, l. 45–55 (Finland) and l. 133–196 (West Germany).

38. RGANI, f. 5, op. 61, d. 59, l. 45–55.

39. RGANI, f. 5, op. 61, d. 59, l. 133–196.

40. In the SRI event attended participants also from Hungary and Czechoslovakia but mainly from the West. Roster of Participants and Schedule: SRI meeting in Vienna November 13–16,1968; Finnish participant Toivo Nordberg's report from the meeting 20.11.1968. A2. Kirjeenvaihtoa, 245 C. Archive of Finnish Enterprise UPM-Kymmene.

41. RGANI, f. 5, op. 61, d. 55, l. 96–147.

42. Archive of the Russian Academy of Sciences (ARAN), f. 579, op. 13, d.162, ll. 72–73. More detailed analysis see Autio-Sarasmo (2011a), 72.

43. As an example of the lively cooperation see e.g. ARAN, f. 579, op. 13, d. 162, ll. 17–34. From the Finnish side see e.g. 'Neuvostoliittolaisen delegaation Suomen vierailu' (Report of Soviet delegation to Finland). TT-komitea: saapuneet kirjeet UMA 1/1–30/6–71. Archive of Finnish foreign ministry (MFA); Matkakertomus matkasta Tallinnaan (Travel report on visit in Tallinn). TT-komitea: matkakertomuksia (travelogue) 1956–1978. Commission of the Finnish-Soviet scientific-technical cooperation (STC), MFA; See also Autio-Sarasmo (2011), p. 72–73.

44. Bystrova, I. V., *Sovetskii voenno-prmyshlennoi kompleks: problemy stanovleniia i razvitiia (1930–1980-e gody)*. Rossiiskaja Akademiia Nauk: Institut Rossiiskii istorii. Moskva 2006, 260.

45. Nokia was one of the most important conglomerates in Finland from the early twentieth century onwards.

46. Häikiö, M., Sturm und Drang. Suurkaupoilla eurooppalaiseksi elektroniikkayritykseksi 1983–1991. Nokia Oyj:n historia. Osa 2, Helsinki: Edita, 2001, 49–52.

47. Häikiö, 52–59, 251–255.

48. See Autio-Sarasmo (2011 a), 74.

49. On the Moscow treaty see e.g. http://www.cvce.eu/obj/en-d5341cb5-1a49-4603-aec9-0d2304c25080 (accessed August 14, 2015).

50. Rudolph, 296.

51. RGAE, f. 9480, op. 9, d. 2509 A, l. 18–26.

52. RGAE, f. 9480, op. 9, d. 2509 A, l. 18–26; RGAE, f. 9480, op. 9, d. 1461, l. 20–28.

53. Wilczynski, 113; See also Amerongen, 129.

54. Rudolph, 302–3; See also RGAE f. 9480, op. 9, d. 1710, l. 98–111.

55. Slama, Jiri and Heinrich Vogel, 'On the measurement of technological levels for the Soviet Economy' in *Economic development in the Soviet Union and Eastern Europe*. Volume 1. *Reforms, technology and Income Distribution*. Ed. by Zbigniew M. Fallenbuchl. Praeger Publishers, New York, 1975, 215; *Vneshnyaya torgovlya SSSR 1922–1981*, Ministerstvo Vneshnei torgovli. Jubileinyi statisticheskii sbornik, Moskva, 1982; See also Rudolph, 274.

56. RGANI, f. 5, op. 66, d. 191, l. 6–237, especially l. 77.

57. Bertsch, G.,'Technology Transfers and Technology Controls: a Synthesis of the Western-Soviet Relationship', in *Technical Progress and Soviet Economic Development*. Ed by Amann, R. and Cooper, J., Oxford, 1986, 117, 120; Soviet government began to conclude various kinds of industrial co-operation agreements with western firms; Holliday, G.,*Technology Transfer to the USSR 1928–1937 and 1966–1975. The Role of Western Technology in Soviet Economic Development*. Westview Press, Boulder, Colorado, 1979, 47.

58. For a full list of West German enterprises see RGAE f. 9480, op. 9, d. 2509 A(1); Sandviken's agreement both in Russian and English RGAE f.9480, op. 9, d.2504, l. 1–7.

59. RGAE, f. 9480, op. 9, d. 2509 A, l. 18–26.

60. Cooperation was established with many Western states. See e.g. the agreement with Swedish Sandviken that was signed in 1975. RGAE 9480, op. 9, d. 2504, l. 1–2.

61. About the East-West activities connected to the Soviet Union and IIASA, see Riska-Campbell, L., *Bridging East and West. The Establishment of the International Institute for Applied Systems Analysis (IIASA) in the United States foreign policy of Bridge Building, 1964–1972*. The Finnish Society of Science and Letters. Commentationes Scientiarum Socialium 75. Helsinki 2011.

62. See e.g. Cooper, 169; *Innovation aspects of the management automation programme in the Soviet Union in Industrial Innovation in the Soviet Union* edited by Ronald Amann and Julian Cooper. Yale University Press, New Haven and London, 1982, 212–241.

63. The CoCom lists were: 1) a munitions list contained military items, 2) a nuclear energy list, 3) an industrial, commercial list. On the industrial list there were products that 'though nominally civilian, had military potential'. Restriction levels were: a total embargo, the quantitatively controlled items and the exchange of information and surveillance list.

64. Jensen-Eriksen, 55–58.

65. Autiio-Sarasmo (2011a), 74. Confirmed by Stefan Widomski. Discussion with Stefan Widomski, the former Senior Vice President International Trade Affairs in Nokia Corp, May 21, 2014.

66. See Amerongen 1992.

67. The concepts of demand and supply as well as push and pull factors are used here only as explanative tool. The aim is not to refer to the classical economic theory (e.g. Marshall, A., Principles of Economics. 8th edition (first published 1890). London: Macmillan and co. 1920) or the push and pull factors used in migration studies (e.g. Everett S. Lee (1966). A Theory of Migration.Demography, 1966,Volume 3, Number 1, Pages 47–57). For another approach to push and pull factors in the case of East Europe

and economic transition, see Johanna Bockman & Gil Eyal: Eastern Europe as a Laboratory for Economic Knowledge: The Transnational Roots of Neoliberalism, in: American Journal of Sociology, Vol. 108, Number 2 (2002), 337–338.

68. See Hanson (2003), 133. Hanson's analysis is based on CIA calculations.

69. See Hanson, P., 'The Soviet Union's acquisition of Western technology after Stalin: Some thoughts on people and connections' in *Reassessing Cold War Europe*. (Eds.) Autio-Sarasmo, S. and Miklóssy, K. Routledge, Abingdon 2011.

70. Holliday, 36.

SEVEN

Stagnant Science?

The Planning and Coordination of Biomedical Research in the Brezhnev Era

Anna Geltzer

Those on top can't, those on the bottom don't want to.
—Soviet-era aphorism

On June 18, 1973, the management and staff of the Institute of Experimental and Clinical Oncology (IECO)—one of the institutes under the jurisdiction of the Soviet Academy of Medical Sciences and the premier cancer research and treatment facility in the USSR—gathered to hear the reflections of an eminent American colleague on Soviet cancer research. The reflections were those of Dr. James Holland, who had spent eight months at the IECO as part of the Soviet-American cooperative program in healthcare that had begun between the two superpowers in 1972 with the blessing of the highest levels of government, as attested to by the signatures of Brezhnev and Nixon themselves. Dr. Holland, at the time Chief of Medicine at the Roswell Park Memorial Institute and "a leading authority in drug development," had gone to Moscow to facilitate the drug exchange program in malignant neoplasms.[1]

The valedictory address was not so much a reflection on Soviet science as a scathing critique of its organization and practices, veiled thinly by the format of suggestion. Holland prefaced his remarks by casting the critique as a life-sustaining intervention on behalf of Soviet cancer research:

> Biology is the study of living things, and one of the characteristics of biological organisms is that they respond to stimuli. When an organism ceases to respond to stimuli, it is a definition of death. Cancer research is one type of living thing. It is a social animal that must respond to stimuli and to new encounters. If it does not respond, it too is dead. I take it as my task to provide some of those stimuli.[2]

The main trouble with Soviet research practices that Holland identified in his address was a lack of communication—between the laboratory and the clinic within the IECO itself, between different institutes within the Soviet Union, and between Soviet scientists and their colleagues abroad. The main problem with the organization of Soviet cancer research was that "the responsibility for all of cancer or of cancer research is not vested in the same place."[3] That is, unlike in the United States, where the National Cancer Institute exercised a great deal of power over cancer research both by providing intellectual leadership in the field *and* by exercising control over the government funding of research, there was no comparably empowered institution in the U.S.S.R. Although the IECO was clearly the intellectual leader in Soviet cancer research, its management had neither the staff nor the funds to provide extramural coordination on a national scale, and no other organization filled the void.

In retrospect, the fact that an expert American observer would diagnose Soviet cancer research as being moribund is not surprising. The year was, after all, 1972—nearly ten years into the rule of Leonid Brezhnev and the period of Soviet history that has been labeled as the period of stagnation, itself interpreted as a kind of moribund state.[4] But the symptoms on which the diagnosis was based do contain surprising elements. The conclusion that Soviet cancer research was hampered by a lack of communication is easy to accept. Like all of Soviet society, the defining characteristic of which for Western observers was that it was closed and controlled, Soviet biomedical science was perceived as isolated and planned. Soviet biomedical scientists were understood to be isolated both from their colleagues abroad—with the result that their science had a somewhat "parochial" character, remaining "outside of the channels of world medical developments,"[5] and their colleagues at home. This perception of Soviet science fits neatly onto the label of stagnation—stagnant science should, by definition, be cut off from the currents of global information exchange, and it's no surprise that it would foster stifling hierarchies.

The conclusion that Soviet cancer research wasn't sufficiently centralized, however, is harder to digest. After all, to Western observers the key feature of Soviet science was that it was centralized and planned. As Mark Field, one of the first Western scholars to undertake a detailed study of the Soviet medical system, observed in his seminal book on the subject, the directionality of the Soviet system

> ...necessitates a strict system of priorities in the investment of the limited resources at the regime's disposal.... This is true, of course, of every society and every cooperative venture, since resources are always limited. And yet in most pluralistic societies the system of priorities is implicit rather than explicit, often spontaneous rather than directed, the result of a multiplicity of decisions and adjustments, as in a market situation, with the role of the polity limited to the maintenance of order and the protection of the public. In Soviet society the presence of an explicit ideology and a series of goals and subgoals, coupled with quasi-absolute political and economic power and control, permits the regime to impose upon the entire society its scale of values, its order of priorities, its timetables, without having to contend with counterclaims and constitutional checks and without fear of antagonizing an electorate.[6]

This directionality applied to the medical system as well, and meant that Soviet biomedical scientists were embedded in an administrative structure that coordinated their activities and set their research agenda in accordance with the needs and priorities of the totalitarian state. At the top of this structure was the Soviet Ministry of Health Protection, which was responsible for "the national direction, the planning, supervision, and financing of health matters."[7] How could such a system be criticized for not being sufficiently centralized and coordinated?

In what follows, I explore this contradiction through an examination of both the institutional structures and the practices of planning and coordinating biomedical research in the Brezhnev period. My account focuses on the Soviet Academy of Medical Sciences—the institution vested with the responsibility for this planning and coordination. I demonstrate that, far from being centralized, the administrative system was an unwieldy, enormously complicated structure full of redundancies, and that planning was not in fact a top-down process but in many ways very much the opposite—contingent on a multiplicity of decisions, subject to a multitude of adjustments, and often explicitly local. Planning often proceeded from the bottom up for two reasons. First, because within the disjointed, overlapping administrative structure that was the Soviet system of health protection, top down planning was simply impractical. And second, because the futility of this task meant that planning functions were continuously delegated—both among and within institutional structures. I then demonstrate that within this quagmire of a system, Soviet scientific planning was, in fact, undergoing a process of revision with new institutional forms emerging during the 1970s whose creators had the ambition to significantly reform the process by challenging the prevailing practices of narrow specialization and achieving the integration of planning and research functions. This portion of the chapter focuses on the history of the Institute of Experimental and Clinical Oncology, and its transformation into the National Oncology Center during the Brezhnev period.

This is, of necessity, a very preliminary account as the history of Brezhnev-era science generally and biomedicine in particular remains largely unwritten.[8] Nonetheless I argue that an examination of these practices can provide useful tools for rethinking the paradigm of stagnation. It vividly illustrates that a single monolithic label cannot adequately characterize this period in Soviet history, and argues that the Brezhnev era was not monolithic not only in time (that is, the Soviet Union was not at all the same in 1970 as it was in 1980) but also in space—that at any given temporal point within its historical trajectory, there were multiple Soviet realities being imagined and enacted.

BIOMEDICAL RESEARCH PLANNING ON A NATIONAL LEVEL

In the Soviet Union, the system of health protection was an integral part of the state structure.[9] This point requires emphasis, as it is one that is frequently lost sight of by Western analysts and observers, who often conclude that because the system of health protection was the subject of planning, it was strictly subordinate to the state and all its employees were nothing more than civil servants required to do the state's bidding.[10] The Minister of Health Protection was a member of the Council of Ministers, which meant that the position was of cabinet-level rank. Here and elsewhere I use the full if cumbersome translation of the Ministry's name or the Russian abbreviation MinZdrav instead of the more common terminology of "Ministry of Health" to draw attention to the important differences between the Soviet system and the public health systems found in the West. What set the Soviet system of health protection apart was that, from its beginnings, it was "established as a unified system combining the preventive (prophylactic) and curative systems under one administration."[11]

The Soviet definition of the concept of prophylaxis requires explanation as well. Although in daily usage the term was pretty much equivalent to the English word 'prevention,' it also had certain epistemic connotations. According to Marxism-Leninism, true prophylaxis was a function of the socialist order—the organization of public life in a way that maximized the health and well-being of the people. Accordingly, pursuing prophylactic goals required a planned, multilayered system which could combine economic, social, and public health initiatives aimed at improving working and living conditions, promoting a healthy lifestyle and raising public awareness and support, and preventing illness and injury.[12] This understanding of prophylaxis was taught in medical schools, stressed in professional publications, and dwelled upon in numerous methodological seminars which were a fixture of professional life at every level of the biomedical research enterprise. To what extent these Marxist-Leninist connotations were internalized by individual actors who comprised the system of health protection is an unanswerable question, but that they were a major component of the Cold War epistemology and as such had an impact on the organization and function of the system of health protection cannot be denied.

The system of health protection had three main goals:

> To develop medical science in order to understand the human organism and its complex relationship to the environment, as well as the possible causes and mechanisms of disease; learning to prevent illness and to use for individual and public prophylaxis all available knowledge, methods and tools; and finally, in case of the appearance of illness provide everyone with universally available and qualified medical help in a timely manner.[13]

Of course, these goals were not fully realized in practice. This does not, however, diminish their practical importance in having a very direct impact on the structure and function of the system.

The top administrative structure of the system was the Soviet Ministry of Health Protection (hereafter MinZdrav). The Ministry was officially responsible for all health-related matters, from the provision of medical care to the population to overseeing the enforcement of public health regulations to guiding the development of biomedical research. The Ministry delegated many of these functions to various specialized subordinate entities. The guidance, development, and funding of much of biomedical research was delegated to the Soviet Academy of Medical Sciences.

Founded in 1944, the Academy evolved into a chimeric organization, combining the features of a learned society (such as a roster of elected full and corresponding members drawn from the elite of the scientific establishment) with those of a technocratic bureaucracy. The Academy was headed by an elected president and the Presidium—essentially a scientific and administrative council whose composition was drawn from the membership ranks. The Academy administration was split into three divisions, each one headed by an academician-secretary who was also a member of the Presidium—the Division of Biomedical Sciences (responsible for the institutes conducting what was termed basic research), the Division of Hygiene, Microbiology, and Epidemiology (responsible for institutes working on problems of prophylaxis), and the Division of Clinical Medicine (responsible for institutes such as the IECO which combined both clinical and research functions).[14]

In 1970, the Academy's mandate was expanded considerably when, by order of MinZdrav, it took over the job of planning and coordinating *all* biomedical research in the Soviet Union from MinZdrav's Scientific Medical Council.[15] The stated goal of the order was, of course, perfecting the centralization and efficiency of planning and coordination, which, according to a report compiled for a meeting of the Academy's Presidium dedicated to reporting on its new functions, suffered from a number of shortcomings. The first was that research questions were formulated within the institutes doing the research. This was especially true of research being conducted at medical schools,[16] and was problematic because "this does not always correlate with the interests of solving relevant scientific problems and searching for new methods."[17] Another issue was that individual institutes pursued too many research problems, which was not conducive to the concentration and effective application of scientific resources. As the report observed, the problem with this was that it led to "continued attempts to solve difficult theoretical problems with weak scientific powers and inadequate modern equipment."[18] Finally—and, from the Academy's perspective, most importantly—there was a disproportionate focus on applied rather than basic research problems. The root of the problem was obvious:

> Inadequate development of theoretical questions can be explained mainly by the fact that many research laboratories are inadequately armed with modern laboratory equipment, there is no uninterrupted supply of reagents. . . . All this sometimes leads to [a situation in which] researchers are basing their plans not on the importance of a given question, but on the capacity of the given laboratory . . .[19]

The impact of this was equally obvious—this situation eventually led to a degradation in the quality of the research staff in these laboratories, and did nothing to advance science.

But although the problems with the current planning and coordination practices presented themselves very clearly, solutions were not nearly as obliging. On the one hand, resolving many of these issues seemed a straightforward matter—if inadequate equipment dragged down the performance of individual laboratories, then the solution was clearly to eliminate the inadequacy through better planning and more efficient use of resources. But the practical implementation of such a solution within the existing system of health protection was rendered effectively impossible by its very structure.

This becomes clear when we examine the Academy's futile attempts to produce an inventory of "all scientific research within the realm of medicine"[20] as a first step in accounting for its activities. In the first of a series of reports produced for the purpose, the attempt yielded the following list:

a. Scientific and technical problems included in the Government economic plan for 1971–1975
b. Scientific and technical problems of other departments included in the Government economic plan for 1971–1975 contracted out to institutions subordinate to MinZdrav and the AMS

c. Research programs within Academy and Ministry institutes approved and subsidized by separate order of the Government Committee on Science and Technology of the Council of Ministers of the USSR
d. Research programs within Academy and Ministry Institutes carried out in accordance with the plan of the AMS for 1971–1975
e. Seventy-five problems of national significance[21]

The list is striking for its vagueness and imprecision. Even if one assumes that for a system insider the distinction between a research program, a scientific and technical problem, and a problem of national significance required no explanation, what the research consisted of, how it mapped onto the 'realm of medicine,' or even exactly which institutions fell within this realm is far from clear.

It seems that whoever compiled the report was not oblivious to this problem, since the next report takes a step back and tries to inventory the system of health protection itself. This attempt is only marginally more successful. The report begins by stating that there are 372 medical institutions in the USSR—278 of them research institutions and 94 institutions of

Table 7.1.

STRUCTURAL ENTITY	*# OF SUBORDINATE RESEARCH INSTITUTIONS*
USSR Ministry of Health Protection	46
USSR Academy of Medical Sciences	30
MinZdrav RSFSR	67
MinZdrav Azerbaijan SSR	11
MinZdrav Armenian SSR	8
MinZdrav Belorussian SSR	9
MinZdrav Georgian SSR	21
MinZdrav Kazakh SSR	9
MinZdrav Kirghiz SSR	5
MinZdrav Latvrian SSR	2
MinZdrav Lithuanian SSR	4
MinZdrav Moldovan SSR	3
MinZdrav Tajik SSR	1
MinZdrav Turkemenian SSR	6
MinZdrav Uzbek SSR	12
MinZdrav Ukranian SSR	42
MinZdrav Estonian SSR	2

higher learning. It does a good job of accounting for the research institutions (see Table 7.1), but can place only twenty-two of the educational institutes within the system hierarchy (those under the jurisdiction of MinZdrav USSR). Moreover, the report does not even make an attempt to keep track of institutions outside the system of health protection that also frequently take up biomedical problems (such as those belonging to the Ministry of Defense or the Ministry of Railways, among others).

As for the research that was being conducted at these institutes, the authors of the report could only provide a rough quantitative estimate about the number of research problems under development:

> Each year in accordance with various research plans in excess of 10,000 separate research projects are completed, with another 30,000 projects in progress. Today it is only possible to approximate the number of ongoing research projects, since the system of universal registration of scientific research has been implemented relatively recently. According to data from the information center of the Government Committee on Science and Technology of the Council of Ministers of the USSR, adequate reporting of research agendas is far from universally practiced by the nation's institutes, including those in our system.[22]

Given that "in all union republics the Scientific Medical Councils of the Ministries of Health Protection carry on their activities in varying structural formats"—that is, that there was not even a standard national administrative template that could make the activities of the republican ministries more transparent to the Moscow-based academics—it is little wonder that even taking an inventory of ongoing research was a herculean task.

Planning and coordinating all biomedical research within the Soviet Union was also a task for which the Academy was ill equipped. The Academy had financial control only over its own institutes, and so had little effective leverage outside this network. To mitigate this problem, the Presidium was pushing for revisions to its charter.[23] Specifically, the academicians requested that the phrasing of the charter be revised so that the Academy would not be positioned as subordinate to MinZdrav, but as the "independent, highest scientific institution in the country that is subordinate directly to the Minister of Health Protection of the USSR, to whom it must annually report its activities."[24]

The Presidium also wanted a more concrete formulation of the section concerning the responsibilities and rights of full and corresponding members of the Academy. It argued that election to the Academy had to redefine the status of the new members:

> For newly elected full members, corresponding members and foreign members, election to the Academy must be the start of a qualitatively new phase in their research and administrative activity. . . . Election must be the beginning of the scientists' participation in the work of the

> Scientific Council, the Problem Commission, the beginning of his taking on new problems and themes. . . . Newly elected members of the Academy must be the main link between the research and educational institutions, including those of the republics, that are not part of the Academy. . . . It is necessary to liquidate the situation in which the research and administrative work of a member of the Academy who does not work within the Academy system does not substantially differ from his work before being elected to the Academy.[25]

This redefinition was necessary so that the Presidium could make specific demands on its members no matter where they were employed so as to enable the Academy to use them as leverage over the institutes not within the Academy system—something that the Presidium found to be currently impossible.

Even if the requested changes had been made, however, there is little reason to suppose that it would have solved the problem, as the Academy would still have little more than moral authority over the majority of the people and institutions that it was supposed to be controlling. MinZdrav could not have been unaware of either the enormity of the task or of how unequal the Academy of Medical Sciences was to its challenges when it divested itself of responsibility for the planning and coordination of research. If the Ministry's goal was indeed to perfect the process of planning and coordination, handing off these functions to a less powerful administrative structure was undoubtedly an ineffective strategy. The benefits of delegating the task, along with the associated paperwork, must have outweighed other considerations.

Planning on the Academy Level

It is, of course, not surprising that the Academy was unable to master a task as large and complex as the planning of all biomedical research in every corner of the Soviet Union. But it is important to realize that the failure was due to more than the enormity of the task. Even on the much smaller, more clearly defined scale of what were known as "problems of national significance," effective control over scientific research continued to elude would-be planners.

The Academy was in charge of planning and coordinating seventy-five such problems. Each one had a dedicated commission composed of current academicians and staff members of various Academy institutes whose job it was to plan and coordinate research on this particular problem nationwide. The commissions had their home base at the Academy institute whose specialty best qualified it to head up the problem (the institute was thus referred to as the head institute). On an annual basis, each commission reported on its own activities and the state of research on the problem it was entrusted with to the structural division of the Academy into whose purview the head institute where the commission was based fell. The divisions compiled these reports, discussed the product at the meetings of their bureaus, and then passed them up the chain of command to the Presidium. The Presidium, in turn, compiled all the divisional reports, reviewed and discussed them, and then reported the results to MinZdrav.

The fact that the problems as well as the institutions and bureaucratic structures involved in carrying out the research and its planning and coordination were clearly delineated did not make the task any more manageable in practice. This becomes clear in examining the transcripts of the various meetings dedicated to this process. For example on March 28, 1975, the Bureau of the Division of Clinical Medicine convened to discuss the fulfillment of the 1974 plan for institutes and problems of national significance coordinated by the Division. There were sixty people in attendance—the Chair and Secretary of the Bureau; fifteen members of the Bureau (all full or corresponding members of the Academy); the directors of two institutes belonging to the Division of Clinical Medicine as well as six Deputy-Directors of Research and nine Scientific Secretaries from other divisional institutes; and twenty-six invited guests from Academy and MinZdrav institutes as well as independent research groups.

A. V. Snezhnevskii, the Chair of the Bureau, opened the meeting by presenting the participants with a clear agenda that focused not so much on the plan and its fulfillment as on the planning and reporting process itself and on how to ensure an equitable representation of both the laboratory and the clinical perspective in this process:

> Before us stands the difficult task of discussing the reports of all the problem commissions coordinated by the Division of Clinical Medicine at once. The discussion must focus on the system of planning and reporting. The job of the problem commissions is to organize research on a particular problem in the country as whole. However this happens in isolation from other, related disciplines which in modern medicine is untenable. At the Presidium, there was talk of creating scientific research *programs* that would allow for the participation of both laboratory and clinical scientists.[26]

But within the confines of the hour-long meeting, there was not even enough time to come to an agreement about which aspects of the planning and reporting process ought to be the focus. Academician A. I. Arutyunov, a member of the Bureau, argued that what needed to be addressed first were problems with terminology. He took particular issue with the term "general theme" which was used in reporting plan fulfillment, arguing that the vagueness of the term distorted the accuracy of the report: "What is a general theme? It can be a theme that itself contains four hundred problems. I don't believe that within a year research has been completed on forty-four general themes."[27]

His junior colleague, corresponding member B. V. Ognev, however, advocated for discussing the criteria used to evaluate research accomplishments, and to begin using international patents and domestic authorship certificates in this capacity: "The goal of the Academy is to create the new, the original, and to go its own way. And for that it is crucial to know the state of world medical science. . . . The presence of discoveries and inventions is the best measurement of the efficacy of research, and we don't have a lot of those."[28] Still other bureau members wanted to forego discussing the planning and reporting process in favor of looking at specific problems, since they had taken the trouble to review the reports on them before the meeting.

Just about the only thing that the meeting participants did agree on was that "it is impossible to illuminate the results of 40 research themes in 50 minutes."[29] Professor V. I. Burakovskii, a corresponding member of the Academy who was serving on the Bureau at the time, fumed that "this form of reporting on all problems [at once] is senseless," and suggested that the division request permission to review each problem individually.[30] That he was not seemingly aware that the division already *did* regularly review reports from individual commissions at its meetings attests to the disciplinary problems at the Bureau, whose members often skipped the meetings.

Although at the level of the Presidium discipline did not present an issue, other problems, such as poorly defined terminology and cumbersome bureaucratic boundaries, remained. For example at a meeting on May 10, 1972, dedicated to producing a report on the outcomes of research on the problems of national significance from the previous year, the Presidium stumbled over the term "physiologically active compound." As S. R. Mardashev, a vice president of the Academy, complained:

> The question of the creation of physiologically active compounds is unclear. . . . Without a definition of what counts as a physiologically active compound it's unclear what needs to be done. This refers to a huge number of different types of substances. I even thought of creating a special council on physiologically active substances. In the physiology problem there are projects on physiologically active substances, in cardiovascular diseases also.[31]

That is, the problem was that the rigid disciplinary affiliations around which problems of national significance were defined made it difficult to administer research that focused on boundary objects—objects such as physiologically active compounds that were present within many different disciplinary communities, even if each community defined the object slightly differently.[32]

Looking closely at the practices of biomedical research planning within the Academy system makes it hard to argue with the salience of the stagnation paradigm. In following the daily work of the Presidium, one gets the sense that the academicians unfortunate enough to occupy positions within it are slowly drowning in paperwork. Though clearly aware of their predicament, they struggle in vain to stay on the surface—their commitment to the paradigm of centralized planning and coordination condemning all their efforts to be counterproductive and result in nothing more than additional paperwork. The only sensible course of action within this system seems to be that adopted by Burakovskii—not to engage in the senseless struggle so that the quicksand may engulf one more slowly.

And yet even within this system, individual administrators were effectively pushing for institutional innovation and reform, and a nuanced understanding of this period of Soviet history is not possible until historians examine their efforts. I will now begin laying the groundwork for such an examination by looking at the efforts of Nikolai Nikolaevich Blokhin, the director of the Institute of Experimental and Clinical Oncology, to build up his field and provide it with an interdisciplinary institutional base. Using transcripts of various meetings of the Presidium of the Academy of Medical Sciences at which Center construction was discussed, I tease out Blokhin's vision for the new institution. Determining to what extent the Center that ultimately came to bear Blokhin's name matched his vision is beyond the scope of this article.

INSTITUTIONAL INNOVATION IN THE CONTEXT OF STAGNATION

Soviet oncology as a separate discipline has its roots at the start of the twentieth century, when the first Institute of Oncology was founded in Moscow in 1903 (the institute eventually came to be named after P. A. Gertsen, who directed it from 1922 to 1934). The institute focused primarily on problems of diagnosis and surgical and radiation treatment, and in 1926 it was joined by another, similar institute in Leningrad.

Although the dominant therapeutic modality at the start of the twentieth century was surgery, active attempts to explore other therapeutic options started quite early, providing a catalyst for further institutional development. For example, efforts at anti-cancer drug development date back to the 1920s, when there were attempts to use the most promising approaches from experimental biology and experimental medicine to uncover compounds that could inhibit tumor growth. The most famous (and infamous) of these efforts was the work of Gregory Ruskin and Nina Kliueva, a husband-and-wife team of microbiologists who developed a biological preparation they termed KR.[33] The preparation showed great promise during animal testing, and made headlines around the world shortly after World War II, when it was touted as a potential breakthrough in cancer therapy. While the preparation was ultimately deemed ineffective during clinical trials, what secured KR's place in history was the political turmoil that engulfed the scientists connected to the project when they were tried before a "court of honor" for divulging state secrets after sharing this work with American colleagues.

The political turmoil around KR did not dampen growing enthusiasm for further research on cancer therapeutics either within administrative circles or the research community. For example, in 1946 the National Scientific Research Chemicho-Pharmaceutical Institute (the Russian acronym, which will be used henceforth, is VNIHFI) received an official mandate to concentrate its drug development in eight areas, one of which was oncology—a surprising level of priority given the postwar medical and economic challenges facing the country.[34] And in 1951 the U.S.S.R. Academy of Medical Sciences expanded Kliueva and Roskin's laboratory into the Scientific Research Institute of Experimental Pathology and Therapy of Cancer.[35] One of the main goals of the Institute was the development of cancer chemotherapeutics, and it was fairly successful, creating two notable drugs within its first three years in operation—sarcolizin and dopan.[36]

Beginning in March 1952, this Institute was under the directorship of N. N. Blokhin—a skilled surgeon and an extremely energetic and ambitious administrator who was the driving force behind its growth and expansion for thirty-five years.[37] The son of a zemstvo physician, Blokhin began honing his leadership skills while studying at the Gorkii Medical Institute in the late 1920s.[38] At the time, medical institutes did not follow a uniform curriculum, and the Gorkii institute was experimenting with team learning. The students in each class were divided into groups of five or six, with the most academically successful being appointed team leader and assuming responsibility for the success of the entire group. Blokhin served in this capacity throughout his initial medical training, and the experience of being vested with a lot of responsibility without enjoying a similar degree of power clearly served him well. In 1952, while serving as chair of the Department of General Surgery of his alma mater, Blokhin was invited to direct the Institute of Experimental Pathology and Therapy of Cancer in Moscow. Also in 1952 he was elected a corresponding member of the Soviet Academy of Medical Science.

Although much of his career up to that point had been devoted to reconstructive surgery, he agreed to take up the post. In March of 1952 the IEPTC was a small, classified institution occupying a wing of the Vladimirskii Moscow Regional Clinical Institute. Despite the fact that his own expertise was clinical, Blokhin focused his early efforts at the institute on the experimental arm of the organization. He organized new laboratories—including a laboratory dedicated to drug development—and assembled a team of leading scientists from all over the Soviet Union to direct them. In 1959, the growing Institute was renamed the Institute of

Experimental and Clinical Oncology (IECO). New laboratories demanded new space, and in 1960 the institute finally got its own building. That same year Blokhin became a full member of the Academy as well as its president—a post he held until 1968 and resumed unexpectedly in 1977.

Since the new building was a former hospital, it was taken over by the expanding clinical division (which started with only sixty beds), while the experimental facilities remained behind in the original space. But only four years later the clinical and experimental arms of the institute were reunited in a newly constructed complex on Kashirskoe Shosse which featured a four hundred-bed clinic, a laboratory building with a vivarium capable of housing eighty thousand animals, an eight hundred-person auditorium and a large library boasting foreign periodicals, and two buildings dedicated to radiation therapy.[39] Impressive as this growth was, it is during the Brezhnev era that the Institute saw its most spectacular transformation—into the National Oncology Scientific Center (VONTs)—a fundamentally new institutional structure within the Academy system which became one of the largest cancer research and treatment facilities in the world, and built up a solid reputation with colleagues abroad.

The creation of the Center began with a resolution of the Council of Ministers in 1969,[40] but neither the architectural designs for the new buildings nor the structure of the new institution had been firmly settled. As late as 1974, in a report to the Presidium on the progress of construction, Blokhin observed that "we still don't have a clear idea about what these centers will be in the Academy system."[41] But while he was quite right that the structure and function of the Center were still in the process of taking their final shape—at the time of his report, even the question of who would lead the new Center had not been formally settled, with Blokhin still occupying only his old post at the helm of the IECO—his own vision for what the Center should be was quite well developed. As Blokhin explained in his report,

> It seems to me these centers have to significantly differ from institutes. Since they are being created to solve the most important problems, they have to be, as a rule, the head institutions in the solution of the main problems of health protection, including gathering statistical data on these problems, implementing the outcomes of research into practice, creating guidelines. The problem commissions have to have these centers as a base. They must be responsible for the coordination, planning and reporting, and also international relations, as well as have a department that is connected to Minzdrav.[42]

In essence, Blokhin wanted to break up the planning process by field, and transfer the related tasks of both the Academy of Medical Sciences *and*

MinZdrav to the new institution. To carry out these tasks, the Center had to be a new structure:

> I think the Center should be a complex of institutes, specialized laboratories and clinics that work together and in that differ from an institute. In the head of each division stands the director, elected in accordance with the Academy Charter, and the director of the whole complex, also elected. A council of directors jointly administers the Center. And in this council you have representatives of other scientific institutions of the country.[43]

Most importantly, this new structure had to be vested not just with broad responsibilities but with effective power, and so Blokhin advocated for allowing the Center to directly control the purse strings of national cancer research through a grant system modeled on that of the National Cancer Institute in the US.[44]

This was an extremely ambitious vision—one that, although it did not give up on the idea of planning, disrupted existing administrative structures entirely and had the potential to actually radically alter practices. It is thus all the more remarkable that the Center was, in fact, built. Although finishing construction dragged on through the decade, the Institute of Experimental and Clinical Oncology effectively dissolved within the new structure in 1975.

RECONSIDERING STAGNATION

Using the practices of biomedical research planning within the Soviet system of health protection as a lens for the examination of the era of stagnation yields a complex, kaleidoscopic image of the period. On the one hand, it demonstrates that the label 'stagnation' has the weight of considerable empirical evidence behind it—the efforts of planning were mired in a cumbersome administrative structure that was choking on its own paper outputs and being strangled by its own processes. On the other hand, it also provides evidence that the system was capable of producing change. Blokhin, after all, was a part and parcel of this system, effectively juggling multiple roles within it throughout his career—that of clinician (he continued to perform surgeries at the Center even after he was forced out of the directorship in 1987), that of institute director, that of academician and government administrator, and that of a spokesman for the Soviet system of health protection both at home and abroad.

While one can make the argument that the development of the National Oncology Center is an exception that only proves the rule, these exceptions require close examination to understand not only the period of stagnation, but what followed as well.

NOTES

1. Memorandum to Assistant Secretary for Health and Scientific Affairs, DHEW, 11 September, 1972. Box 6, Folder: Dr. James Holland; Records of the Office of the Assistant Secretary for Health, 1950–1992, Record Group 514, National Archives at College Park, MD.

2. James Holland, "Reflections on Soviet Cancer Research," June 18, 1973; Box 5, Folder: Dr. James Holland, 1; Records of the Office of the Assistant Secretary for Health, 1950–1992; Record Group 514; National Archives at College Park, MD.

3. Ibid., 6.

4. See the introduction to this volume.

5. Mark G. Field, *Soviet Socialized Medicine: An Introduction*, (New York: The Free Press, 1967), 183.

6. Ibid., 10.

7. Ibid., 77.

8. The history of Soviet medicine generally has only recently begun to receive attention from historians. See Susan Gross Solomon, ed., *Doing Medicine Together: Germany and Russia Between the Wars* (Toronto: University of Toronto Press, 2006); Krementsov, *The Cure*; Tricia Starks, *The Body Soviet: Propaganda, Hygiene, and the Revolutionary State*, (Madison, WI: The University of Wisconsin Press, 2008). There have also been several dissertations at the university of Chicago that remain unpublished: Christopher Burton, 1999, "Medical Welfare during late Stalinism: A study of Doctors and the Soviet Health System, 1945–1953" and Michael David, 1999, "The White Plague in the Red State: The Control of Tuberculosis in Russia, 1900–1941", Ben Zajicek, 2009, "Scientific Psychiatry in Stalin's Soviet Union: The Politics of Modern Medicine and the Struggle to Define 'Pavlovian' Psychiatry, 1939–1953." The body of scholarship produced on the subject in Russia is also quite small—although the Soviet period is covered in some sweeping history of medicine texts (see M.B. Mirskii, *Meditsina Rossii X-XX vekov: ocherki istorii*, (Moskva: Rosspen, 2005), there have been very few historiographies dedicated to the period published.

9. In this, the Soviets followed a long history of Russian government regulation and even provision of medical care—the first administrative structure charged with regulatory functions, the *Aptekarskii prikaz*, was instituted in 1581, and its functions and structure expanded and evolved in response to the needs of the state (see Mirskii *Meditsina Rossii*). The Soviet innovation consisted in reconceptualizing healthcare provision as a key function and obligation of the government.

10. See Field *Soviet Socialized Medicine* and also Mark G. Field, *Doctor and Patient in Soviet Russia*, (Cambridge, MA: Harvard University Press, 1957). Also Michael Ryan, *Doctors and the State in the Soviet Union*, (New York: St. Martin's Press, 1990).

11. Odin Anderson, "A review and impressions of the health services in the USSR, the month of September, 1972, Moscow and Leningrad," Folder: Anderson, Odin W (Daniels). Records of the Office of the Assistant Secretary for Health, 1950–1992, Record Group 514, Box 6. National Archives at College Park, MD.

12. M.I. Barsukov, ed., *Ocherki istorii zdravoohraneniia SSSR: 1917–1956*, (Moskva: Medgiz, 1957).

13. D.D. Venediktov, *Sovetsko-Amerikanskoe sotrudnichestvo v oblasti zdravoohraneniia*, (Moscow: Meditsina 1977).

14. "Razvitiye meditsinskoy nauki v SSSR," Archives of the Academy of Medical Sciences (AMS), Moscow. F. 9120 Op. 2 d. 6370.

15. AMS F. 9120 Op. 2 d. 6370.

16. Although education and research functions were theoretically separate in the institute system, in practice faculty at the medical schools also conducted research. For faculty members already holding doctorates, research was a way to maintain their prestige and break up the routines of teaching; for more junior faculty members, research was a way to advance up the career ladder.

17. "Spravka o meropriiatiah po organizatsii sistemi planirovaniia, prognozirovaniia i koordinatsii nauchnih issledovanii po problemam soyuznogo znacheniia, kuriruemym AMS F. 9120 Op. 2 D. 6596, l. 9.
18. AMS F. 9120 Op. 2 D. 6596, l. 9.
19. AMS F. 9120 Op. 2 D. 6596, l. 10.
20. AMS F. 9120 Op. 2 D. 6596, l. 3.
21. AMS F. 9120 Op. 2 D. 6596, l. 3.
22. AMS F. 9120 Op. 2 D. 6596, l. 20.
23. AMS F. 9120 Op. 2 D. 6596, l. 34.
24. AMS F. 9120 Op. 2 D. 6596, l. 35.
25. AMS F. 9120 Op. 2 D. 6596, l. 36.
26. "Protokol №5 zasedaniya Byuro otdeleniya klinicheskoy meditsiny AMN SSSR ot 28 marta 1975 goda." AMS F. 1 Op. 3 D. 1269 l. 185.
27. AMS F. 1 Op. 3 D. 1269 l. 185.
28. AMS F. 1 Op. 3 D. 1269 l. 186.
29. AMS F. 1 Op. 3 D. 1269 l. 187.
30. AMS F. 1 Op. 3 D. 1269 l. 186.
31. "Otchet o vypolnenii problemno—tematicheskogo plana za 1971 god po problemam vsesoyuznogo znacheniya, kuriruyemym Prezidiumom AMN SSSR." AMS F. 9120 Op. 2 D. 6357, l. 137.
32. Susan Star and James Griesemer, "Institutional Ecology, 'Translations' and Boundary Objects: Amateurs and Professionals in Berkeley's Museum of Vertebrate Zoology, 1907–39," *Social Studies of Science* (1989),19/3: 387–420.
33. Nikolai Krementsov, *The Cure: A story of cancer and politics from the Annals of the Cold War*, (Chicago: The University of Chicago Press, 2002); V.D. Esakov and E.S. Levina, *Stalinskie 'Sudy Chesti': delo 'KR,'* (Moscow: Nauka, 2005).
34. Mary Schaeffer Conroy, "The Soviet Pharmaceutical Industry and Dispensing: 1945–1953," *Europe-Asia Studies*, Vol. 56, No. 7 (Nov., 2004), pp. 963–991. The mandate probably came from MinZdrav, which had jurisdiction over this institute, though Schaeffer Conroy does not specify the source.
35. At the dawn of its existence, the Institute was a secret institution. N. G. Blokhina, *Akademik Nikolai Nikolaievich Blokhin: vrach i chelovek*. (Moskva: Meditsina, 2001).
36. "Dolgosrochniye prognozy na 15–20 let razvitiia vazhneishyh napravlenii meditisinskoi nauki, tom 1," AMS F. 9120 Op. 2 D. 6270.
37. Prior to this appointment Blokhin was working in his native city of Gor'kii, where he received his medical training.
38. This and other biographical data comes from N.G. Blokhina, *Akademik Nikolai Nikolaevich Blokhin: Vrach i chelovek*, (Moskva: Meditsina, 2001).
39. N.G. Blokhina, *Akademik Nikolai Nikolaevich Blokhin: Vrach i chelovek*, (Moskva: Meditsina, 2001).
40. "O rassmotrenii zadaniya na proyektirovaniye stroitel'stva nauchno—eksperimental'noy chasti Onkologicheskogo nauchnogo tsentra AMN SSSR." AMS F. P9120 Op. 2 D. 6365.
41. "Stenogramma zasedaniya prezidiuma Akademii Meditsinskikh Nauk SSSR 27 marta 1974 goda." AMS F. 9120 Op. 2 D. 6807 l. 25.
42. AMS F. 9120 Op. 2 D. 6807 l. 25.
43. AMS F. 9120 Op. 2 D. 6807 l. 26.
44. "Protokol №4 zasedaniya Prezidiuma Akademii Meditsinskikh Nauk SSSR 26 yanvarya 1973 goda." AMS F. 9120 Op. 2 D. 6597.

EIGHT

If You're Going to Moscow, Be Sure to Wear Some Flowers in Your Hair (and Bring a Bottle of Port Wine in Your Pocket)

The Soviet Hippie "Sistema" and Its Life in, Despite, and with "Stagnation"

Juliane Fürst

The Soviet hippie system—*sistema*—has its origins somewhere on the Maiakovskaia Square in central Moscow. Its founding fathers (and to a lesser extent, mothers) were a bunch of longish-haired, hippie-ish youngsters who liked hanging out, chatting about music, drinking port wine, and provoking passing members of the public. They revelled in the fact that they felt free and careless—freer than their more conformist contemporaries and more careless than their parents and grandparents who worked and lived within the Soviet system—often in high-ranking and powerful positions. These youngsters despised the grey and dull character of Brezhnev's Soviet Union. They rebelled against a pervasive sense that nothing would ever happen and nothing would ever change. They were attracted by the gentleness of a movement that rejected hierarchy and violence. They thought that music and love could change the world—their personal one and the big, global one. It was an unlikely time to see the emergence of a Western-inspired subculture that was anti-American yet rested on American attributes. And it was an unlikely environment to bring about a "system"—a term associated with order, organization and, not least, the official Soviet structures. Yet, within a few years, the Moscow sistema had become a Union-wide association of hippies and like-minded people, who had built up a network of communication, information, mutual aid, and ritualistic practices that stretched from Novosibirsk to Lvov, from Ufa to Tallinn, and many points in between. The sistema, while never formally founded or officially defined, proved incredibly durable in the face of persecution and rapid political change. Arguably the sistema is still alive today, even though most of its protagonists speak of it now in the past.[1]

The hippie sistema with its dynamic of rebellion, differentiation, innovation, and clear Western inspiration sits uneasily with the common understanding of the term "stagnation." What was stagnating about young Muscovite men and women falling for the new idea of making the world better through love and peace; putting beads in their hair and ribbons around their wrists, turning themselves into objects of art by wearing colorful, self-tailored dresses, jeans with painted and stitched flowers and jackets and coats bearing the insignia of the international 1960s counterculture? How could the Moscow hippies and their linked milieu of the emerging Soviet rock music scene be called dull when they became local legends to their audience? How repressive could a system be that allowed hippies to make Gorky Street and several other points in the city their own—maybe unhappily and reluctantly so, but apparently without resorting to a Stalinist purge?

Yet the emergence and development of the Soviet sistema says a lot about the time and nature of stagnation. Indeed, it might be a useful prism to redefine the term, remove it from its original economic context, and give it a new life as a concept that is useful both in its primary sense as well as a metaphor for its idiosyncratic consequences. For, while the world of the hippies and their sistema was not stagnating, it was created on the basis of many of the implications of stagnation and developed in ways that were specific and fitting to the realities of it. The attraction of the Soviet hippie movement, as it was emerging in the 1960s and growing in the 1970s, was to no small extent due to the fact that young people *perceived* the world around them as stagnating. They might not have used the very term *zastoi*—and indeed it rarely even appears in the interviews conducted in recent years—but they describe an atmosphere that is associated with a country in which nothing is changing and nothing seems to be likely to change. It is the same general consensus that "everything was forever until it was no more" that is so aptly analyzed in Aleksei Yurchak's eponymous book.[2] This generation—which Yurchak termed the "last Soviet generation"—differed markedly from the so-called Thaw generation who came of age in the late 1950s and 1960s, whose general outlook was much more optimistic about the future of the country they lived in, eager for reform and keen to be actively involved in the process of change.

By the late 1960s, and even more so in the 1970s, the general mood favored the avoidance of involvement, hope was considered, naïve and reformism was akin to activism or dissidence, both of which were considered signs of either careerism or pathological social behavior.[3] The lure of the official communist youth program, mainly, but not solely, presented by the Komsomol had long faded. The social mobility that had advanced this generation's parents and grandparents seemed elusive to this new breed of Soviet people who imagined their future in terms of connections and engrained privilege rather than individual achievement and new opportunities. There was not even the drama of obvious and drastic repressive action on behalf of the state, which had kept Stalinist society tense and intense. Instead Brezhnev's young Soviets saw corruption, lies, and entrenched interests everywhere. They did not believe that they could change the system or even their lives. A young member of a commune in Leningrad in the late 1970s succinctly summarized the prevailing sentiment: "I am sick of it all," she exclaims in a small cartoon painted by her boyfriend. "*Mne vse nadoelo.*"[4] Regardless to what extent these perceptions of "stagnation" were borne out by reality, their power rested on the fact that they were commonplace not only in the minds of the young but in the imagination of most of Soviet society.[5] Yet, the perception of stagnation bred the opposite of stagnation—social movement.

This chapter will follow the fate of the Soviet hippie movement (which was only one of the many areas in which the 1970s developed an active scene parallel to the public sphere), in particular its sistema, and its interlinked and interdependent relationship with the epoch in which it lived and flourished. It will trace the origins of the movement in the late 1960s in the circles of Moscow's elite offspring (even though concurrently and independently hippies started to appear in the Baltic states) and examine how and why the Moscow hippies solidified in a system. It will investigate how the sistema became ritualized and formalized in the following years, broadening its membership base and intensifying its character. Over the following years the sistema became less an offshoot of the international hippie movement and increasingly an entity in its own right, based on the realities of late socialist everyday life and in constant dialogue with its possibilities and weaknesses. Ultimately, this article will argue that the Soviet sistema of hippies offers an interesting and insightful window into the complex mechanisms of stagnation—a window that both showcases the borders of late socialist society, in so far as it illuminates a group at (and often outside) the margins of society, and offers general observations of what it meant to live in and with stagnation. In short the sistema emerges as an entity that was peculiar to stagnation, yet at the same time redefines the term, giving it a more complex and—ironically—more dynamic meaning.

There is no academic history of the sistema. During Perestroika there was considerable interest in the contemporary sistema by progressive

Soviet sociologists.[6] The movement was sufficiently "underground" not to be well-represented in state sources (at least not in any that are available at the moment). There have been attempts by various hippie webpages (hippi.ru; domikhippi.ru) to piece together some history of the movement, but these are skewed by the fact that contributors only know their small share of the chronicle of events in their specific location and that different factions within the movement vie for "authenticity." The following chronology has hence been painstakingly pieced together from interviews, memoirs, and some documents. As far as possible I have verified specific information through corroborating evidence, but at times evidence was conflicting or only provided by one person. I have indicated as far as possible such instances in the footnotes, when I had to use author's privilege to accept a version of events over another. The result is a first attempt to historicize the sistema. It is necessarily incomplete and at times chronologically vague, but it rests on the evidence of more than 120 interviews, many more than are cited specifically in this chapter.

HOW THE "SISTEMA" WAS BORN

The sistema was born in Moscow, yet its conception undoubtedly occurred in the West. Of course it had its local subcultural predecessors such as the *stiliagi*, style-enamored jazz fans of the 1940s and 1950s, and quasi-Beatniki, who ran underground poetry circles in a variety of locations in the 1960s. But there is a surprising consensus among contemporary witnesses that what turned Soviet youth into hippies was what was happening in San Francisco's Haight Ashbury, London's Hyde Park, and many other places around the world. It was the Soviet Union's own media empire that provided first glimpses into the world of Western flower power. In 1967 the journal *Rovesnik* ran a mostly sympathetic piece on a wave of free-spirited flower children in London turning against their capitalist parents, even if they ultimately described them as victims of their consumerist system. [7] *Pravda* followed the same year with an even more unequivocally positive article about the antimaterialist, anticapitalist, peace-loving hippie dropouts of New York.[8] These articles were read from Lvov to Vladivostok, and a multitude of youngsters started to weave beads into their hair, grow their hair, paint flowers on their faces, and hang around in public spaces, which they named Love Street and such.[9] In Moscow, young people did not have to rely solely on articles in the press. If you lived in the center, maybe went to one of the prestigious faculties of MGU, belonged to the wider intelligentsia, there was a high chance that you knew somebody who traveled to the West for professional reasons, that you or your friends possessed items that came from the capitalist world, and that your knowledge of the fabled world on the other side of the Iron Curtain was more firsthand than for most people. It is no coincidence that the Soviet sistema of hippies started out in the center of the Soviet Union, Moscow and, more precisely, in the very heart of the capital and its political establishment.

The very earliest signs of Moscow hippiedom can be detected in 1966/1967, when bands of singing and guitar-playing youngsters with longish, Beatles-like hair started to congregate in the *truba*—the tunnel that led from the Western entry of the Hotel *Natsional* to the Red Square.[10] Inspiration supposedly came from the fabled Masha Shtatnitsa (in real life Marina Izvekova, whose adopted name came from the Russian word *Shtaty* for United States) who, as daughter of diplomatic parents, arrived back in Moscow in 1966 from New York as a full-blown hippie and bearer not only of colored ribbons and peace signs, but of a treasure trove of knowledge of how to be and what it meant to be a hippie.[11] From 1968 onward, the movement mushroomed. When Artemy Troitsky returned from Prague in 1968, he found that Moscow was a much more happening place than the Czechoslovakian capital deep in the throes of liberalization. "The hippie thing refashioned our youth in the blinking of an eye."[12] But the rebellious socialist "brethren" played an important role of transmission. It was the children of Czechoslovakian diplomats (whose embassy was located on the *Maiakovskaia*) who alerted the *tusovka* meeting at the square to the pleasures that could be found outside the socialist world, underlining the fact it was status that drove information channels. The Czechoslovakian youth invited their Moscow friends to drink and jam in the nearby embassy's cellar bar and watch Western films in the embassy's cinema.[13] They shared Czech newspapers with them, which wrote liberally about the Beatles and other bands, hipsters and hippies, Europe's new left and Czechoslovakian reform attempts. These happenings came to an abrupt halt when all diplomats were called back in November 1968 in the wake of the crackdown on the Prague Spring. Yet the Moscow hippie movement was only just beginning.

The composition of the new trend was indicative of those at the forefront of disaffected youth in the Brezhnev period. A great number of them were children of privileged parents, who lived close to the Kremlin around Gorky Street and the Arbat. Some, such as Vasilli Stalin, grandson of the *vozhd*, or Anastas and Alik Mikoian, grandchildren of Politburo longtimer Mikoain, came from seriously famous families with connections to the highest echelons of power. Many like Sasha Boradulin, son of the famous Soviet photographer Lev Boradulin, and Sasha Lipnitskii, stepson of Khrushchev's and Brezhnev's personal translator, were members of the MGU journalism faculty, which was a hotbed for privileged youth.[14] Their friend Tatiana Strelnikova's father was the *Pravda* correspondent in New York. A fellow *zhurfak* member became one of the most colorful early hippie leaders in Moscow: Sveta Barabash, better known as Ofelia. Her mother was an English teacher for Military Intelligence. Via her first husband Igor Dudinskii she was linked to the circle around the so-called Smogisty, a union of young poets, and a visitor to Moscow's Bohemian salon run by Iurii Mamleev.[15] Moscow's premier hippie couple Sasha Penannen and Sveta Markov, who, until their emigration in 1974, hosted a hippie hangout and tailoring atelier in their apartment on Prospekt Mira, had all of Moscow's disaffected youth through their door, including nonconformist artists, rock stars, ballet dancers, career criminals and Moscow's morphine and opium addicts. Sveta's party-loyal and *apparatchik* mother lived in the same apartment. Sveta's deceased father had been the chief curator of the Lenin Museum on Red Square.[16] Among the hippies from the city center were also the son of Bulat Okudzhava and the son of Tukhachevskii's right-hand man, who himself had been born in a gulag at Kolyma. This too was a sign of the times: the descendants of perpetrators and victims of Stalin's crimes shared the same space and the same interest, united by their common alienation from official Soviet life.[17]

However, it was another young man who proved to be most influential for the development of the *sistema.* Iura Buriakov, or Solntse (Sunny), is widely considered to be the leader and founder of the Moscow *sistema,* which, in its early years, also went by the name *sistema Sol'ntse* or, because of the geographical location of its meeting places—*tsentrovaia sistema.* It is not clear if Solntse ever studied or worked in a proper profession—nobody ever recalled him doing so. But he was supremely well-connected. Solntse was simply known by everyone. His peers describe him as funny, an engaging conversationalist, an extremely good and elegant rock 'n' roll dancer, and a lady's man, who never said no to a measure of alcohol.[18] His sociability embodied the *sistema.* It was Solntse who supposedly decided to bring structure to the loosely connected hippies across town, all of whom had only a few things in common: they loved music, they disliked authority, they favored Western fashion, and they knew of Solntse and his *tusovka.* How the curious term *sistema* came about remains shrouded in mystery. Sol'ntse's friend Soldatov claimed he came up with the term to describe the recently established connection between Moscow and Riga hippies. The Baltic hippies had indeed been in touch with each other for years. But it was left to the Moscow visitors, who ventured into the Soviet Union's "little Europe" for the first time in 1969, to formalize these connections with a proper concept. In our interview, Soldatov implicitly acknowledged the idiosyncrasy of using a term that was widely known to describe the very entity they so despised. He described the new formation as "non-Komsomol" (*akomsomol'skii*) and "not an organization, but a network." Similarly Senia Skorpion, another hippie whose roots go back to the early 1970s, immediately referred to the "official" system in order to describe their own: "They had their system, we had ours."[19] (The possibility of parody or self-irony remains hazy: one of the original terms, *sol'nechnaia sistema* [solar system], also includes a certain over-dramatisation of the Soviet hippie movement.) According to Soldatov, it was a way of expressing "I know you, and you know me."[20] Another eminent hippie of the first hour, Ofelia, later developed the idea and described the *sistema* as not merely a union of people but a different "system of living." A term of differentiation, it was also a more unique, less global identity, with the term *sistemny* soon being as prominent as the term hippie among the Soviet non-conformist community (and in places like Leningrad, the preferred way for people to describe themselves).[21] Yet for the first five years of its existence it remained primarily a Moscow term. Here they knew not only the *tsentrovaia sistema* but also the *Ismailovskaia* and *Baumanskaia sistema* (referring to different Moscow neighborhoods), and possibly several more. But no matter how many and where local hippies met, those who were serious eventually drifted to the center—to Sontse's *sistema*, even when it was already clear that its charismatic founder of the *sistema* had turned into little more than a drunk.[22]

Central to the functioning of the *sistema*—whether central or local—were commonly accepted and reliable meeting spaces. In the center they were a variety of places on Gorky Street and, in the early years, the *Psichodrom*. This space, the old MGU courtyard, was representative of the student background of the Moscow hippie movement and also indicative of its intellectual roots. It had served already as an important space for the Smogisty and could trace its pedigree as a place of youthful nonconformism even further back in time.[23] From around 1968–1969 onwards it became a place for hippies, semihippies and hangers-on from the surrounding faculties and other institutes of higher education: some devotees were otherwise diligent *otlichniki*, some were simply present by coincidence, some liked the fashion, others the look of the girls.[24] Parallel to the new visibility in open spaces, the hippies also continued the time-honored tradition of the 1950s and 1960s *kompanii* to turn private apartments into quasi-salons. Aleksei Romanov's (later member of the group Mashina Vremeni and then leader of Voskresenie) place at the Petrovka became one-such legendary space, as was the Markov's apartment on *Prospekt Mira*. With its painted walls and deliberate lack of furniture, their apartment served as one of the major assembly spaces for the larger Moscow underground. Yet the Markovs were not complete dropouts. Alexandr was an architect, while Sveta worked as a coveted seamstress, supposedly making costumes for the young Alla Pugacheva.[25] She also dressed many members of the Moscow hippie community and their rock musician friends.[26] In their salon different generations of nonconformists assembled, with veteran *stiliaga* Aleksei Kozlov as well as the newly emerging rock music elite such as Igor Digtariuk in attendance.[27] It was the heady mixture of new music, radical philosophy, and the spirit of the times (with Czechoslovakia, Vietnam, Paris, and Woodstock all contributing to the overall feel) that propelled enthusiasm for the idea of love, peace, long hair, and flowery frocks. By the early 1970s, Moscow was home to several hundred, possibly even several thousand, hippies. Even the Moscow Komsomol city committee, which was likely to err on the conservative side, reported that by 1971, it had several hundred hippies in its card database—supposedly (mis)labelled HIPI—at the Komsomol control point underneath the *Berezka* hard-currency shop on Gorky Street.[28]

The early hippies were as much a product of opportunity as design. There was an absence of policy and control governing daily life for youth in those twilight years after Khrushchev and before the more regulated 1970s—less because liberal forces were at work, more because attention was not focused on the new phenomenon of rock and pop and its accompanying fashions. The Beatles were banned, but hundreds if not thousands of student bands played their songs (and those from many other Western groups) on makeshift electric guitars and bad drum sets in youth and culture clubs all over the country. Songs were distributed on X-ray plates; visitors and travelling parents brought in early tape recordings and records from the West. Large swathes of the student population adopted a fashion style they believed to be hippie-ish. Long-haired youngsters openly loitered on Gorky Street and around the Moscow University.

The press remained largely silent in the face of the emergence of this new movement. In the absence of guidance or prohibition, young people were surprisingly at ease following their fancies. In the late 1960s and early 1970s being a hippie—or fancying oneself a hippie—was not a big deal—and not a major commitment. Tatiana Strel'nikova, daughter of the *Pravda* correspondent in the United States, testified that she and her friends felt "absolutely free to do anything." Photographs of the time, too, show her and her friends in surprisingly daring outfits, looking more like 1960s revellers than socialist citizens.[29] That was partly because she belonged to the small stratum of extremely privileged youth in Moscow whose parents had good connections. Partly, however, it was a sign of the innocence of the times. Vasia Long, Volodimir Boriarintsev, recounted a similar ease and laissez-faire attitude in his memoirs. Long, a regular at the Moscow hippie scene, described a hippie day of lazing around that culminated in him and a good number of other young people (including some British tourists) crashing a concert of the enormously popular group *Rubinovaia Ataka* laid on by helpless Komsomol organizers. When the evening got too wild, the authorities pulled the plug—literally, by switching off the electricity. When the officials left, the party resumed.[30]

It seemed as if the official Soviet Union had not made up its mind what to do with the new wave of youth culture. The fight against jazz music, which in the 1940s and 1950s had spawned the subculture of the *stiliagi*, had recently been declared as over. Jazz was incorporated into the official Soviet musical canon. There seemed to be limited appetite to attempt to curb the emerging rock music scene through another vain struggle. Indeed, the then legendary band *Rubinovaia Ataka* was asked by the Komsomol Central Committee to play at one of their evenings. When they started out with soft Soviet estrada numbers, the apparatchiki demanded the Rolling Stones and Jimi Hendrix.[31] Officially billing themselves as student bands, these groups played under the radar—or at times with the sanction—of the authorities. In reality, they filled clubs every evening and made not insignificant amounts of money. Finally, the general inertia on the part of the authorities was supported by the fact that the Western hippies were an anticapitalist, anti-American phenomenon, whose situation in the Soviet normative world was yet undefined. Indeed, there is some anecdotal evidence that negotiations took place between some of the hippie leaders and Komsomol officials. Supposedly a plan to create a hippie agricultural commune in Moldavia was on the table. The legendary hippie demonstration of June 1, 1971, to be discussed below, is also said to have had the permission of the Moscow authorities.[32]

However much of these rumors is true, the relative calm in which early Moscow hippies existed testifies to a less well-known aspect of "stagnation." It offered surprising spaces of freedom. Young people knew where the boundaries were. They also knew that, while the state still had teeth, borders and boundaries did not shift as quickly and unpredictably as they did during Stalin's time. Undefined territory was free to be tested—and filled with new concepts such as the *sistema*. Yet, this situation was to change when the Moscow hippies took another step toward asserting their presence. When the Moscow *sistema* organized an anti-Vietnam demonstration, the official system reacted to what it considered to be trespassing on its territory. Political opinion-making, unlike hippie-ish dress codes, was a state matter and hence not subject to the politics of a reluctant and vaguely hostile tolerance that had governed the Soviet regime's relationship with its hippies so far.

HOW THE SISTEMA WAS FORCED TO GROW UP

From the very beginning, the early Moscow hippies seem to have harboured a desire to be more than a loosely knit group of like-minded friends in hippie dress. After all, they were products of the Soviet educational system, albeit rebellious ones, who imbibed with their upbringing both a sense of striving for purpose and a habit of adherence to a calendar of rituals and practice. The *Zeitgeist,* and not least their Western idols, shared the conviction that "being a hippie" was not just a "lifestyle fad," but indeed a movement capable of changing life, politics, and even human nature. For all their rejection of official norms and involvement in politics, Moscow's young hippies were partial to the Bolshevik ideal of serving a higher mission and proselytizing their new "faith."

The adoption of the Day of the Defense of the Rights of Children as a special hippie holiday can thus be read as both an act of adopting convenient bits of the Soviet ritualistic calendar and/or as a deed of defiant parody, brilliantly inversing the Soviet reading of the day by declaring hippies to be flower children and thus the true subjects of celebration. It is unclear when the day was observed for the first time. Yet in 1971 it became one of the milestones of Soviet hippie history. It was on this day that the Moscow hippies planned to hold a demonstration against the Vietnam War and its child victims. While certainly modeled on similar hippie actions in the West, the plan also demonstrated once again a desire to consolidate the Moscow hippies as a coherent force—regardless of whether the demonstration's inception was a provocation or not. It was to make the Moscow hippies both part of the global counterculture (a big part of which was built on opposition to the Vietnam War) but also visible and unified among the local nonconformist youth—and in the process challenge the Soviet authorities on their very own playing field. After all, the peace campaign for Vietnam was also on official Soviet flags, yet the means—a demonstration—was not.[33]

In a much more informal manner, a similar set of ambiguous motivations had already been demonstrated by the 1969 "great walk," which saw several hundred hippies wander from the *Psichodrom* to the *Maiak*, shed their shoes and continue barefoot down Gorky Street past the Hotel *Natsional* to the Lenin library, then down to the river and up again to the Hotel *Rossiia*, where they settled down on a piece of grass next to a small church. People played the guitar, while others sang—mainly Beatles tunes. Somewhere during the march, it was decided that this march was in protest of the Soviet intervention in Prague a year earlier, since the following day was the Day of the Tank Drivers. According to one participant, by the time the barefooted hippies had reached the church, they numbered close to the five hundred followers.[34] Again, the action betrayed both Western inspiration and Soviet traces. The barefoot element was a homage to the American hippie model; the walk down Gorky Street a parody of the public ambulation customary at Soviet holidays. The guitar playing and singing of Beatles songs, too, had both Western connotations and associations closer to home, where bards and songwriters had been the (sub)cultural backbone of a previous generation of youth. The conscious subversion of an official holiday into a commemoration commensurate with the ideals of the hippie movement showcased the complex interplay between the young Moscow hippies and their Soviet heritage and habitat.

Three years later the idea of a mass gathering and processional walk took hold again among the Moscow hippie community.[35] No one knows where the idea of an anti-Vietnam demonstration came from originally.

Some tell of Komsomol leaders, who came and planted the idea in the heads of those sitting at the *Psichodrom;* some attributed the idea to Sol'ntse. There is no doubt, however, that Solntse fully embraced the plan and promoted its organization. He began recruiting his friends and acquaintances to the endeavor at short notice—and according to some sources even obtained permission from *Mossoviet* and/or the Trade Unions.[36] This time the character of the demonstration was much more purposeful with preprepared placards and slogans and a defined marching route from the *Psichodrom* to the American embassy on the Garden Ring. The dissident *samizdat* publication *Chronicle of Current Events* speaks of a leader unveiling a sign in English "Make Peace not War" and of several other banners.[37] Yet the KGB was also better prepared. Before the demonstration could even get off the ground, the courtyard of the *Psichodrom* was locked and everybody was herded into waiting buses. Other would-be participants of the demonstration, who had assembled on Gorky Street, were picked up by police at Pushkin Square; some others observed the action from afar and quickly ran away.[38] The perceived leaders were whisked away in Volgas, the rest in normal buses.[39] Most of the arrested hippies—the majority of whom were students at MGU—escaped with a mere warning and registration with the police; others found themselves imprisoned for disorder for fifteen days, and some ended up in the closed wards of the psychiatric hospitals (including Solntse himself, who had not shown up at the agreed meeting space thus inviting widespread speculation concerning his betrayal).[40] Many more found themselves suddenly force-recruited into the army the following year when Nixon came to Moscow and the streets were cleaned of the embarrassing Soviet flower children.[41]

The shift of space reflected a shift in the participants and character of the movement. Students were now much less likely to be among the hippie crowd, and the second wave of Moscow hippies already counted very few among their followers who studied or worked in a profession (or, if they were students, they soon ceased to be so). Those who populated the hippie hangouts after 1971 were far fewer in number than the first wave of the late 1960s, but they were much hardier. The crackdown after the demonstration resulted in a professionalization of the Soviet hippies. Soviet hippie life was now too dangerous and risky an adventure for the casual hippie—even though the weekend hippie continued to exist. If one still had a foot in the official system, true participation in the hippie system was a constant danger to one's livelihood. The consequence was that the core of the hippie movement dropped out of mainstream society to a much larger extent. They populated the jobs that were to become the subject of Boris Grebenshikov's much cited songs about the generation of courtyard and storage attendants (*pokolenie dvornikov i storozhei*).[42] They worked in theaters, as models in art schools, and in the rock music scene.

The loss of the student hippie and the "professionalization" of the remaining hippies also meant an intensification of certain pastimes such as excessive drinking and general loitering among and alongside the semi-underworld of the *strit*. There was no more talk of demonstrations and hippie politics—at least not among the crowd that assembled around Solntse, who himself drank constantly, still commanding respect among his crowd but giving little ideological guidance anymore. The memoirs of Vasilii Boriantsev and Vasilli Kafanov describe a world that was jolly, irreverent, norm-breaking, and liberating to its participants, but fuelled by excessive amounts of alcohol, especially port wine, and saturated with encounters of the sexual kind. It resembled a bachelor party than a world based on the lofty ideals of love and peace. Kafanov wittily pointed out that he and his friends were indeed united by "love"—the physical variety, which drew them into each other's arms in house entrances, courtyards, and people's apartments.[43] Boriantsev stresses the experience of *kaif*—the collective sensation of joy in the face of the good life, which was made up of wine, women, and fun.[44]

Some hippies found that the *sistema* was not to their liking anymore.[45] Kozlov describes his encounter with the people from the *tsentrovaia sistema* in the flat of Sveta Markova and Sasha Penannen on Prospekt Mira with disdain. Many of the first wave of hippies moved on to new shores. Masha Shtatnitsa had returned to civilian life. A number of the musicians such as Stas Namin and Andrei Makarevich were concentrating on their musical careers, gradually leaving the world of the *strit* in favor of travelling the country on tour.[46] Jewish hippies like Shekspir (Lev Polev) and Ssha Borodulin took the opportunity to emigrate to Israel. The Markovs were expelled in 1974 (some claim they bought Jewish documents while the Western press talked of their expulsion), looking for the hippie life in San Francisco. In his *samizdat* journal, *Alternativy* Tsen Baptist dates the end of the Soviet hippie movement to 1973, even though he himself was a confessed hippie to the very end of his life in postsocialist Russia.[47] In the same year, Sol'ntse was stabbed by a fellow hippie in an argument over a girl, sending shock waves through the community.[48] Yet it would be wrong to say that the movement was in decline. The *sistema* was not dying. Indeed, its heydays were still ahead.

HOW THE *SISTEMA* BECAME A PARALLEL WORLD

It took a new generation of hippies to give *sistema* a more definitive sense of self, even though it continued to make the lack of definition one of its hallmarks. A dictionary of *sistema* slang published sometime in the 1980s defines *sistema* as "its own morals, aesthetics, ethics, ideology, literature, painting, music, religion, lifestyle, thought and God knows what else."[49] It was not by literary deliberations that the *sistema* was shaped (indeed there is little evidence that before the compilation of the 1980 dictionary anyone attempted to put the idea of the *sistema* into words), but rather by its practices. In the mid-1970s, a new crowd joined the "old" hippies on the *strit,* who now assembled in two distinct places, reflecting a certain degree of not only spatial but also ideological separation between groups. A drunken Solntse and his jolly crowd reigned at the *Pushka* (Pushkin Square), highly visible and the first point of contact for travelling hippies from elsewhere. At the café Aromat, nicknamed Babylon, on the Boulevard Ring, just off Gorky Street, a more arty crowd hung out, loosely led by Ofelia and her group Hair (*Volosy*). They shunned the port wine but adored the effect of narcotics, with which they liberally experimented. It was to this place that a new breed of hippies, in search of new ways of life, were drawn, among them Sergei Moskalev, who quickly advanced to become one of the leaders and developers of the all-Union *sistema*. The *sistema,* while still orientating itself around Western models, increasingly became a world of its own and, in the process, acquired Soviet rather than global overtones, even though the two directions partially overlapped, especially in their desire for self-improvement and community building.[50] This process of simultaneous distancing itself from the Soviet system, while at the same time reflecting many late-socialist hallmarks was particularly visible in the sistema's practices and rituals. Space was an important factor in establishing *sistema* identity.

The designation of fixed meeting points was both a way of taking possession of their city and a subversion of the official public sphere. The hippie practice of sitting around was, in essence, a negation of the officially prescribed purposefulness of life, so prized in Bolshevik ideology. To mark their territory, hippie spaces were given names that grounded them in local hippie culture but also expressed a yearning for "elsewhere." Kaunas and Tallinn both had 'Love Streets,' Vilnius the "Bermuda Triangle"; in Moscow, Gorky Street was christened the *strit,* a secluded place on Pushkin Square the "Dacha," the shop *Russkoe Vino* turned into *Rashn Vein*. In Leningrad, the metro entrance of Nevsky Prospect and Canal Griboedova was known as *mikroklimat*. The most famous of all bohemian hangouts was the legendary Café Saigon on Nevskii prospekt, referring back to the old hippie cause of anti-Vietnam protest (even though its attendees were by no means solely hippies). The marching routes between the various places of assembly added movement to the static nature of loitering. Wandering was the logical extension of hanging out. The practice of travelling that was soon to be at the core of the *sistema* flowed from here.

Ever since Moscow hippies had discovered in 1969 that the Baltic States had their own lively scenes of flower children, Riga, Tallinn and Vilnius were placed firmly on the hippie map. The South, especially the Crimea, was another favorite summer destination. A few brave souls, such as the legendary Moscow hippie Skorpion, went as far as Siberia, where, to his surprise, he found a fully functioning hippie community in Irkutsk, who had perfected the art of "plane-hopping."[51] For many years, there was little attempt to channel the travelling hippies toward one destination or along predetermined routes. Yet, gradually, being on the road and moving between *sistema* strongholds became a marker of hippie life and a goal in itself. For the new generation of hippies, who arrived at the Café Aromat in the middle of the decade, travel had become ritual. Destination and mode of travel assumed the characteristics of a Christian pilgrimage or Islamic haj, with only certain types of place and transport deemed to advance hippie conscience. Sergei Moskalev explained that there were hierarchical stages of hippiedom, which, while never explicitly discussed, were achieved through travel first to Leningrad, then to the Baltic and ultimately to Central Asia.[52] Those in the know, knew where and how to go (hitch-hiking, or on the Moscow-Leningrad route suburban trains with no ticket). Those who did not were destined to remain hangers-on or freshmen—so-called *pionery*.[53]

In later years, the Soviet hippies resembled swarms of birds migrating from one place to another in rhythm with the seasons, living their life according to their own calendar—starting with the First of May in Tallinn on the Gorka and ending in September with a return to their home bases. The Lithuanian hippie Jakimavičius describes these yearly wanderings, which possessed identity-defining significance on two levels: the experience and the narrative—the so-called hippie *telegi* (tales):

> The hippies would show up in Vilnius in autumn and stay awhile. Then they'd take off and hitch-hike to Saint Petersburg or the Crimea or they'd take a month off and hang out in the psychiatric hospital. Then they'd show up again in the Bermuda Triangle. We'd meet, drink coffee, red Bulgarian wine, smoke Prima cigarettes, and they'd talk nonstop about their adventures, about everything that they'd been through while they were away.[54]

The increasing mobility of Soviet hippies meant that the *sistema*'s connections and reach became increasingly extensive. The travellers passed information along the hippie highways. This could be phone numbers for good contacts, locations of apartments where one could crash, or political and social gossip. The *sistema* hippies were among the best-informed people in the country, not least because the movement's tentacles reached into the milieu of religious dissenters, political dissidents, and nonconformist artists and musicians. Hippies in the various *sistema* hot spots—most notably Moscow, Leningrad, Tallinn, Riga, Vilnius, Minsk, and Lvov—stopped thinking of themselves as individual *tusovki* but as part of one big enterprise—a *sistema* of networks, information exchange, and cultural distinction. It also started to reference back to its own history more frequently than to Western idols. That was partly because even the

Soviet hippies sensed that the Western hippie moment was fading fast in the mid-1970s, while their own *sistema* was still in the ascent.

From 1976, there were various attempts to hold a proper hippie summer camp, somewhere out of reach of the KGB, police, and Komsomol. The first trials on the Gulf of Finland near Leningrad and in Vitrupe in Lithuania failed after just a few days, but in 1978 the *sistema* found a permanent summer home in Gaia near Riga. Although set up by Misha Bombin, a long-standing Riga hippie (and active dissident) of Russian ethnicity, this camp was never a local enterprise, but a truly "Soviet" community.[55] Every year for more than a decade, hundreds if not thousands of hippies from all across the Soviet Union would travel to the woodland on the river Gaia and camp for a few days, weeks, or even months, exchanging news, discussing religion (both Orthodox and more Eastern varieties), and hanging out in a place they considered separate from Soviet life. The late 1970s and early 1980s were the heydays of the *sistema*, when, in the words of two of its leaders, Misha Bombin and Gena Zaitsev, the association of hippies was "a state within a state."[56]

In 1978 the *sistema* rallied hippies from all across the Soviet Union to the gates of Iasnaia Polana on Tolstoi's one hundred fiftieth birthday (where they were denied entry). Its members marked the shooting of John Lennon on the Lenin Hills in Moscow (where a good number of people were arrested).[57] It also started to celebrate its own history, resurrecting the 1st of June tradition, assembling first at the Psichodrom and later in the park of Tsarytsin.[58] Furthermore, it had self-appointed organizers—Sergei Moskalev in Moscow, Gena Zaitsev in Leningrad, and Misha Bombin in Riga—who tried to establish rules both for behavior in the summer camp (no drugs) and, more generally, for what it meant to be a hippie. It also harbored dissent, with 1982 seeing two Gaia camps in existence—one with and one without drugs—and with some hippies rebelling against the existence of the rules and leaders. It survived the repression of the Olympic year and emerged into the new decade of the 1980s with yet another new generation of members, who took the *sistema*, its practices, and rituals into the Perestroika years and beyond. With its organizational structure, defined rituals, and even its internal dissent, the *sistema* acquired in many ways a very Soviet face, while at the same time embodying a quintessential non-Soviet way of life. It was precisely in this tension that the *sistema* reveals itself as a true product of late socialism.

SISTEMA AND "STAGNATION": PARADOX OR SYMBIOSIS?

Both terms—*sistema* and stagnation—are evidently paradoxes in themselves. Both imply notions of order and rigidity, yet both seemed to harbor the opposite as well—a certain anarchy as well as an ability to generate change. Is it coincidental that the period of "stagnation" brought about the *sistema*—a vibrant and long-lived counterculture that shaped young people's taste in fashion, music, and ideals? Is it by chance that the hippie movement in the Soviet Union opted to create a *sistema*—an entity that in term and association seems contrary to usual hippie aspirations? Clearly, "stagnation" and *sistema* have a complex interrelationship both affirming and challenging each other.

On a very simple level, the existence of the *sistema* proves that stagnation cannot be a term that is applied literally to all aspects of society. Clearly, there was significant activity for some subjects of Brezhnev's stagnant times. Even if one restricts one's view to the very inner circle of hippies, one finds a considerable amount of energy and creative force, which produced fashion, art, music, and literature, not to mention a new approach to the question of how to navigate the Soviet system: creating an increasingly parallel world (and the hippies were by no means the only ones engaged in the construction of refuges from the Soviet world). If one lifts one's eyes a bit further, it becomes apparent that the hippies did not live in a vacuum. Indeed, the question of where to draw the boundary between hippies and youth hanging around them is impossible to answer. Not all of the people sitting at the *Psichodrom* or at the *Maiak* and *Pushka* would have considered themselves hippies. Some only came because they wanted to talk music, others liked the girls (or the boys), yet another contingent came out of curiosity, mixed a little with the regulars (even married some of them), and then returned to more normal lives. Others only glimpsed them from afar, yet carried that memory back toward their more ordinary lives.

If one looks at the wider hippie world—rock musicians, underground poets and artists, *fartsovschiki,* drug dealers, and small-time criminals—the image of a stagnant society crumbles even more comprehensively. Indeed, for many people the 1970s were the most moving decade of their life. Rock music went viral, creating both a vibrant market for Western music as well as its own local scene. Fashion—even mainstream fashion—changed more rapidly than in any other Soviet decade. What had been decidedly non-conformist (and hippie-ish) in the early 1970s—jeans or other trousers with wide legs; long hair; colorful, long-collared shirts—was decidedly mainstream by the end of the decade. Underground art became a force that could, at least in the cities, be enjoyed by many. And not all of it was due to activities below or parallel to the official structures. Reluctantly, but steadily, the Soviet system tried to adapt to the new challenges. By the end of the decade the bands of former hippies Andrei Makarevich (*Mashina Vremeni*) and Stas Namin (*Gruppa* Stasa Namina, formerly *Tsvety*) were playing in official concert halls. The Soviet textile industry produced items that would have been unimaginable a decade before. And the record company *Melodiia* was producing both Western and Russian rock.

Yet does this mean that the force of the *sistema* does away with the term stagnation? A closer look demonstrates that stagnation still has a role to play in illuminating and explaining late-socialist society, even its most marginal sectors. It was the perception of *zastoi*—and it is important to note that the term is used here in the sense of "being stuck in the status quo" and a certain ennui—that made the new hippie idea coming from the West so attractive to late-1960s youths, who—not unlike their Western counterparts—had become disillusioned with the virtues of the system they inhabited and craved a different approach to life. While in the West, the flower children objected to the capitalism and imperialism of their surrounding environment, Soviet youth wanted to escape the petrified and empty phrases that accompanied their and their family's daily life. In both East and West the perception of stagnation was crucial in breeding the movements of the 1960s and 1970s.

Once the regime had decided that hippies were enemies to the ruling order, hippies felt the power of the regime—sometimes through relatively harmless means of temporary arrest and spells in the psychiatric hospitals, sometimes through the brutal force of beatings and forceful administration of painful medicinal measures.[59] Inadvertently, the persecutions that hippies experienced created a subcultural type, who, ironically, despite being more divorced from the rest of Soviet society, was better equipped to live in Soviet society. He (more often than she) was less tied to the normal Soviet life, prepared for physical and financial hardship, and since he rarely spent too much time in one space, more difficult to track and pin down. He had a better sense of his identity and created an increasingly parallel world, in which he disappeared during the season, while taking advantage in the winter of the strange employment opportunities the system offered—boiler rooms, art schools, courtyards, and so on.

It was thus only logical that the hippies were keen to formalize this commitment in a system of values, rituals, and practices. The *sistema*, while not initially designed as such, proved an adequate, possibly the only adequate, answer to the system—the official world of order, conformity, and repression. But it was also precisely this world that helped the *sistema* to live as long as it did. The failings of the official system ironically produced an environment that was well suited to the hippie lifestyle and survival. The combination of economic dysfunction and a general commitment to a socialist welfare state created a world in which one could indeed live with little care for money and few material possessions (even though hippies often did go hungry and found themselves down to their last kopecks).[60] The "sistema ask," which often involved spinning yarns to passers-by in order to get a few kopecks, bottle collecting, boiler room jobs, and so on furnished a living for those who had little desire to be part of the real Soviet world. However, just as Yurchak has concluded for the St. Petersburg *Mitki*, total rejection ultimately meant total acceptance of the system.[61] The hippies took the Soviet system as it was and used it to create their own world, which shamelessly lived on—and off—the deficiencies of late socialist reality. The hippies made use of the Soviet system for feeding the masses by plundering *stolovye* (canteens) and other state-owned providers (as did, of course, almost everybody else). They used the Soviet Union's underdeveloped economy to earn small change through odd jobs, or big money through trading deficit items. They forged identity through difference, which was easily achieved in a society clothed by the Soviet textile industry and socialized by a propaganda monopoly. They created their own spaces, making use of the rudimentary—and thus open to interpretation—infrastructure that Soviet official life provided. The Saigon or Aromat could not have existed in a world with a Hard Rock Café, but hippies could make use of the simple cafés and bars with the nondescript chairs that made up Soviet hospitality.

The hippies, their *sistema*, and stagnation hence formed a paradoxical symbiosis. The *sistema* was what it was because it existed within the restraints and opportunities that stagnation provided. The hippies both responded to stagnation by creating a world that was dynamic, but parallel, to the official system, but they also challenged it by pushing constantly the boundaries of the self-imposed isolation of their *sistema*. On a more philosophical level, hippies and stagnation, or better societal perception of stagnation, also suited each other in their joint worldview that knew no linear trajectory and no future. The hippies' self-perception as eternal flower children and their refusal to grow into "proper" adults was facilitated by the era's atmosphere of eternity, in which nothing would ever change.[62] The extent to which stagnation and *sistema* depended on each other becomes evident when considering their simultaneous decline and demise. In the end it was not the KGB that killed off the *sistema*, but Gorbachev's Perestroika and the sanctioning of all those things that had before been special to the *sistema* and its wider circle. As Sergei Moskalev said: "What was there left to protest? It was all there."[63] With the end of the Soviet Union came the cold wind of capitalist reality, stronger drugs, and shock-therapy-induced poverty. The 1990s witnessed the death of a great number of hippies. Slowly and inevitably the *sistema* ceased to be of relevance to those who once carried it forward. For a while its memory was entirely buried under the hardship of postsocialist life and the multitude of new trends and fashions. These days it exists as a memory on numerous webpages devoted to the Soviet hippie community and in the minds of those who witnessed its rise and fall. Freedom in the Western sense—so desired by the Soviet hippies—proved the death of the *sistema*. Ultimately, the *sistema* needed stagnation to live.

INTERVIEWS

Sergei Lysenko (Baske), Moscow, interviewed Moscow 16.7.2010
Sergei Batovrin, Moscow, interviewed New York, 24/25. 5. 2011
William Brui, Leningrad, interviewed London, 16.10.2011
Sergei Bol'shakov (Liutik/Ryshii), interviewed Moscow, 8.3.2012
Oleg Burian (Khobbo), Leningrad and Moscow, interviewed Moscow, 25. 4. 2009
Iurii Fokin, Moscow, interviewed San Francisco, 24.9.2010
Andris Grinbergs, Riga, interviewed Riga, 10. 4. 2009
Aleksandr Iusevo (Sasha Khudozhnik), Moscow, interviewed, 10.7.2009
Eizens Ivanov, Riga, interviewed Riga, 9.4.2009
Maksim Kapitanovskii, Moscow, interviewed Moscow, 8.9.2011
Natasha Kurshak, Moscow, interviewed Amsterdam, 29.3.2012
Natasha Kazantseva, Moscow, interviewed Moscow, 9.9.2011
Maksim Kapitanovskii, Moscow, interviewed Moscow, 8.9.2011
Galina Lisina (Khavira), Cheliabinsk and Moscow, interviewed Cheliabinsk,
Günther Meyer, Leningrad, interviewed Hamburg, 17.12.2012
Sergei Moskalev, Moscow, interviewed Moscow, 24.4.2009 (I); 10.1.2013 (II)
Stas Namin (Anastas Mikoian), Moscow, interviewed Moscow, 9.7.2009
Alik Olyseevich (Woodychild), Lvov, interviewed
Roma Osipov, Moscow, interviewed Moscow, 10.9.2011
Sasha Penannen, Moscow, interviewed San Francisco, 8.9.2015
Lev Polev (Shekspir), Moscow, interviewed Jerusalem, 2.8.2011
Sandris Riga, Riga and Moscow, interviewed Riga, 9.4.2009
Sergei Rybko (Iura Terrorist), Moscow, interviewed in Moscow, 26.4.2009
Senia Seniavin (Skorpion), Moscow, interviewed Moscow, 10. 7. 2010
Vladimir Soldatov, Moscow, interviewed Moscow, 30.5.2009
Sergei (Sorry), Moscow, interviewed Moscow, 26.4.2009
Vladimir Tarasov, Moscow, interviewed Jerusalem, 3.8.2011
Artemy Troitsky, Moscow, interviewed New York, 7.3.2013
Vladimir Widemann (Kest), Tallinn and Moscow, interviewed London, 19.6.2011,
Aleksandr Zaborovskii, Moscow, interviewed Moscow, 14.7.2010
Gena Zaitsev, Leningrad, interviewed Voloshovo, 3.6.2009

NOTES

1. My research rests almost entirely on more than a hundred interviews conducted with former Soviet hippies and a smattering of memoirs. There is a surprising dearth of state documents on the hippies and they are hard to track down. Those, which have been obtained, have proven of little value, even if of KGB provenance, since they are either very general in their description or merely serve to demonstrate the lack of knowledge officials had about the movement.

2. Aleksei Yurchak, *Everything was Forever until it was no more: The Last Soviet Generation* (Princeton, 2006). There is some overlap in the people, who feature in my and Yurchak's work, but Yurchak sets out to explain a whole generation, while I approach this era through the prism of an outlier community, which showcases both the extent of 'non-normality' possible and the significance these outliers had nonetheless for the era overall. There is still limited research on late socialist subjectivities, but while the model of 'stagnation' as a blanket term is under assault, its subjective importance has been confirmed even by Yurchak's critics, who agree that the "rich proliferation of interior worlds" is directly linked to the perceived narrowness of the official, collective vision of the Soviet regime. Benjamin Nathans, Kevin Platt, 'Socialist in Form, Indeterminate in Content: The Ins and Outs of Late Soviet Culture,' *Ab Imperio* Nr. 2, 2011, 303. The feeling of living in a non-changing world is also expressed by many of Don Raleigh's interview subjects, who in terms of age belonged to a cohort that is better known as the Thaw Generation. Don Raleigh, *Soviet Baby Boomers: An oral history of Russia's Cold war Generation* (Oxford, 2012).

3. Yurchak, *Everything*, 102–108. See also Nathan and Platt, Socialist,' pp. 301–324..

4. Private Archive Feliks Vinogradov

5. See descriptions of late Soviet society offered by Christopher Ward, Brezhnev's Folly: The Building of BAM and late Soviet socialism (Pittsburgh, 2009); Sergei Zhuk, Rock and Roll in the Rocket City: The West, Identity, and Ideology in Soviet Dniepropetrovsk, 1960–1985 (Baltimore: John Hopkins's University Press, 2010). This is not to say that genuine enthusiasm in official culture was dead (for example Ward's BAM volunteers were often propelled by genuine enthusiasm) or that idealism gave way to complete cynicism (this period also saw the emergence of the so-called New Left in the political underground), but in comparison to previous periods non-engagement seems to have been the preferred option, especially among young people.

6. A few Western and Russian scholars have written on the *sistema*, but always with the *sistema* of the 1980s in mind. In English see John Bushnell, *Moscow Graffiti: Language and Subculture* (Boston, 1990), 117–124. Hilary Pilkington, *Russia's Youth: A Nation's Constructors and Constructed* (London, 1994), p. 230. For a participant-sociologist account see Tat'iana Shepanskaia, *Sistema: Teksty i traditsii subkul'tury* (Moscow, 2004); For Perestroika era work see among others Aleksandr Zapesotskii, Aleksandr Fain, *Eta neponiatnaia molodezh': Problemy neforma'nykh molodezhnykh ob'edinenii* (Moscow, Profizdat, 1990). M. Rozin, 'The psychology of Soviet hippies,' *Soviet Sociology* 2 (1), 1999, 44–72. There has been discussion of local hippie groups, which did not focus on the *sistema* very much (Risch) or which pertained to groups not included in the sistema (Svede). There is also a growing, non-scholarly memoir literature, much of it online

7. "Deti s tsvetami i bez tsvetov," *Rovesnik*, 1967. Another very influential article was Genrikh Borovik, 'Khozhdenie v stranu Khippilandiu,' *Vokrug Sveta* Nr. 9, 1968, pp. 25–32.

8. Iurii Zhukov, 'Pis'ma iz Ameriki: Khippie i drugie,' *Pravda*, 6.4.1967, p. 4.

9. For these early hippies see interviews with Soldatov, Grinberg, Bombin, Brashman, Olysevich, Futermann. See also William Risch, *The Ukrainian West: Culture and the Fate of Empire in Soviet Lviv* (Cambridge, (Mass.), 2011), 237–246. Mark Swede, 'All you need is Lovebeads: Latvia's Hippies Undress for Success,' in Susan Reid and David Crowley, *Style and Socialism: Modernity and Material Culture in Post-War Eastern Europe,*

(Oxford: Berg, 2000), 189–208, for early non-sistema Lviv and Riga hippies respectively.

10. Interview Zaborovskii; Kazantseva.
11. Interview Zaborovskii, Kazantseva
12. Artemy Troitsky, *Back in the USSR: The True Story of Rock in Russian* (London, 1987), p. 23. Interviews Soldatov, Zaborovskii, Troitsky.
13. Interview Soldatov
14. Interviews Strelnikova, Lipnitskii
15. SMOG stood for *Samoe Molodoe Obshchestvo Geniev* (Youngest Society of Geniuses) or *Smelost,' Mysl,' Obraz, Glubina* (Fortitude, Thought, Image and Depth). On Ofelia's link to SMOG see interview Kazantseva
16. Interview Sasha Penannen
17. Interview Zaborovskii
18. See for example interviews Soldatov; Kest, Lipnitskii; Sorry, Skorpion
19. Interview Skorpion
20. Interview Soldatov
21. Interviews Gena and Vova Zaitsev
22. Interviews Skripach, Tarasov, Miakotin
23. Vladimir Aleinikov, *SMOG-roman poema* (Moscow, 2008), p.8.
24. Interview Kazantseva, Namin
25. Interview Sergei Moskalev II
26. On Romanov see interview Strelnikova, on Prospekt Mira see interviews Kapitanovskii, Riga, Batovrin
27. Aleksei Kozlov, *Kozel na sakse—it tak vsiu zhizn . . .* (Moscow, 1998), 263–264.
28. TsAOPIM, f. 635, op. 1, d. 2858, ll. 18–19; for a much higher estimate of between 2–3000 see interview Batovrin, New York, 24/25.5.2011. Others put the number closer to a few hundred, Interview wit Bol'shakov, Moscow. Much of it centers on the question of definition. Some deny the term 'hippie' at all. Interview Stas Namin, Doktor.
29. Photographs Private Archive Strel'nikova
30. Vasilli Bariantsev, *My—Khippi* (Moscow, 2004), p. 9
31. Interview Kapitanovskii, Baske. This could, of course, be a tale spun by the two band members, but it fits with the fact that love for rock music far transcended the rebellious youth scene, just as love for jazz had reached far into the echelons of the Komsomol in previous years.
32. Interview Batovrin
33. Julie Hessler, "The Soviet Public and the Vietnam War: Political Mobilization and Public Organizations, 1965–1973," unpublished manuscript. A similar demonstration by international students in 1965 was also violently broken up.
34. Interview Zaborovskii, Kazantseva. Personally, I doubt the number of 500, but it is eminently possible that over a hundred people had assembled. Sveta Markova cited a number of 30 in a 1970s interview, but it is not entirely clear she is speaking of the same event. Jochen Kaufmann, 'Moskau wirft seine Hippies raus,' *Münchner Merkur*, July 26, 1975.
35. Moscow was indeed not the only place where there were ambitions to enter the public sphere. In Sevastopol, too, hippies planned a demonstration of this kind. In Tallinn, the local hippies organized a congress in 1970 to which they invited their Baltic neighbors. However, it too, was intercepted by the KGB. Interviews Futermann, Ludmilla, Dormidontov, Loit.
36. Interviews with Soldatov, Sorry, Batovrin, Kazantseva, Lipnitsky, Kapitanovskii, Litvinenko ; see also documentary 'Vo vsem proshu povinit' Bitlz,' documentary film by Maksim Kapitanovskii, Moscow, 2007.
37. *Khronika Tekushchikh Sobitii*, Nr. 20, 20.7.1971,http://www.memo.ru/history/diss/chr/index.htm, accessed 29.1.2013
38. Interview Soldatov. The Chronicle also places Sontse at the Pushkinskaia, as do other witnesses, yet nobody saw him there in person. Khronika, Nr. 20,http://www.memo.ru/history/diss/chr/index.htm, accessed 29.1.2013

39. *Khronika Tekushchikh Sobitii*, Nr. 20, 20.7.1971,http://www.memo.ru/history/diss/chr/index.htm, accessed 29.1.2013

40. Interviews with Soldatov, on Sol'ntse's time in the Psychiatric wards, see interviews with Sorry, Batovrin

41. Interview Kapitanovskii

42. To satisfy the requirements of the authorities, many hippies had some sort of official job or worked only during the winter, but in general, there was no career within the Soviet system anymore. This contrasts with the first wave of hippies, who studied at university or other institutes of higher education and at times even had very respectable jobs.

43. Interview Kafanov

44. Boriantsev, *My Khippie*,

45. Interviews Zaborovskii, Kapitanovskii

46. Stas Namin these days distances himself from the hippie movement, even denying its existence. He quickly made it big in the official music world. Interview Namin; Andrei Makarevich, however, makes much of his hippie credentials in interviews and memoirs. . . ..

47. Private Archive Tatiana Teplisheva.

48. Interview Soldatov, Litvinenko

49. Zapesotskii, Fain, *Eta neponiatnaia*, p. 98. Since the internet has become an important forum for former Soviet hippies, there have been more attempts to define *sistema* retrospectively—some of which contain factual historical mistakes. See the long and interesting essay published in 2002 onhttp://www.altruism.ru/sengine.cgi/8/4(accessed 20.3.2014), which is clearly written by someone who was active in the 1980s *sistema*; short and only partially informed on one of the main hippie forums:http://hippy.ru/f59.htm.

50. William Risch has observed a similar development in the early Lvov hippie community before it ever came into contact with the *sistema*. Here too the counter culture could not resist incorporating certain Soviet values and practices. William Risch, "Soviet 'Flower Children': Hippies and the Youth Counter-Culture in 1970s L'viv." *Journal of Contemporary History* 40.3 (July 2005): 565–584.

51. Interview Skorpion

52. Interview Moskalev

53. Interview Moskalev

54. Seewww.versus.lt/var/ezflow_site/storage/original/application/ac2d5865fc87e2748574a4d0ed778ef1.pdf(accessed, 31.1.2013)

55. This is the picture of the *sistema*, which was encountered by the Soviet sociologists in the1980s, who started to observe the phenomena. See footnote 1.

56. Bombin and Zaitsev used these words independently of each other in interviews. However much has been written in the press and online by both of them and it is thus not clear if this terminology was employed then or has been shaped since then.

57. Elena Kharo, 'Delo Lennona,' *Kampus* (11), December 2009, pp. 56–58. Interview Khudozhnik.

58. There is a famous picture in the archive of many of the *sistema* hippies, which shows a restaging of the meeting place in the courtyard of the MGU on 1st of June 1978. (Archives Kiss, Moskalev, Olysevich). As a result of police harassment from 1979 onwards, the Moscow hippies started to assemble in Tsaritsyn, where they still meet every year now.

59. The accounts of hippies of their spells in psychiatric wards differ vastly, but treatment could be brutal with insulin shocks and forced sedation. Interview Azazello, Tania Ivanova. An interesting insight is also given by the recently published medical file of Alexander Dvorkin, who was forcefully hospitalized several times for his hippie life-style.http://www.alexanderdvorkin.info, accessed 11 October 2014.

60. The testimony of an outsider is illuminating here. Günther Meyer, a West German, who was friendly with the Leningrad crowd, asserted how astonished he was at

the asceticism of their friends, who often had literally only crumbs in their pockets. Interview Meyer

61. Yurchak, *Everything*, 239

62. While this phenomenon is partially explored in Yurchak's *Everything was Forever* (2006), I owe the concept of no-futurist temporality' to Anna Fishzon, who analyzed this phenomenon in animated films of the Stagnation era. Anna Fizhzon, "Re-Animating Stagnation: the Queer Times and Magical Spaces of Late Socialism," unpublished manuscript.

63. Interview Moskalev II

NINE

Norton Dodge in Lianozovo

Transnational Collaboration and the Making of the Soviet Unofficial Artist[1]

Courtney Doucette

In early September 1974, Soviet artist Oskar Rabin and Soviet art critic Alexander Glezer sent a letter to the head of the Moscow Artists' Union (MOSKh) asking to hold an outdoor art exhibit in mid-September. The request was unusual because Rabin was not an official artist, meaning he did not belong to the Soviet Artists' Union, nor did his painting exhibit the tenets of socialist realism, the only legally sanctioned aesthetic form in the USSR.[2] According to his work card, he was employed as a low-ranking railroad engineer. In his free time, he painted dark and gloomy images with elements of abstraction. The head of the Artists' Union wrote back that by law he could not prohibit the event, for the Soviet Constitution permitted freedom of speech, but he could not recommend it, either. Rabin and Glezer moved forward with their plan. They distributed invitations to their friends, and the thirteen artist-participants put the final touches on their work.[3] On September 14, 1974 Rabin and Glezer met with an old acquaintance, Christopher Wren, correspondent for the *New York Times*, to ensure publicity for what would be the first public exhibit of non-socialist realist art by Soviet artists in the USSR since 1932.[4]

At twelve o'clock noon on September 15, 1974, the artists arrived at Beliaevo Park on the outskirts of Moscow and got to work staging their paintings and other artworks. At the edge of the field lurked several bulldozers. It was unclear why they were there—perhaps preparing to do work in the park, maybe sitting idly until the workweek resumed. Spectators trickled in for the show that was scheduled to last for four hours. As the audience became increasingly robust, noise came from the edge of the field: the bulldozers had started their engines. The machines turned toward the exhibit and charged the crowd. The teeth of the ploughs shredded artwork and sent Glezer flying through the air. Altercations broke out between the drivers and exhibitgoers. One driver knocked Wren's front tooth out. The city police arrived on the scene and arrested several artists, including Rabin, who was held in custody until September 18 for public disturbance. Bulldozer operators, who were allegedly assigned to "clean up" the park that day, gathered the remaining art and threw it away.

The September events in Beliaevo Park generated an enormous scandal in Cold War Western presses. The *New York Times* played a particularly active role.[5] Foreign embassies began to take a greater interest in the role of art in Soviet society as well. "[WE] WILL KEEP DEPARTMENT INFORMED ON THIS MATTER IN VIEW OF POSSIBLE CONFLICT WHICH COULD AGAIN GENERATE MUCH PUBLICITY UNFAVORABLE TO THE SOVIETS," the American Embassy wrote to the US Secretary of State in early 1975.[6] The scandal forced the Soviet government to take special action, too. Officials sanctioned another exhibit in Izmailovo Park several weeks later and ultimately held the Moscow City Police responsible for the violent outburst at Beliaevo. In the long run, the scandal resulted in clearer legislation on unofficial art. The Soviet Artists' Union created a leftist branch of the Moscow Union of Artists (*Levyi MOSKh*) that regulated exhibits of nonsocialist realist art over the next decade.

One of the remarkable if also often overlooked aspects of the Bulldozer Exhibit, as the events of September 15, 1974, have become known, is that from the very start it was a transnational affair. Even before the event took place, Rabin and Glezer involved foreign journalists, including Wren, to report on the exhibit because they thought that reports in the media made the event legitimate. It was clear that no mainstream Soviet newspaper would cover the event, and so the organizers invited foreigners. In the aftermath of the event, having those foreigners there, some of whom suffered permanent physical injuries, transformed a suppressed art show into an event known the world over. Foreign governments took interest in the event, used it as propaganda, and ultimately leveraged change in the Soviet government's relationship to artists who were not recognized by artists' unions. These points are just a small part of a much larger story about international entanglement in the development of Soviet unofficial art.

We can get at the bigger story by looking at specific interactions between artists and foreigners, including journalists, art connoisseurs, and especially art collectors. The American economist Norton Dodge came to rank among the most prolific non-Russian collectors of Soviet unofficial art. Arguably, he was even more significant than Alberto Sandretti, Dina Vierny, Camilla Gray, and others, for between 1962 and the end of his life in 2011, he amassed one of the largest collections of Soviet unofficial art in the world. His collection included works from Russia as well as the Baltics and Central Asia. One of his favorite artists happened to be Rabin, the organizer of the Bulldozer Exhibit, and the circle of Moscow artists to which he belonged: the Lianozovo group. Tracing the history of this art collector, this artist group, and, to the extent the sources permit, the interactions between them illuminates the long prehistory of the Bulldozer Exhibit and provides a telling case study in the equally long transnational history of Soviet art. It also illuminates an important process in Soviet art: the coming into being of the unofficial artist. The Soviet unofficial artist was produced not simply by a repressive state that drove nonconformist art underground but by interactions between Soviet artists and foreign art connoisseurs from the late 1950s through the early 1970s.[7]

Lianozovo, in the words of poet Genrikh Sapgir, "was not a group. It was a teacher, and it was students."[8] It began in the early 1950s, in the dark last years of Stalin's rule and the period of uncertainty following his death in 1953. The teacher was Evgenii Kropivnitskii, an artist, poet, and musician, and his first students included Rabin in art and Sapgir in poetry. The teacher and his pupils gathered at Kropivnitskii's barrack in the Moscow suburb Dolgoprudy, where he lived with his highly artistic family, including his wife Olga Potapova, daughter Valentina Kropivnitskaia (who later married Rabin), and son Lev Kropivnitskii. The family embodied the dynamic and paradoxical early history of the Soviet Union. Evgenii was a key member of the well-known Soviet avant-garde group the Jack of Diamonds, and Olga, too, was a well-known figure among 1920s revolutionary artists. In the 1940s, their only son served on the front in World War II before beginning his studies at an art institute in Moscow. As a student in the 1940s, he was brought to trial for "political activity" and sentenced to ten years in a hard-labor camp in Kazakhstan.

It was during the bleak years following Stalin's death that Norton Dodge first began thinking about visiting the Soviet Union. At the time, he was a graduate student in economics at Harvard University, where he was working on a Ph.D. thesis on machine production in the USSR. He wanted to conduct first-hand research in the Soviet Union. Fearing that the Soviet Embassy would not grant him a visa on his own application, he convinced his father, the president of a liberal arts college in Oklahoma, to apply for a visa to study the Soviet education system and to take him along as a research assistant. The plan worked. The two received visas to travel and even special permission to visit Soviet collective farms.[9] As a researcher Dodge was both conniving and inventive. When visiting collective farms he wrote down the number stamped on each tractor engine as a way to assess the number of farm machines produced in the USSR. Ultimately, this research did not amount to a dissertation, but Dodge completed his degree at Harvard and wrote his first book about women in the Soviet economy. He selected this topic because, in terms of gender parity in the workplace, he believed that the Soviet Union provided a shining example for the capitalist West.[10]

When Dodge left the Soviet Union in 1955, members of the Lianozovo group, of whom he had no knowledge at the time, began to expand in size to include artists Vladimir Nemukhin, Lydia Masterkova, and Nikolai Vechtomov and poets Igor Kholin and Vsevolod Nekrasov. Relative stability was interrupted only by an unexpected turn of political events in 1956. Speaking behind closed doors at the Twentieth Party Conference, First Party Secretary Nikita Khrushchev delivered the so-called "Secret Speech" in which he blamed Stalin for the "cult of personality" that resulted in unnecessary violence during his rule. Though he delivered the speech behind closed doors, his words leaked into society at large. People began to talk, if only in hushed tones, and former prisoners began to return home, including Lev Kropivnitskii.[11]

Around the same time, Kropivnitskii's circle moved its gatherings from Dolgoprudy to a suburb south of Moscow, Lianozovo, where Rabin lived and from which the group took its name. At the time, Rabin's employer—the railway company—provided him housing in a barrack, which until 1956 had been a dormitory in a women's concentration camp. The setting was grim, yet the young intellectuals were excited about words and images and looked to each other for stimulating companionship. They set up private exhibits, with each home providing a personal museum. Residents pinned up their own artwork on the walls and entertained small audiences well before the 1974 events at Beliaevo. They invited their friends and even had guest books where they could sign and comment on the art.[12]

Khrushchev's "Secret Speech" was not a full-out condemnation of the previous leader but a critical assessment and an invitation to purify the methods for building Communism. In an effort to create the social circumstances necessary for advancing toward the bright future, the First Party Secretary launched a broad housing campaign to give every Soviet family their own apartment, including those who lived, like the Kropivnitskiis and Rabin, in wartime barracks and former prison dormitories. Over the next decade one-third of the entire Soviet population—some 84.4 million people—moved into new residential dwellings.[13] A decade and a half out from the end of World War II, Soviet leaders welcomed unprecedented levels of international cultural exchange in Soviet cities. In 1956 Moscow welcomed an exhibit of Picasso's work, the first public exhibit of foreign abstract art in the Soviet Union since 1932. Soon thereafter, a Cezanne exhibit came to Leningrad.

These events were mere rumbles compared to the cultural earthquake of July 1957, when the Sixth World Festival of Youth and Students opened in Moscow.[14] A small fraction of "the Festival," as it was popularly called, included exhibits in Gorky Park of over four thousand works by artists from more than fifty-two countries.[15] It was the first time that many festival-goers saw foreign artwork, especially artwork from non-socialist countries. The opportunity to see abstract art transformed Lianozovo artists. Upon seeing it, the artist Vladimir Nemukhin "was simply quiet, he couldn't speak." He reported that "Oscar [Rabin] was still making sketches" at the time of the Festival, but after seeing the exhibits "he threw out his sketches. Threw them out immediately and forever." Lydia Masterkova had an even stronger reaction. "After she returned," Nemukhin commented, "on the second or third day [she] painted abstractions in gouache. I felt it as her entire being changed—her eyes, her face, she became a different person."[16]

In the midst of dynamic developments in Moscow, Dodge planned a second trip to the USSR in 1962. On this trip and subsequent visits, he received visas by traveling with groups of academics on trips organized by American universities and sponsored by Intourist, the Soviet travel agency. On his first trip to the Soviet Union, Dodge was hardly interested in art. It was a chance encounter on his second trip that peaked his curiosity. The first artist he met was the roommate of an American friend, Peter MacDonald, who was studying abroad at Moscow State University. MacDonald's Soviet roommate was interested in drawing pictures for himself—pictures that had no commonalities with socialist realist works. The second person to introduce Dodge to unofficial art was George Costakis, an enigmatic figure who held a Greek passport, worked at the Canadian Embassy, and was frequently consulted by the Soviet government. Costakis was well known for hosting soirees for artists of all kinds. He also collected avant-garde art. His house was a museum of works that were not shown anywhere else in the Soviet Union. He gifted Dodge his first piece of unofficial art in 1962.[17]

On the same trip, Dodge's friend MacDonald offered to introduce him to artists themselves. There was a private apartment exhibition of abstract art, which Dodge believed to be the first in Moscow since the 1920s. It turned out to be hosted at the home of one member of the Lianozovo group, which had hosted many such exhibits throughout the 1950s. Dodge deeply admired "a small abstract work on paper by the nearly blind nonconformist artist Vladimir Yakovlev." "Before leaving," he wrote, "I was able to acquire the uncharacteristic work plus a suitcase-sized work by [Lev] Kropivnitskii, titled *Outer Galactic Logic* [(1960)]."[18] This chance encounter marked a long relationship between the Lianozovo group and Dodge, and more importantly, transformed the young economist's purpose for traveling to the Soviet Union. Traveling through Intourist meant that each day abroad would be planned out. Dodge skipped as many required activities as possible. Each chance he got, he would find a pay phone, for which he vigilantly saved his two-kopeck coins, to call the artists whose numbers he received from friends at the embassy. He would then hire a private car to take him close to the artist's residence, but never too close, to avoid informers reporting his whereabouts to the militia who might connect him to artists he visited. He always took a flashlight with him to navigate dark hallways and attics. On each trip he stifled these activities only when tour guides threatened to report him to the KGB.[19]

That same year of Dodge's second visit, 1962, a famous exhibit took place at the Manege Exhibition Hall off of Red Square. Entitled "Thirty Years of the Moscow Artists Union," it was to display the best artwork produced in the Soviet Union since 1932, the year socialist realism became the only legal style in the Soviet Union and all artists, if they wished to be recognized by the state as such, had to join an artists' union. Twelve years before the Bulldozer Exhibit, the Manege, too, resulted in scandal. The night before Khrushchev's planned visit, exhibit organizers invited artists of the Beliutin School, the only group of unofficial artists older than Lianozovo, to display their work in a single exhibition room. The artists agreed. The next day, Khrushchev visited the exhibit and scolded the artists for ideologically problematic work. "It's shit!" he screamed.[20] It is unclear if Dodge's second visit to the Soviet Union was just before or after this event, but either way, it certainly would have given him the feeling that the painting Costakis gave him was important and that he should continue to collect unofficial art.

Other events also compelled Dodge to pursue a collection. The confrontation at the Manege directly resulted in two Party decrees of December 1962 and March 1963 attempting to define clearer guidelines for ideologically acceptable art. Two years later, in September 1965, the Soviet government brought a trial against writer Andrei Sinyavsky and translator Yuli Daniel, accused of publishing materials abroad under the pseudonyms Abram Terz and Nikolai Arzhak, respectively. The courts sentenced Sinyavsky to seven and Daniel to five years of hard labor in camps in Mordovia (east of Moscow). This trial politicized many writers in Moscow, who only later adopted the word "dissident" (*disident*), taken from the English, to describe themselves. Dodge did not entirely separate the fate of writers and artists. "Dissident literary works were widely read and studied in the West, and figures such as Boris Pasternak and Evgenii Yevtushenko had become well known," he stated in one interview, "but nothing comparable was happening in the visual arts. I felt that someone should try to develop a similar record for the visual arts."[21] In short, he saw artists as writers whose courage and resilience had not yet been recognized. The 1964 trial thus gave Dodge another reason to collect Soviet unofficial art in earnest.

Between 1962 and 1977, Dodge returned to the Soviet Union ten more times, making a total of twelve trips. At this time, he usually traveled with a translator, with whose help he amassed the foundational part of his collection. Out of fear for the artists more than himself, Dodge did not record the dates he collected each piece. He destroyed many of his notes on meetings with artists before he left the Soviet Union because he was worried that authorities at the border would confiscate them. Many of his early works came from Lianozovo artists, who in interviews recalled meeting Dodge in Moscow, though over time the details of their meetings had evaporated. Thus the historical record is shrouded in mystery. With the exception of the first meeting between Dodge and Lianozovo artists, which took place in 1962, it is impossible to reconstruct a detailed picture of the meetings between the two parties or the gradual development of their relationship over time. Yet by comparing the ideas at the heart of Dodge's collection and artists' creative production, we begin to see similarities and differences between the collector and artists, and the ways in which understanding and misunderstanding were at the heart of the creation of Dodge's collection.

At least three principles guided Dodge's purchases for his collection. Most importantly, he sought out art that demonstrated, in his words, "a tendency toward an emotional, passionately conservative attitude toward the past."[22] Like Dodge, the Lianozovo artists fashioned themselves protectors of a conservative social order. They were not 1920s revolutionaries. We see this in their search for a more truthful, uncorrupted, older order, as well as the gender dynamics between members of this group. The search for something more "truthful" and "real" took place particularly when the artists traveled around the Soviet Union—not because they believed their Soviet surroundings were a hoax but because they were deeply inspired by what appeared to them to be a world "untouched" by politics, not to mention war. In 1962, Lev Kropivnitskii wrote his wife Galina from Vologda, a medieval Russian city northwest of Moscow: "We went to a museum which was built on [the grounds of] a former monastery. There was a wonderful Sofian cathedral of the sixteenth century and a bell tower with (illegible word) bells." He noted that the bells had been "touched [by] neither Peter nor his successors."[23] Similarly, when Valentina and her family toured Central Asia, women "in nationalist garb" were a different kind of untouched belles. They looked "very beautiful and harmoniously brought together the beauty of the contemporary modern city (*sovremennogo modern goroda*) with southern nature." The men were quite different from the women: "The men are dressed mainly in European [garb], only the old Turkmeni men are sometimes in nationalist clothing," she noted.[24]

Valentina's comment on gender points to a way in which artists and foreign art connoisseurs overlapped with one another in spite of their differences and, perhaps, misunderstandings. Dodge was initially compelled to study the Soviet Union as an economist because he believed the United States had much to learn from the place of women in Soviet society.[25] His admiration of the radical gender politics of the Soviet Union motivated his first book *Women in the Soviet Economy: Their Role in Eco-*

nomic, Scientific, and Technical Development (1966). Yet in terms of art, he was looking for works that embodied political conservatism. Part of Lianozovo's conservatism included traditional gender roles. Art historians often ask why there were so few women among groups of unofficial Soviet artists. In an interview artist Tatiana Levitskaia, wife of Borukh Steinberg, one of the thirteen participants in the Bulldozer Exhibit, answered: "We were watching the children."[26]

Valentina's letters from Paris confirm Levitskaia's answer. When describing what she did with each day in letters to her brother Lev, she often wrote about completing the chores around the house while her husband and son painted, after which she would start on her own artwork. The deeply gendered dynamic of the Lianozovo Group is also evident in a comparison of Valentina and Lev's letters to their father. Valentina mostly wrote about her family, her health, and her father's health, and there was much greater pressure on her to visit her father and care for him, especially after her mother passed away in 1971. Meanwhile Lev wrote about literature and art and God. In 1956 before visiting with the woman he had married in Kazakhstan, he wrote to tell his father not to comment on her clothing, because it would make her self-conscious, and not to read poetry to her, because she wouldn't understand it.[27]

A second area in which the creative projects of Dodge and Lianozovo converged was in what they believed should be the subject of painting. Dodge was looking for certain themes—themes he believed would not be recognized as the proper subject of art by the Soviet government, including overtly political, religious, and erotic art. Both were drawn to the topic of religion, as is suggested in the paintings by Rabin in Dodge's collection. The Kropivnitskii archive provides further evidence of the artists' interest in religion. They frequently visited churches and sought out religious relics in museums. Writing from Perm in 1964, Galina (Lev's wife) raved to her husband about the ancient sculpture on display at the museum as well as paintings of Christ.[28] In 1966, Lev took up icon restoration.[29] The same year he wrote his father: "Relating to whether or not God exists. For me [He] exists. For you [He] exists. For Pushochka [He] exists. For Galiushechka [He] exists. For (illegible word) [He] exists." But, he continued, "for everyone [He] is different. If each [person] connects his understanding about Him to a different subject (for ex. with ceremonies, churches, icons or something else), that's his business."[30] His idea of who God was did not resemble Orthodox tradition.

The origins of the theme of religion in the work of Lianozovo artists are unclear. One possibility is that religious tradition was passed down through the generations, despite the fact that it was illegal and socially taboo. Another possible origin may be camp culture, particularly in the case of Lev.[31] As Solzhnitsyn suggested in his description of camp life, religion flourished in places where many other personal freedoms ceased to exist.[32] The Kropivnitskii archive suggests there were several links between Lianozovo and the camps in addition to Lev. Evgenii's archive includes a short autobiography of Valentin Sergeevich Petrov, a musician, who was freed after finishing his sentence on September 8, 1955. The following day he wrote his life story in a somber tone and with great economy of words: his life from birth to that day occupied just over one page.[33] Regardless of the origins, it is important to note the different ways Dodge and the artists read religion in the Soviet Union. For Dodge, religious themes in art constituted an affront to Soviet ideology. But for the artists, religion did not necessarily contradicted Soviet values. Religion appeared to be part of their search for truth and their appeal to traditional Russian culture.

The third point on which the projects of Dodge and the Lianozovo artists converged was that selling one's work constituted an important part of the artistic project. One of Dodge's main goals was to help develop a private art market in the Soviet Union. "The nexus that is necessary for the development of an interest in some sort of art movement was missing," he stated. "Much of the nexus is involved around the mechanism able to make the artist able to survive and produce. This did not exist in Russia."[34] Perhaps the most important example of this point is Rabin, the first unofficial artist to live entirely from the sales of his art. As incomplete a story the archive tells about Rabin, correspondence in the Kropivnitskii Collection suggests that he was behind many of the meetings between buyers and artists. Of his eleven letters and telegrams in the archive, five of them invite Lev and Evgenii to gatherings of people "whom it would be good for them to meet."[35] Rabin never stated whom they would meet or why they should come, but given Rabin's special connection to the art market, one can surmise that these were meetings, probably with foreigners, to sell artwork. Letters from Lev to his father and wife sometimes mention Rabin's gatherings as well.[36] In 1963 Lev wrote his wife about developments in his work: "I completed a watercolor (the fourth in your absence) and five gouache drawings. I've moved on to this kind of technique because this is 1) portable, [and] 2) cheap."[37] Like Rabin, Lev does not say he's preparing to sell his artwork, but that he's making it so that it's "portable" suggests he had sales in mind. Later artists would say art for sale was made "for the suitcase," that is, small enough for foreign art connoisseurs to carry their purchases out of the country without having to get special permission.

Despite their concern for a deeper truth, did the Lianozovo artists end up catering to the desires of foreigners who wanted to buy their art? Over time some of the themes Dodge looked for became more common. This was especially the case with overtly political themes. As Dodge himself noted, he "did not find much of this until the 1980s."[38] Moreover, some artists believed that the artists who succeeded at making sales were committed to making interesting art. In the 1970s, unofficial art became pejoratively known as "art for export."[39] But artists were no different from other Soviet citizens in their need for money. After World War II, the Soviet economy again became heavily cash oriented. Two money reforms—one in the 1950s, the other in 1962—then greatly devalued the ruble.[40] A significant portion of the letters Lev and Galina wrote to each other while one person was away on vacation was devoted to business and money matters. In the same letter in which Lev announced his shift to cheaper and more portable art, he noted that he spent thirty-six kopecks for three soft cheeses, fifteen kopecks for bread, seven kopecks for tea, and ten kopecks for butter.[41] The meticulous attention to all parts of their budget suggests a widely shared concern with money. This family was not trying to get rich so much as make ends meet.

While in many ways Dodge and the Lianozovo artists pursued kindred projects, there were misunderstandings between the two sides, too—ways in which the artists were not the countercultural figures that Dodge saw them as. One important difference concerns semantics. While Dodge distinguished unofficial art from official art based on its relationship to socialist realism, the Lianozovo artists used different categories. For them, there was a difference between art that was "interesting" (*interesnoe*), "sincere" (*iskrennoe*), "modern" (*sovremennoe*), and "new" (*novoe*), and art that was none of those things. The difference between artists and art connoisseurs came down to those who "understood" (*ponimaiushchie*) and those who did not. In 1967 Lev reflected on exhibits of French, English, and American modern art that had been in Moscow over the few years previous. He noted that many viewers "who didn't understand new art went and got upset." Lev felt sorry for "the poor [people], unable to take pleasure in one more aspect of multivalent art." He took it upon himself to explain to them what the art meant and why it was good, but ended by vowing never to waste his breath again.[42] Despite the difference between Dodge and the artists on this point of vocabulary, the difference helps explain why the artists were so drawn to people like Dodge: their interest in "interesting," "modern," "new" art suggested that they understood!

In a similar vein, the artists, unlike Dodge, did not see their work as political, especially in the period before the Bulldozer Exhibit. In 1967, Lev engaged his father in a debate over the late imperialist society of Russian artists, the Wanderers (*Tvorishchestvo peredvizhnykh vystavok*). He wrote: "I deeply love this movement, like a Russian person who loves his own history." But he took issue with one particular aspect of the Wanderers' art: "[T]hey showed only one side of life and from only one side," he wrote. "They were political (in the contemporary sense of the word. . .) and accordingly depicted life."[43] In contrast, Lev and other Lianozovo artists saw their art as a site not of political but of deeply individualistic activity. When his family moved to a new apartment, Lev told his father that a new apartment was good, but that only art could plumb the depths of the human soul: "One thing is clear—a person aspires to save and lengthen life. And he aspires to spiritual perfection. These are facts. Plainly put, a good apartment can help in the first regard, comprehension of art—the second."[44] The emphasis on cultivation of the self is also evident in the highly unique style that each artist cultivated. The dark hues of Rabin's paintings differ sharply from the frolicking rabbits characteristic of Kropivnitskaia's sketches. Both differ from Nemukhin's abstractions with playing cards, which bear little resemblance to Masterkova's abstractions. No two Lianozovo artists would have been mistaken for each other based on their style.

Though the artists rejected a political identity before 1974, their relationship to politics changed starting with the Bulldozer Exhibit. We should not assume, however, that after they were politicized by the Bulldozer Exhibit they came to see politics in the same way as art connoisseurs from the Cold War West. Valentina's remarks on Parisian politics evokes the difference. In a letter to her brother, she remarked: "Oscar went to class at the Sorbonne [but] returned—there are strikes, demonstrations and the devil knows what there as well. In general there are a lot of strikes here. The post office strikes as does the railroad, the subway, the trams, the gas company and everything. [. . .] There are demonstrations of protest very often."[45] It is no wonder, in light of this comment, that the Lianozovo artists never came to see the Bulldozer Exhibit as a "protest" against the government, but as exercising their constitutional rights.

Dodge took his last trip to the Soviet Union in 1977. Each time he flew to Moscow his wife worried about her husband and his safety. He himself had become so fearful that he decided it would be his last trip.[46] It is difficult to assess the level of danger Dodge faced. Most Cold War Westerners who visited the Soviet Union exited unscathed, though in 1963 Frederick Barghoorn, a Yale professor, was arrested for attempting to carry art out of the Soviet Union and released only under pressure from U.S. President Kennedy.[47] Dodge also noted the increasing pressure put on those he associated with most on each trip, namely the artists. After the Bulldozer Exhibit in 1974, Rabin, Glezer, and others were regularly harassed by the authorities. In 1975 Glezer emigrated to France, where he opened the Russian Museum in Exile in Montgeron. In the late 1970s Rabin, his wife Valentina Kropivnitksaia, and their son Alexander Rabin wanted to travel abroad, though they loved their homeland too dearly to move—all the places they had visited and written each other about in their letters. The Soviet authorities initially rejected their application for an international passport. Then, in 1978, they had a stroke of luck: they received all documents necessary to travel in France for several weeks. Then, while they were abroad, the Soviet government revoked their citizenship. They never returned home.

Some years later, writer John McPhee asked Dodge why he collected Soviet art in the face of fear and danger. Dodge replied: "The Americans were not interested because art historians like dead artists, dealers want a steady supply, and critics review exhibits, they don't go off digging up artists. Museums don't collect artists unless they have been anointed by having many shows with good reviews. I felt it was left to an economist who goes to Russia. I thought, If anybody's going to do it, I guess I'll have to. That's why I was first attracted. The people who should have been doing it weren't doing it; and I thought, If the right people aren't doing it, then who else but me?"[48] When he discontinued his travels to the Soviet Union in 1977, he decided for the first time to put his unique collection on display. The show "New Art from the Soviet Union: The Known and the Unknown" opened in 1977 at the Arts Club of Washington in Washington, D.C., and then traveled to the Herbert F. Johnson Museum of Art at Cornell University in Ithaca, New York.[49] The exhibit was one more reason Dodge never returned to the Soviet Union: it left no ambiguity about his real intentions for traveling there.[50]

From 1977 on, Dodge expanded his collection with the help of intermediaries who traveled regularly between the USSR and the United States. He also purchased works from the ever-growing community of Soviet artists in emigration in New York and New Jersey. He was particularly fond of the Moscow Conceptualist artist duo Vitaly Komar and Alexandr Melamid after their arrival in New York in 1978. Dodge's respected place in the community of Soviet artists became evident in 1979. That year he was the only non-Russian art connoisseur featured in Komar and Melamid's artistic performance "The Corporation of the Buying and Selling of Souls," staged in New York and, with the help of their former students, Moscow simultaneously. In the United States, the exhibit poked at the commodification of life under capitalism. In the Soviet Union, the sale of souls evoked Gogol's *Dead Souls* and the Russian Imperial context, in which male serfs who headed households were referred to as "souls" (*dushi*). Dodge's soul sold for nearly three hundred rubles in Moscow—the highest-priced soul on the Soviet art market and a staggering sum in comparison to Andy Warhol's soul, which brought in just one penny in New York. Dodge's soul was sold to Tatiana Kolodzei, who often translated for the American collector in the Soviet Union, and who later opened her own museum of Soviet unofficial art in New Jersey.[51]

By the late 1980s, Dodge's collection was by far the largest of its kind in the world. At this time his interests in unofficial art expanded beyond the Soviet Union to the United States, which, he contended, had its own community of artists who were regularly blocked from showing their work in public venues.[52] At the same time, he sought a new home for his collection of Soviet art. Up until then he had kept it at his home, Cremona Farm, in Mechanicsville, Maryland. But the works needed proper storage and documentation, and the collection deserved to be on permanent display. Dodge had had offers from the Metropolitan Museum and the Museum of Modern Art to buy specific pieces in the collection, but he preferred to keep the collection together.

A firm believer that study and analysis would markedly improve his vast collection, Dodge approached several American universities about donating it there. He tried Columbia University, the University of Wisconsin, Madison, and the University of Maryland. Nothing came of these conversations, in most cases because they could not accommodate the entire collection.[53] In 1991, the Soviet Union collapsed, Dodge found a new home for the works at Rutgers, the State University of New Jersey, where his works complemented the large Riabov Collection of Russian Art at the Jane Voorhees Zimmerli Art Museum. Museum directors committed to building a new wing for the art Dodge gathered, and Francis Lawrence, President of Rutgers, envisioned the rich art collection as the beginning of making the University a center for Russian studies. Dodge ensured scholarly research by including funds for a research curator, graduate students, publications, and exhibitions. A permanent exhibit showcasing his collection opened in 1995. He remained actively involved in stewarding the collection, holding a seat on the board of the Zimmerli and visiting New Jersey regularly.[54]

When Dodge passed away in November 2011, he left behind an immeasurable imprint on the history of Soviet unofficial art. Indeed, it is in many ways thanks to him that there is a record that allows the study of this subject. His legacy is evident in the artists themselves, many of whom, like Rabin and Glezer, emigrated to the West in the 1970s, 1980s, and 1990s, because they believed the audience for their works existed. What they found, however, was that few artists enjoyed economic success abroad and that their Western audience preferred "underground art"—a moniker not applied to art produced after the Soviet collapse or in exile. The legacy of foreign collectors also remained in the very identity of the unofficial artists, who, looking back on Soviet times, came to be seen and, in some cases, saw himself as a hero. "Soviet nonconformists helped create and enlarge the cracks in the Soviet totalitarian edifice that finally brought the system crashing down," wrote Dodge.[55] The artist as political activist and dissident is an important element in the identity of some unofficial Soviet artists today, but the creation of that identity has a complex and often unexamined history. It was not simply the product of state repression. Transnational exchange between artists and collectors like Norton Dodge also played a critical role in bringing into being the Soviet unofficial artist as we know it today.

NOTES

1. I am indebted the artists and art collectors, including Norton Dodge, who met with me in 2011 as I pieced together Dodge's interactions with Soviet artists from 1962 to 1977. Our conversations greatly enriched my understanding of Soviet history and

Soviet art. Many thanks as well to those who read and commented on drafts of this paper, including Yelena Kalinsky, Jochen Hellbeck, Belinda Davis, Nathan Long, and participants of the Seminar in Modern European History at Rutgers, the State University of New Jersey.

2. Scholars and art critics use the terms "unofficial," "nonconformist," and "dissident" to describe Soviet artists who did not paint in the style of socialist realism or, in some cases, did not belong to the Artists' Union. These terms are politically loaded and originated in the Cold War West. In this paper I avoid "nonconformist" and "dissident" because artists themselves take issue with these words. I instead use "unofficial," which is also imperfect, but is the term that most artists prefer and captured an important profession distinction made in the Soviet Union between those who belonged to the Artists' Union and those who did not.

3. "Priglasitel'nyi billet na vystavku 15 sentiabria 1974 goda," in *Iskusstvo pod bul'dozerom*, ed. Alexander Glezer (London: Overseas Publications Interchange Ltd., n.d.), 123. When the invitation was printed, the participants included Oscar Rabin, Evgenii Rukhin, Vladimir Nemukhin, Lidia Masterkova, Nadezhda El'skaia, Yurii Zharkii, Alexander Rabin, Borukh Steinberg, Alexander Melamid, Vitalii Komar, V. Sitnikov, V. Vorob'eva and Igor Kholin.

4. See Timeline for the Bulldozer Exhibit in *Primary Documents: A Sourceook for Eastern and Central European Art since the 1950s*, eds. Laura Hoptman and Tomás Pospiszyl (New York: Museum of Modern Art, 2002), 65–72.

5. For articles published on both sides of the Iron Curtain, see "Materialy pressy" in *Iskusstvo pod bul'dozerom*, 47–120.

6. For copies of two letters written by the American Embassy to the US Secretary of State, see *Primary Documents*, 74–75.

7. This argument is consistent with recent historical literature on the Cold War. These works and others revise the traditional argument that during the Cold War, the Iron Curtain constituted an impermeable border between East and West and show instead the porousness of the Iron Curtain. For the Soviet case, see, for example, Susan E. Reid, "Who will beat Whom? Soviet Popular Reception of the American National Exhibit in Moscow, 1959," *Kritika* 4 (Fall 2008), 855–904. For Europe more broadly, see Simo Mikkonen and Pia Koivunen, *Beyond the Divide: Entangled Histories of Cold War Europe* (New York: Berghahn Books, 2015).

8. "Mushketery ee velichestva svobody: Beseda Aleksandra Glezera i Genrikha Sapgira" ["Muskateers of Her Highness Freedom"] (16 January 1995), in *Lianozovskaia gruppa: istoki i sudby. Sbornik materialov i katalog k vystavke v gosudarstvennoi tret'iakovskoi galeree, 10 marta—10 aprelia 1988; Tabakman Museum of Contemporary Russian Art (New York), 15 May—15 June 1998*, ed. Alexander Glezer and Genrikh Sapgir (Moscow: ZAO "Rasters," 1998), 3.

9. Norton Dodge, "Notes on Collecting Soviet Nonconformist Art," in Alla Rosenfeld and Norton Dodge, eds., *Gulag to Glasnost: Nonconformist Art from the Soviet Union* (New York: Thames and Hudson, 1995), 10.

10. Norton Dodge, *Women in the Soviet Economy: Their Role in Economic, Scientific, and Technical Development* (Baltimore: Johns Hopkins Press, 1966). Several years later, Dodge published a second book more to the point of his critical view on women in the American capitalist economy: Norton Dodge and Robert Tsuchigane, *Economic Discrimination against Women in the United States: Measures and Changes* (Lexington, MA: Lexington Books, 1974).

11. Miriam Dobson describes the uneven path to downsizing the Stalinist prison system between 1953 and 1961 in *Khrushchev's Cold Summer: Gulag Returnees, Crime, and the Fate of Reform after Stalin* (Ithaca: Cornell University Press, 2009). Historians continue to debate the extent to which there was a "thaw" in Soviet history following Stalin's death and even after Khrushchev's "Secret Speech." Also see Denis Kozlov, *The Readers of Novyi Mir: Coming to Terms with the Stalinist Past* (Cambridge: Harvard University Press, 2013).

12. See, for example, "*Kniga otzyvov o vystavke Evgeniia Kropivnitskogo 12.1958," (vystavka prokhodivshaia v kvartire kompozitora Andreiia Volkonskogo zimoi 1958 g.)*, Rossiiskii gosudarstvennyi arkhiv literatury i iskusstv [hereafter RGALI], F. 3135, OP. 1, D. 125.

13. Susan Reid, "Communist Comfort: Socialist modernism and the Making of Cozy Homes in the Khrushchev-Era Soviet Union," *Gender and History* 21:3 (2009), 469.

14. See Chapter 1, "Soviet Internationalism," in Eleonory Gilburd, "To See Paris and Die: Western Culture in the Soviet Union, 1950s and 1960s," Ph.D. dissertation, University of California, Berkeley, 2010.

15. Matthew Jesse Jackson, *The Experimental Group: Ilya Kabakov, Moscow Conceptualism, Soviet Avant-Gardes* (Chicago: University of Chicago Press, 2010), 19.

16. Vladimir Nemukhin, Interview with Andrei Erofeev, reprinted in Irina Alpatova, ed., *Drugoe Iskussvo: Moskva, 1956–1988* (Moscow: Galart, 2005), 28.

17. Dodge, "Notes on Collecting," in *Gulag to Glasnost*, 10.

18. Dodge, "Notes on Collecting," in *Gulag to Glasnost*, 10.

19. *Ibid.*, 12.

20. Boris Zhutovskii, *Kak odin den': pamiat' priroda iskusstvo*, Vol. 1 (Moscow: OAO Tipografiia "NOVOSTI," 2011), 122–133; Susan Reid, "In the Name of the People: The Manege Affair Revisited," *Kritika* 6:4 (2005), 673–716.

21. Interview with Norton Dodge, in *Soviet Dissident Artists: Interviews after Perestroika*, ed. Renee and Matthew Baigell (New Brunswick: Rutgers University Press, 1995), 25–26. Also see Dodge, "Notes on Collecting Nonconformist Soviet Art," in *Gulag to Glasnost*, 9.

22. Alison Hilton and Norton Dodge, Preface to *New Art from the Soviet Union: the Known and the Unknown* (Washington, D.C.: Acropolis Books, Ltd., 1977), 7.

23. Letter from Lev Kropivnitskii to Galina Kropivnitskii, 3 August 1962, RGALI, F. 3091, Op. 2, D. 10, L. 1.

24. Letter from Valentina Kropivniskaia to Evgenii Kropivnitskii, 14 September 1976, RGALI, F. 3135, Op. 1, D. 79, L. 28.

25. Dodge, "Notes on Collecting," in *Gulag to Glasnost*, 10.

26. Conversation with Tatiana Levitskaia, 5 July 2011.

27. Letter from Lev Kropivnitskii to Evgenii Kropivnitskii, 4 July 1956, RGALI, F. 3135, Op. 1, D. 67, L. 14.

28. Letter from Galina Kropivnitksaia to Lev Kropivnitskii, 23 December 1964, RGALI, F. 3091, Op. 1, D. 135, L. 35–36.

29. Letter from Lev Kropivnitskii to Evgenii Kropivnitskii, 27 October 1966, RGALI, F. 3135, Op. 1, D. 67, L. 22.

30. Letter from Lev Kropivnitskii to Evgenii Kropivnitskii, 21 June 1966, RGALI, F. 3135, Op. 1, D. 67, L. 21. Lev did not always feel so strongly about his spirituality—in 1971 he wrote his father: "I have even begun to believe less in God"—but throughout the artists' lives, they cultivated an interest in religion. See Letter from Lev Kropivnitskii to Evgenii Kropivnitskii, undated [1971], RGALI, F. 3135, Op. 1, D. 70, L. 22.

31. It is, however, not surprising that religion continued to exist in the Soviet Union. For an exploration of how official position on religion changed over time, see Victoria Smolkin-Rothrock, "The Ticket to the Soviet Soul: Science, Religion, and the Spiritual Crisis of Late Soviet Atheism," *The Russian Review* 73 (April 2014), 171–197.

32. See, for example, Alexander Solzhenitsyn, *One Day in the Life of Ivan Denisovich* (New York: New American Library, 2009).

33. *Zagalovok dela: Avtobiografiia (Petrov Valentin Sergeevich)*, RGALI, F. 3091, Op. 1, D. 255.

34. McPhee, *The Ransom of Russian Art*, 93.

35. Letter from Oscar Rabin to Lev Kropivnitskii, 30 March [c. 1966], RGALI, F. 3091, Op. 1, Ed. khr. 193, L. 6.

36. Letter from Lev Kropivnitskii to Galina Kropivnitskaia, undated [1969], RGALI, F. 3091, Op. 2, D. 10, L. 26.

37. Letter from Lev Kropivnitskii to Galina Kropivnitskaia, 25 August 1963, RGALI, F. 3091, Op. 2, D. 10, L. 7–8.

38. Interview with Norton Dodge in *Soviet Dissident Artists*, ed. Baigell et al, 35.

39. Martina Weinhart, "Comprehensible Incomprehensibility; Moscow Conceptualism and the Western Viewer," in *Die Totale Aufklaerung Moskauer Konzeptkunst 1960–1990/Total Enlightenment Conceptual Art in Moscow 1960–1990*, ed. Boris Groys et al (Ostfildern, Germany: Hatje Cantz Verlag, 2008), 73.

40. On post-war money reform, see Kristy Ironside, "The Value of a Ruble: A Social History of Money in Postwar Soviet Russia, 1945–1964" (Ph.D. dissertation, University of Chicago, 2014).

41. Letter from Lev Kropivnitskii to Galina Kropivnitskaia, 25 August 1963, RGALI, F. 3091, Op. 2, D. 10, L. 7–8.

42. Letter from Lev Kropivnitskii to Evgenii Kropivnitskii, 17 November 1967, RGALI, F. 3135, Op. 1, D. 69, L. 10–11.

43. Letter from Lev Kropivnitskii to Evgenii Kropivnitskii, 1 December 1967, RGALI, F. 3135, Op. 1, D. 69, L. 14–15.

44. Letter from Lev Kropivnitskii to Evgenii Kropivnitskii, 1 February 1967, RGALI, F. 3135, Op. 1, D. 69, L. 14–15.

45. Letter from Valentina Kropivnitskaia to Lev Kropivnitskii, 14 October 1980, RGALI, F. 3091, Op. 1, Ed. khr. 131, L. 45–46.

46. Dodge, "Notes on Collecting," in *Gulag to Glasnost*, 16.

47. Bruce Lambert, "Frederick Barghoorn, 80, Scholar Detained in Soviet Union in 1963," *New York Times* (26 November 1991), available athttp://www.nytimes.com/1991/11/26/obituaries/frederick-barghoorn-80-scholar-detained-in-soviet-union-in-1963.html(accessed 19 August 2015).

48. John McPhee, *The Ransom of Russian Art*, 93.

49. The catalog for this exhibit is Alison Hilton and Norton Dodge, *New Art from the Soviet Union: the Known and the Unknown* (Washington, D.C.: Acropolis Books, Ltd., 1977).

50. Dodge, "Notes on Collecting," in *Gulag to Glasnost*, 16.

51. Natalia Kolodzei, "Raznye sud'by khudozhnikov russkoi immigratsii v Amerike," in *Russkoe ART zarubezh'e, vtoraia polovina XX-nachalo XXI veka*, ed. Zinaida Starodubtseva (Moscow: Gosudarstvennyi Tsentr Sovremennogo iskussva, 2010), 57; *Kvartirnye vystavki, 1956–1979* (Moscow: Rossiiskii gosudarstvennyi gumanitarnyi universitet, 2005).

52. Dodge wrote that Soviet nonconformist art teaches Americans that "we must keep constant guard against those forces and persons who seek to suppress freedom of expression in our own society. This freedom is a precious heritage with which we have long been blessed and which we must never take for granted but always cherish and defend." See Dodge, "Notes on Collecting," in *Gulag to Glasnost*, 35.

53. McPhee, *The Ransom of Russian Art*, 178.

54. Phillip Dennis Cate, "Introduction" to Rosenfield and Dodge, eds., *Gulag to Glasnost*, 7.

55. Dodge, "Notes on Collecting," in *Gulag to Glasnost*, 35.

TEN

Changing Dynamics

From International Exchanges to Transnational Musical Networks

Simo Mikkonen

The focus of this chapter is on the Soviet Union's musical networks with Finland during the Brezhnev era, particularly after the period of Thaw. The standard periodization of the Soviet era in relation to arts sees the Thaw era being followed by a period of more strictly enforced ideological conformity.[1] In music, a feeling of stagnation seemed to be embodied by composer Tikhon Khrennikov, who remained the general secretary of the Soviet Composers' Union right from the Stalin era until the end of the Soviet Union. Under his leadership, the Union fought avant-garde and other modernist tendencies in music.[2] Meanwhile, the realities of art production and the official party line were increasingly distant from each other. However, despite this idea of artistic stagnation in the domestic sphere, a lot was happening in the realm of foreign cultural connections. By taking examples from connections between Finland and the Soviet Union, this chapter aims at understanding the changing dynamics and multifaceted nature of artistic networks of the Brezhnev era. It will be argued that organizations and individuals in the West who were allowed to be in touch with their Soviet counterparts were increasingly less Communist-inclined. Ideology, in general, became less present in artistic exchanges during the Brezhnev era than ever before since the Stalin era.

The changes brought about by the period of the Thaw with regard to Soviet foreign cultural connections have been documented, and there continues to be a growing body of literature on this topic.[3] Under Stalin, foreign connections had been exclusively tended and controlled by the Communist Party and Soviet security organs. Connections were few and limited to the necessary diplomatic ties, or few highly publicized contacts with foreign communists or Soviet sympathizers.[4] Access of the wider Soviet public to foreign connections was highly limited, and the Communist Party strictly controlled the images conveyed of foreign countries. Even so, the postwar era brought former émigrés back to the Soviet Union as repatriates; many Soviet citizens had, for the first time, been outside Soviet borders, either as soldiers in the army or as workers. However, the authorities quickly intervened to suffocate foreign influences with the anticosmopolitan campaigns of 1946 and 1948.[5]

In contrast to the Stalin era, the quantitative expansion of foreign connections in the post-Stalin era was indeed remarkable. The Soviet Union engaged capitalist governments by establishing bilateral agreements on cultural exchange, and increasing travel and tourism to capitalist countries. What took place can be described as the emergence of Soviet cultural diplomacy.[6] Bilateral agreements on cultural exchange with Western countries during the Thaw resulted in an expansion of connections between the Soviet Union and the surrounding nonsocialist world.[7] Khrushchev himself engaged the West in his rhetoric, and sought examples from the West in his attempts to modernize the country.[8] Toward the end of his leadership, this agenda and, more generally, the period of Thaw, have been seen to have come to an end. However, an important watershed with regard to the arts emerged in 1962, when the Kremlin's reformist wing, which had allowed more space for the arts and nurtured foreign cultural connections, started to face increasing difficulties.[9] For arts and artists, renewed connections with the West had been most welcome. The return of stricter policies thus threatened once again to stifle artistic expression.

An important aspect of Soviet foreign networks concerns the extent to which Soviet travelers were subject to limitations when abroad. It would seem that these limitations were more severe before a trip than during it.[10] In order to travel to the West, Soviet citizens had to go through several security checks, and their travel rights could be suspended at any time without any explanation. However, things changed for Soviet citizens after crossing the border. Even if Soviet security organs aimed at arranging tourist groups so that a KGB-hired "nanny" would prevent undesired contact with foreigners—and individual artists usually had "personal secretaries" for similar purposes—these precautions were only partially efficient. Source materials indicate that in Finland, for instance, surveillance was far from complete.[11] Cases in this chapter suggest that in foreign artistic connections, circumventing surveillance was fairly common and easy, and furthermore, surveillance was sometimes completely lacking.

The musical intelligentsia and their networks provide an interesting case study of the changes that took place in the East-West connections of the Brezhnev era. The relevance of connections with the West was greater for Soviet artists and artistic life than for the average citizen, but they were also easier to come by for artists. Artistic intelligentsia in the Soviet Union had privileges and an elite status.[12] Not everyone was allowed to travel, especially when it came to individual artists who usually had to be prominent in their own field before they could be considered to be sent to the West. Still, when groups like Moscow's Bolshoi Opera or the Leningrad Symphony were sent on tour, they easily included well over a hundred artists. Hardly all were stars. Furthermore, foreign connections established during the Thaw era continued to expand through the 1960s and 1970s, and travel became more commonplace. Contacting Western artists became easier, and, sometimes, occasional connections led to deeper cooperation. Thus, in contrast to the Thaw, when state-to-state-level connections rapidly expanded, the expansion during the Brezhnev era took place in the less visible realm of people-to-people and other informal connections that will be referred to in this chapter as transnational networks.

Finland was important to the Soviet Union for several reasons, making it an ideal country for investigating the transnational networks of the Soviet artistic intelligentsia. Finland's accessibility to the Soviet Union was unique among Western capitalist countries. This was partly a result of a shared border, but the fact that Soviet citizens could not seek asylum in Finland also played a role. Unlike other Western countries, Finland returned asylum-seekers back to the Soviet Union.[13] Finland thus became a top tourist destination in the West for the Soviet Union, enabling several other types of connections that were more limited elsewhere.[14] The proximity to Leningrad also played a role. Fairly cheap and daily train connections, from both Leningrad and Moscow, eased the establishment of connections. After 1964, Helsinki also connected with Tallinn, the capital of Soviet Estonia, by a ship that took mere hours. Finally, there was a Soviet-Finnish friendship society, which was among the biggest civil societies in Finland. It was also different from its counterparts in other Western countries where such societies were smaller in size and consisted mostly of leftists.[15] The changing role of the Finnish-Soviet society in Finnish-Soviet networks hints to the much broader phenomena of artistic East-West networks during the Cold War era.

This chapter is based on oral history, supplemented with archival materials collected from Russia and Finland. Interviews were conducted with people who were actively in touch with their Soviet counterparts. Rather than occupying official or political roles, these people were musicians, pedagogues, and secretaries in companies and organizations that dealt with foreigners as part of their duties. Such interviews are very important for providing information about the functioning of connections with the West, about motivations for participating in such networks, as well as explaining possible salient changes during perestroika. Interviews connected to artistic exchanges were mainly gathered in Finland, mostly from Finnish citizens.

ON TRANSNATIONALISM

To understand the change in Soviet foreign artistic connections after the thaw, it is crucial to understand the difference between international relations and transnational networks. The traditional field of international relations tends to emphasize diplomacy and state-to-state relations, which, in the case of the Soviet Union, often results in underlining of ideological and political objectives. Seen in this light, Soviet foreign connections appear as a strictly controlled area with little space for individual maneuvering. It is becoming increasingly apparent, however, that the dynamics of Soviet foreign activities notably changed during the decades after Stalin. Yet, the implications of these changes are still too poorly understood. Instead of concentrating on diplomacy and state-level actions, the transnational approach takes us toward individuals and organizations, their perspectives on the movement of people, goods, ideas, and practices over the Soviet border.

The term "transnational" is used in this chapter primarily to distinguish international (state-to-state) connections from lower-level (people-to-people) connections. It helps us to consider the motivations and objectives of the individual actions behind the ideological and political facade.[16] In the case of the Soviet Union, the line between the party and the individual is rarely clear-cut, but this does not mean that it did not exist or that it is not worth pursuing. It has been underlined that the rupture between the official and individual objectives increased during the Brezhnev era, making this dividing line interesting.[17] If we take the Thaw and compare it to the Brezhnev era, the traditional narrative emphasizes the return to conservative values and a stricter control over foreign connections, limitations in travel, increased KGB control and surveillance.[18] The transnational approach to foreign countries is also important because of the changes between the individual and the public in the Soviet Union. A majority of the studies on the changes in individual and public spaces have focused on the Khrushchev era, but it would seem unlikely that the gap between the personal and the public closed after the Thaw.[19]

Transnationality, a key concept in this chapter, has been a point of discussion within the field of history for more than two decades, but it has found its way to the field of Soviet history only recently.[20] Since then, however, the transnational approach has quickly gained ground. Anne Gorsuch's *All This Is Your World*, which discusses Soviet tourism, is among the few books that examines Soviet foreign connections in the post-Stalin era with a clear transnational focus. Several other works have also suggested that looking beyond international relations and reaching toward individuals and organizations could reveal aspects from the Soviet Union that have so far been overlooked.[21] This new research on the Soviet Union and its changing place in the world underlines the need for further study on the Soviet Union with a transnational perspective. The majority of existing studies address earlier Soviet periods, underlining the need to examine transnational networks during the Brezhnev era when foreign connections had started to become commonplace.

The problem with the transnational approach vis-à-vis the Soviet Union is that much of the literature on transnational history is largely derived from the U.S. context.[22] Unlike the United States, though, the Soviet Union was never a nation-state. Still, it was the center of the communist "second world," and the crucial boundary here is not necessarily the Soviet border, but rather the systemic borderline between economic, ideological, and political systems. Differences between the East and the West were simultaneously real and imaginary.[23] Finland, with its position between the East and the West, offers a particularly fruitful area to look at the functioning of Soviet transnational networks. While Finland was a Western capitalist democracy with full access to Western markets and cultural currents, it also harbored close ties with the Soviet Union. For the Soviet Union, friendly ties to a capitalist country underlined the benevolence of the Soviet foreign policy and seemed to support Soviet propaganda about the imperialist and warmongering West. However, the Finnish-Soviet connections also underline that the picture is much more complicated and often less ideologically colored when looked beneath the surface.

The transnational approach is not a method as such, but it does guide the selection of sources as well as the type of information derived from them. Official documents in the Soviet-era archival material pose certain problems from the transnational perspective. Archives were controlled by the Communist Party, and documents there tend to reiterate the official perspective. The lack of a functioning civil society in the Soviet Union also limits what is available in the archives concerning subgovernmental connections. Oral history interviews, however, help in providing the necessary gateway past the official barrier. Still, it is not easy to tell apart the official Soviet objectives from those of individuals. Internationalism as an idea striving beyond national rivalries[24] was present to a certain extent in the Soviet Union. For example, one openly stated aim of the Soviet government was to introduce foreign cultures to the Soviet public.[25] This aim mixed internationalism with the actual desire of many people to get in touch with the world outside the Soviet Union. This, naturally, complicates the picture by making the aims of the State and the Party multilayered. It is not necessarily easy to dissect personal aims from those of the Party.[26]

Distinguishing between these differing aims by way of interviews can be tricky, especially since the interviews conducted for this study were made decades after the actual events. However, the interviews uncover personal experiences and motivations, which are usually lacking in the archival documents. By combining different source materials, it is possible to avoid one-sidedness and strive toward more comprehensive conclusions about the nature and implications of Soviet transnational networks. Thus, from the methodological point of view, combining oral history with archival evidence is highly important. Even if the selected archival material presents the viewpoint of individuals and indicates points of social change, the interviews provide not only a good way to cross-check such findings, but also necessary data on the personal experiences related to transnational networks.

The Soviet Cultural Diplomacy and the Thaw

The most dynamic phase concerning Soviet cultural diplomacy took place during the first post-Stalin decade. It also forged the basis for the Soviet's approach to foreign cultural exchanges that continued—and even increased—during the Brezhnev era. By the mid-1950s, the Soviet Union had started to establish and rebuild its foreign connections outside the immediate socialist sphere. While this change had important repercussions for international relations, such connections also implied the participation of Soviet citizens. The partial opening of the borders allowed many the chance to build connections with the world outside the Soviet Union. Different exhibitions, a steady flow of foreign visitors, and tourism from the Soviet Union all increased the chances of connecting with foreign artistic currents as well as colleagues. While connections in the 1950s were still small, mass tourism already became a phenomenon in the 1960s, and different forms of exchange grew continuously. Khrushchev-era foreign cultural operations are important, then, in pointing out the quantitative change from the Stalin era cultural connections that touched only a selected few. After Stalin, Soviet artists started to swamp concert halls and musical competitions, and Soviet works of art filled exhibition halls and museums in the West. A country that had kept its borders closed, fiercely blocking foreign influences, suddenly started to interact with the surrounding capitalist world.[27] Yet, the stated purpose was not so much a dialogue with the West as competition in which the USSR participated to prove its superiority and, in this way, to win over foreign populations. The opening up of possibilities for artistic exchange was primarily a tactical rather than a strategic change.

Two major organizational changes in the Soviet bureaucracy illustrate the changes in the Soviet's approach to foreign artistic connections before and after the Thaw. They also help in explaining the change in dynamics of these connections. Until 1957, foreign cultural connections had been tended to by the All-Union Society for Cultural Relations with Foreign Countries (VOKS). This organization was originally established in 1925 to coordinate contacts between Soviet cultural workers and their colleagues in the West. It kept alive limited connections, mostly with communists and leftists who were willing to be in touch with the Soviet Union.[28] However, by 1957, the Communist Party felt that VOKS had become restrictive and outdated; it decided, then, to restructure the organization and expand its scope.[29] This was done by replacing VOKS with two new organizations. Most of the old VOKS was restructured into what became the Union of Soviet Societies for Friendship and Cultural Contacts (SSOD); this segment took care of all the friendship associations and was in touch with its foreign counterparts (in this case, the Finnish-Soviet Society). The other, and more major, change was the establishment of the State Committee of Cultural Ties with Foreign Countries (GKKS) by the Soviet Council of Ministers, which signaled actual changes in the Soviet's approach to foreign cultural exchanges. This powerful committee parceled out its authority from the Ministry of Foreign Affairs, but also, to a certain extent, from the Ministry of Culture, Radio Committee, and other Soviet organs dealing with foreign cultural ties. Throughout the Thaw, this committee exercised vast powers over cultural exchanges and artistic connections to foreign countries. It took care of much of the foreign propaganda, but also controlled matters pertaining to foreign travel, closely coordinating with other parts of the government and Party organs.[30] The Chairman of this new committee was Yuri Zhukov, a reform-minded Soviet official and editor of *Pravda,* who had spent several years on assignments outside the Soviet Union in the 1940s and 1950s. Under Zhukov, the GKKS assumed a less rigid role in cultural affairs than its predecessors, VOKS and the Ministry of Foreign Affairs.

The GKKS's actions seemed less aggressive and generally embodied the Khrushchev administration's ideas about openly competing with—but, to some extent, also learning from—the West. These ideas led to the mutual exchange of artists, students, professionals, and tourist groups, as well as printed materials and cultural artifacts. The arts took a lead in such foreign exchange during the Thaw. Frederick Barghoorn, a U.S. contemporary, described aptly that Soviet cultural diplomacy was a systematic exploitation of cultural material, symbols, persons, and ideas in reaching its foreign political objectives.[31] Indeed, the Soviet Union initiated and signed agreements of bilateral cultural exchange in the latter half of the 1950s with most capitalist countries.[32] Agreements were often left fairly open, without strict definitions about cooperation, in order to prevent their Western counterparts from controlling actions on their side.[33] Furthermore, the Soviet government often dealt with prominent individuals in the West and with private companies rather than with capitalist governments.[34] This was logical, as companies and individuals were believed to have less political and ideological ambitions than governments in exchange projects. Yet, as a result of the Thaw era agreements, lasting bonds between many Western and Soviet art professionals were made possible in the form of mutual networks.

CHANGES AFTER THE THAW

Cultural exchanges with European countries were easier for the Soviet Union than with the United States, which was more expensive, more averse to the Soviet Union, and farther away. Therefore, the official exchange of artistic troupes between the United States and the Soviet Union had been almost nonexistent before the U.S.-Soviet Cultural Exchange Agreement (1958) was signed. The development of different forms of exchange and mutual projects was rapid until 1962, after which Soviet cultural diplomacy experienced changes; development more or less ceased with security concerns overcoming progressive agendas.[35] The passing of the Thaw was not only manifested in the fading dynamism of Soviet cultural operations, but also in the GKKS itself. Yuri Zhukov had to resign in 1962, and his powerful committee started to wane, assuming merely routine tasks instead of actively seeking new forms of engagement and opportunities for exerting cultural influence.[36] Finally, the whole committee was terminated in 1967, and its powers were returned to other government institutes, starting with the Soviet Foreign Ministry.

Still, the sidelining of the GKKS did not result in a decrease in exchanges with the West. On the contrary, while the forms of state-to-state exchange remained unchanged, quantitatively exchanges actually increased substantially after the Thaw. Between 1957 and 1961, when the Soviet Union actively sought cultural connections with the West and developed new forms of interaction, the average number of groups exchanged between the Soviet Union and the United States was 1.6 per year. From 1962 to 1973, this same average increased to 2.75 per year.[37]

Even if the quantitative change was tangible, the qualitative change was even more so. This change did not take place at the state level, where the Ministry of Foreign Affairs simply took back its authority from the GKKS, but rather at the lower levels. Official bilateral exchange programs of the Thaw produced connections—particularly artistic connections—that started to develop on their own, often along lines not set forth by the Communist Party. Instead of ideological and political aims, artists were pursuing their own personal and professional motivations. Connections that had been a part of state-to-state agreements ended up becoming a part of East–West transnational networks where individual and professional aims mattered more than international relations or diplomacy.

Finnish-Soviet Connections

The key problem in detecting this qualitative change is that it occurred slowly. The SSOD, which continued to exist from the Thaw throughout the Brezhnev era, is illustrative of this. While Friendship organizations lived on after the Thaw, they were left with mostly routine tasks with little political importance. This is particularly visible in the case of Finnish-Soviet connections. The Finnish-Soviet Society was assumed to be, like many other friendship organizations in the West, politically and ideologically inclined toward the Soviet Union. It has been assumed that Friendship organizations leaned toward communism and working for Soviet foreign policy objectives.[38] While this was certainly true during the Stalin era, things had started to change when travel to the Soviet Union became more commonplace and programs of cultural exchange were initiated.

The Finnish-Soviet society had started to actively nurture connections between Finnish civil society and numerous Soviet organizations, particularly after the mid-1950s. Although Finnish communists had sought such connections before the Thaw, the Soviet Union had been reluctant. The Finnish-Soviet Society was one of the biggest civil society organizations in Finland, with about 5 percent of all Finns as its members in the late 1940s. Furthermore, it was not completely associated with communism even if leftists were over-represented in the society. During the Stalin era, its primary function had been to act as a propaganda channel, distributing Soviet information, educational material and Soviet films.[39] However, its role changed significantly from the mid-1950s.

As cultural exchanges between Finland and the Soviet Union took shape in the mid-1950s, the society became active in organizing all kinds of cultural connections. These activities ranged from exhibitions to tours of Soviet artists in Finland, tours of Finnish artists in the Soviet Union, to student and professional exchanges, as well as the exchange of information and materials. Throughout the thaw, the Finnish-Soviet Society was actively in touch with its Soviet counterpart. In the 1960s, however, connections to the Soviet-Finnish Society started to become increasingly routine; for ideologically and politically important questions, the Finnish-Soviet Society began to turn to the Soviet Foreign Ministry and Soviet Embassy in Helsinki. The role of the Soviet-Finnish Society, and its relationships with Finns became mostly formal, ritualistic, and unimportant.[40] The SSOD was no longer dynamic, it was unable to provide enough results, and for important tasks, there were more significant players around.

During the Brezhnev era, the Finnish-Soviet society started to facilitate connections between numerous Finnish and Soviet organizations, societies, and even individuals. As cultural connections between Finland and the Soviet Union increased, the society assumed the role of a mediator, rather than pursuing its own programs, or working as the Soviet's mouthpiece in Finland. The society engaged in building bridges between Finnish and Soviet organizations and individuals without setting ideological or political preconditions, instead helping any Finnish organization or individual willing to contact their Soviet counterparts. For this purpose, it offered translation and expert services, which usually meant finding the right officials and actors within the Soviet government and the Party for those who were not used to Soviet bureaucracy.[41]

CONTENTS OF ARTISTIC EXCHANGES

From the grassroots perspective, Soviet foreign connections experienced notable changes during the Brezhnev era. At the governmental level, the political dimension of East-West cultural exchanges never quite vanished, but their significance for individuals increased and adopted new forms. For example, while the Soviet leadership aimed at creating benevolence toward Soviet policies through artistic exchange, Soviet artists who took part in these exchanges often used this opportunity to travel to access international trends in art and further their own professional agenda. Sometimes there were very concrete souvenirs, like in the case of Gershwin's *Porgy and Bess*, which was performed by the Estonian National Opera in Tallinn in 1967. This American score was unavailable in the Soviet Union but available in Finland, where it was photographed and brought to Tallinn.[42] Interviews with two women, who for several decades took care of Soviet artists' visits and practical issues in Finland, underlined that while high-profile artists often had tight schedules while in Finland, they always had time not only to socialize and make friends with Finnish artists, but also to shop for everything from bed mattresses to saunas and stoves, sometimes finding it hard to fit everything they had bought into their train compartments when heading back.[43]

When the freedoms of Soviet travelers in Finland are examined in detail, it turns out that they could generally move about more freely than their travel programs would suggest. The discrepancy between what Soviet travelers were supposed to do and what they actually did has been addressed by Anne Gorsuch.[44] The difference in personal and official motivations in foreign connections was notable, with political and ideological objectives often pushed to the background. Soviet leaders believed they could control and manipulate individual objectives toward their political aims, but with the expansion of tourism in the Brezhnev era, this became impossible.[45] The same dichotomy that applied to tourism prevailed in artistic connections: while the Soviet leadership always reasoned the exchanges in political and ideological terms, the conduct of the travelers often did not follow the ideological contours. What might seem like political and ideological fare in archival documents turns out to be something very different when examined in detail. This dichotomy also began to emerge in the Finnish-Soviet Society description of artistic exchanges. While such exchanges were initially described in ideological terms, by the Brezhnev era this had vanished almost entirely, transforming instead into purely professional terms.[46] Loyalty to state and party aims started to become less and less relevant.[47]

Finnish-Soviet Musical Networks

It is clear, then, that Finnish-Soviet artistic networks became rather multifaceted and the role played by individuals grew in the 1960s. Individuals, rather than governments, started to initiate exchange projects. One such person was Finnish conductor Onni Kelo. Born in 1930, Kelo had begun his studies in Helsinki; by the 1950s, he began to seek training that was unavailable in Finland. He eventually managed to get into the Leningrad Conservatory through a path opened by the Thaw. At the time, the conservatory still had very few Westerners. After initial difficulties, and learning Russian, Kelo passed through the conservatory's famous conductor class in the late 1950s. Kelo was not politically active, and he briefly studied in the Netherlands before Leningrad. Kelo was one of the first to lead the way for numerous Finnish musicians and conductors after him who went to nearby Leningrad to further their studies.[48]

While studying at the world-class Leningrad conservatory was important for certain prominent Finnish musicians, even more important, considering transnational networks, were Kelo's later actions. During his time in Leningrad he had managed to build extensive networks, which he put to effective use upon returning to Finland. In the 1960s, Finland had a serious lack of skilled music teachers in several key instruments, such as the violin. When Kelo assumed the position of music director for the northern Finnish city of Oulu, he encouraged the local music school to get a visiting teacher from the Soviet Union where world-class pedagogues were aplenty. One of the first such teachers was Tatiana Pogozeva, a high-profile Moscow pedagogue and mother of violin virtuoso Igor Bezrodnyi.[49]

Pogozeva arrived in Oulu in 1967, and in the course of a few years, initiated a transformation of Finnish violin pedagogics, rebuilt according to her blueprint.[50] The fact that a regional Finnish music institute of little national repute managed to hire her for two years aroused great interest in Finnish music circles. Soon, many other regional music institutes followed Oulu's lead—for instance, Jyväskylä, which would engage one or two Soviet teachers every year until the end of the Soviet Union.[51] Several other interviewees also underlined the transformative effect of Soviet pedagogues on Finnish music pedagogics since Pogozeva's initial visit. Her pioneering role brought numerous other pedagogues to Finnish regional music institutes throughout the 1970s and 1980s. Many of the visiting teachers were hard-driving, committed to their students, and worked very systematically. This had an effect on their Finnish colleagues, too: Finnish teachers were said to improve their own teaching after seeing their Soviet colleagues work so hard with their students.[52]

Pogozeva's posting to Finland was by no means obvious. While Finland had received Russian-speaking teachers from the Soviet Union before, there was no active exchange of pedagogues between the countries in the 1960s, especially not for longer durations. Kelo's crucial role in the process has been remarked upon by several prominent Finns. Kelo himself modestly notes that being in the right place at the right time had helped. According to Kelo, when Tikhon Khrennikov, the influential head of the Soviet Composers' Union, was visiting Finland, Kelo—who could now speak Russian—was invited to meet him. The two developed a rapport, and when Kelo told Khrennikov about his problem of finding a proficient violin pedagogue to fill a vacant position, Khrennikov hinted that he could help. Soon, Kelo was encouraged to contact Goskontsert, the Soviet concert organization that dealt with music tours and concert visits, which led to Pogozeva being hired.[53] Consequently, the benefits of hiring a high-profile Soviet music pedagogue in a regional town were noted across Finland.

Along with Finnish music education, the exchange of performing artists—a more typical feature of cultural exchanges in the Cold War era—was experiencing changes. Initially, the exchange of artists was something that the Finnish-Soviet Society had tried to set in motion ever since the war between the Soviet Union and Finland ended in 1944. At the time, there was little that VOKS could, or was willing to, do. Early in 1945, the foremost Soviet artistic troupes, the Red Army Choir and Dance Ensemble and the Moiseyev Dance Company, along with several prominent Soviet artists visited Finland. Post-1945, however, such exchanges became few and far between. The Finnish-Soviet Society tried to pull all strings possible, even approaching the foremost Finnish concert organizer, Fazer Concert Office, requesting a list of foreign musicians visiting Finland in 1948. The document was sent to VOKS: it listed Danes, Dutch, Spanish, Americans, even "two negro singers," but not a single Soviet.[54] It was reasoned that Finnish musicians and audiences would orient to the West unless some kind of Soviet presence was created.[55] The answer given for this, as well as numerous other similar letters during the Stalin era, was: "We will look into this issue later on."[56]

By the mid-1960s petitions for Soviet artists forwarded by the Finnish-Soviet Society were hardly ever turned down. However, the role of the society had already changed from an initiator into a mediator. Initiatives for inviting Soviet artists came from individuals such as Kelo, or from organizations like the Fazer Concert Office, who had often been in dealings with their Soviet counterparts, either at international festivals, in Finland, or during their own trips to the Soviet Union. Onni Kelo had, in fact, recommended using the Society as a mediator as he was certain that when Soviet organizations were contacted by a trusted Finnish partner, their approach would be taken more seriously.[57] The Finnish-Soviet Society had the best connections and the means to get their Soviet colleagues involved.

However, the Finnish-Soviet Society and Soviet organizations like Goskontsert merely facilitated these connections. Many Finnish artists met their Soviet counterparts and used official channels to invite them to Finland. In many cases, matters were usually settled through personal communication even before Goskontsert was involved.[58] Similar cooperation was organized in many other areas, ranging from theater to scholarly and other professional fields. Music, however, being a field that is less dependent on spoken language, was among the most active.[59]

In part, Finland's success in attracting Soviet performers was based on the aforementioned law that prevented Soviet citizens from defecting to Finland. As a result, Finland was used as a launch pad for Soviet artists before they could travel further West. The case of the celebrated piano virtuoso, Sviatoslav Richter, perhaps best exemplifies this. The KGB had denied Richter travel to the West throughout the 1950s; finally, in 1960, the KGB yielded to pressure and allowed Richter to visit Finland. Only after that was Richter allowed to travel freely to the West.[60]

Many other high-profile musicians followed the same route, resulting in Finland enjoying the benefits of cultural exchanges with the Soviet Union extensively. This lead to a curious phenomenon: small localities in Finland began to offer high-profile concerts and teachers than even the capital city of Helsinki could not. Festivals and symphony orchestras in Turku and Jyväskylä were among the first to regularly bring Soviet performers, and tiny communities, such as Kuhmo in the north, soon followed. Festivals brought Soviet performers not only to perform, but also to conduct master courses, usually in the summer when schools were closed.[61]

Organizers of Finnish festivals or music institutes that sought Soviet performers or pedagogues often knew neither the Soviet bureaucratic system nor Russian. Thus, contacting Soviet organizations directly was typically an overwhelming task for them; people like Onni Kelo who could communicate directly with the Soviets were a rarity. While Soviet artists quite often spoke other languages—most often German, which was also fairly commonly spoken in Finland at the time, or sometimes French or English—Soviet organizations were rarely willing to operate in languages other than Russian. Certain Finnish organizations like the Fazer Concert Office managed to build working connections with Goskontsert by using German and English, but such organizations were constantly in touch and persons from both organizations already knew each other.[62] With organizations that dealt with each other more infrequently, the Finnish-Soviet Society came to facilitate correspondence with the Soviet

Ministry of Culture and Goskontsert. The initial role of the Finnish-Soviet Society in establishing connections was often a major one, but it diminished as connections became more commonplace. When Finnish and Soviet professionals came to know each other, they usually agreed on details and logistics through personal correspondence, only after which they would contact official organizations. Usually, the Finnish counterparts contacted Soviet organizations requesting the services of a certain Soviet individual, even in cases where the original initiative came from the Soviet side.[63]

NETWORKS IN ACTION

It is easy to understand the political reasoning for sending high-profile Soviet performers abroad. The Soviet Union used its foremost musicians as cultural ambassadors who were also believed to prove Soviet Union's cultural superiority.[64] The reasons for sending teachers to Finland for long periods since the late 1960s are more complicated. Potential problems could occur when Soviet pedagogues or musicians would spend extended periods in Finland, socializing with and meeting Finnish and Western colleagues. This was precisely what happened, and there is no indication that the Soviet authorities tried to prevent interaction in any way. Teachers who came to Finland were practically without any kind of surveillance, and they rarely met Soviet officials during their stay.[65] The same applied to performers, even though they were at least nominally appointed "nannies" when they came to Finland for days or for weeks at a time. According to the interviewees, these high-profile performers could visit their Finnish colleagues in their summer cottages, and travel around without any difficulty.[66] The Soviet authorities naturally could recall their citizens (which was rarely done, even in the case of teachers), and the possible prolonging of agreements was also subject to negotiation. Teachers often came only for one year, but there were cases, such as viola teacher Viktor Repik, where pedagogues taught in Oulu for up to four years in a row.[67]

Since defections were not possible, this likely made Soviet security organs much more relaxed about Soviet citizens visiting Finland as compared to other capitalist countries. Thus, Pogozeva and Bezrodnyi were frequent, and much desired, visitors in Finland throughout the 1970s.[68] The same was true with many other top Soviet musicians, such as Dmitry Bashkirov, Mikhail Khomizer, Liana Isakadze, Oleg Kagan, and several others who greatly enriched Finnish musical life.

The motivation for these high-profile musicians to visit Finland was not the country's art scene or that its musicians were more accomplished than elsewhere in Europe. Rather, Finland was accessible, and it offered a welcome respite for artists coming from the hectic pace of Leningrad or

Moscow. Sparsely populated Finland—with a population the size of Leningrad, or half of Moscow—offered something that was difficult to come by elsewhere. The Kuhmo Festival, for example, which frequently featured prominent Soviet artists, took place in a secluded area, one hundred kilometers towards Russia from the closest town of Kajaani (thirty-five thousand inhabitants). Since 1970, the Kuhmo Festival has drawn top musicians from all around the world. During the Cold War, the festival disregarded politics, allowing musicians from the East and the West to meet each other far away from their daily pressures.

The initiative unleashed by the dynamic phase of Soviet cultural operations during the Thaw to use Soviet musical prominence to conquer foreign audiences bore fruits. By the Brezhnev era, the Soviets were certainly conquering audiences—except not as representatives of the Soviet system, but as individuals and music professionals. The Soviet musicians hardly ever mentioned politics during their visits to Finland. The political framework did affect their actions and limited their ability to visit Finland to a certain extent, but it did not have much effect on what they did when abroad.[69]

Networks that were created as a result of individual visits sometimes grew beyond the individuals themselves. Tatiana Pogozeva, the violin pedagogue, made many friends in Finland. Her son, Igor Bezrodny, became a famed violin virtuoso, a Stalin Prize laureate (1951), and a frequent visitor to Finland. Furthermore, when Pogozeva died in 1981, Bezrodny settled in Finland, first partly and then permanently. He was a professor at the Moscow Conservatory for almost forty years while continuing to teach in Finland, and the head conductor at the Turku Philharmonic Orchestra from 1986 to 1990. He died in Helsinki in 1997.

Even if a great majority of Soviet artists who visited Finland during the Brezhnev era never planned to stay, it seems that the artistic intelligentsia became increasingly alienated from Soviet ideology. Some immigrated to Finland, but most decided to stay in the Soviet Union.

CONCLUSION

The reasons for the Soviet authorities' decision not to limit cultural exchanges after the Thaw are unknown. Perhaps they considered expansion of cultural exchanges to be a mistake of sorts, as they retracted some of the reforms related to Soviet cultural diplomacy during the Thaw. While they had foreseen the undesirable consequences of such cultural exchanges, they also saw that the benefits were greater. This led to the expansion of foreign cultural ties. The major expansion and actual creation of Soviet cultural diplomacy was based on the assumed appeal of the Soviet system. For Khrushchev, the international presence of the Soviet Union and the embellishment of its public image were top priorities. In their fierce ideological competition with the United States, the Soviets believed they could win over foreign populations by proving their superiority in the cultural arena. To this end, a series of cultural operations were inaugurated, bureaucracy was amended accordingly, and Soviet organizations adopted highly active roles throughout the Thaw. Through exchange programs, Soviet scientists, scholars, artists, and, in some cases, even ordinary people were able to establish foreign ties to an unparalleled level. This resulted in the Soviet people having a newfound access to Western influences in ways unimaginable during the Stalin era. However, a clampdown on arts and intelligentsia ensued in 1962. Simultaneously, the development of cultural influences as part of the Soviet foreign policy came to an end. Yet, this did not suppress foreign connections. Exchanges did continue to take place throughout the Brezhnev era, but the dynamism was no longer present; operations became routine-like, allowing new forms of interactions to surface outside the government control.

The dichotomy between official and unofficial—or governmental and transnational—connections manifested in the artistic ties between Finland and the Soviet Union, though the line between the two is often thin and blurred. Examining the evolution of cultural connections reveals that, over time, individual and professional aims became much more prominent than those of the Soviet government and party. In fact, politics and ideology played a continually decreasing role in the artistic connections between Finland and the Soviet Union during the Brezhnev era. The role of the Finnish-Soviet Society illustrates this change rather well, as it transformed from an ideologically and politically active organizer into a facilitator with little influence on the actual content of cultural exchanges.

Even if the Soviet government and the Communist party were crucial in enabling foreign connections throughout the Soviet era, their roles became increasingly more passive. Permissions to travel could be revoked, and people abroad could be asked to return, but these permissions were rarely ever used. The dynamic approach of the Soviet Union in the field of cultural diplomacy turned into a routine that allowed artists the freedom to travel and interact with foreigners. Artists could then build networks and further their own professional interests during the Brezhnev era.

At the governmental and international level, it may seem that the artistic connections in the Soviet Union had stagnated. However, at the transnational level, we can see how new personal and professional connections developed and became more dynamic. This hardly supports the picture of a culturally stagnated state. What was for the Soviet leaders a battle of the hearts and minds, for many Soviet individuals was primarily just a chance to go abroad and pursue their personal and professional goals. Seen through the lens of the transnational approach, foreign artistic connections during the Brezhnev era look quite dynamic and vibrant.

NOTES

1. For discussion about the thaw, its periodization, and significance, see Denis Kozlov and Eleonory Gilburd, The Thaw as an Event in Russian History. In Denis Kozlov and Eleonory Gilburd (eds), *The Thaw: Soviet Society and Culture during the 1950s and 1960s* (Toronto: University of Toronto Press, 2013). For the relationship of artistic intelligentsia and post-Thaw, see Stephen Lovell and Rosalind Marsh, "Culture and Crisis: The Intelligentsia and Literature after 1953." In Catriona Kelly and David Shepherd (eds), *Russian Cultural Studies: An Introduction* (Oxford, 1998), 65–66.

2. Gerard McBurney, "Soviet music after the death of Stalin: the legacy of Shostakovich." In Kelly & Shepderd, *Russian Cultural Studies*, 124.

3. See, e.g. Anne Gorsuch, *All this is Your World. Soviet Tourism at Home and Abroad after Stalin* (Oxford: Oxford University Press, 2011); Kozlov & Gilburd, *The Thaw*.

4. Michael David-Fox, Showcasing the great experiment: cultural diplomacy and western visitors to the Soviet Union, 1921–1941 (Oxford: Oxford University Press, 2012); Katerina Clark, Moscow, the Fourth Rome: Stalinism, Cosmopolitanism, and the Evolution of Soviet Culture, 1931–1941 (Cambridge, MA: Harvard University Press, 2011),

5. In music, anti-Westernism culminated in 1948 in the so-called antiformalist campaign, which was basically about fighting abstract modernism and Western tendencies. See e.g. Kirill Tomoff, *Creative Union: The Professional Organization of Soviet Composers, 1939–1953* (Cornell University Press, 2006), 140–8.

6. Nigel Gould-Davies, The Logic of Soviet Cultural Diplomacy, *Diplomatic History* 27 (2003), no 2, 193–214; Simo Mikkonen, "Winning Hearts and Minds? Soviet musical intelligentsia in the struggle against the United States during the early Cold War" in Fairclough, Pauline (ed.) *Twentieth- Century Music and Politics* (Farnham: Ashgate, 2013); Mikkonen, Simo "Introduction" in Mikkonen, Simo & Suutari, Pekka (eds) *Music, Art and Diplomacy: East-West Cultural Exchanges and the Cold War* (Farnham: Ashgate, 2016).

7. Soviet relations with the West are typically examined in the field of international relations, often from the western point of view. See Yale Richmond, Cultural Exchange and the Cold War: Raising the Iron Curtain (University Park: Penn State Press, 2003); Victor Rosenberg, Soviet-American Relations, 1953–1960: Diplomacy and Cultural Exchange During the Eisenhower Presidency (Jefferson: McFarland & Co. 2005). More balanced approach can be found in David Caute, The Dancer Defects: The Struggle for Cultural Supremacy during the Cold War (Oxford: Oxford University Press, 2003). Implications of increased connections to the West during the Thaw have been addressed in Stephen V. Bittner, The Many Lives of Khrushchev's Thaw: Experience and Memory in Moscow's Arbat (Ithaca: Cornell university press, 2008); Vladislav Zubok, *Zhivago's Children: The Last Russian Intelligentsia* (Oxford: Harvard University Press, 2009).

8. Rosa Magnusdottir, "Be careful in America, Premier Khrushchev!" Soviet perceptions of peaceful coexistence with the United States in 1959. In *Cahiers du monde Russe* 47 (2006), 1–2, 109–130.

9. Susan Reid, In the name of the People: the Manege Affair Revisited. In Kritika: Explorations in Russian and East European History vol. 6, 4 (2005), 673–716;

10. Gorsuch, *All this is your world*. Gorsuch has pointed out, that Soviet travelers actually had more freedoms than has previously been supposed. On how people in the West were able to meet Soviet travelers, see also Mikkonen, Stealing the Monopoly.

11. Interview with Märta Gartz-Kuokkanen (worked for Fazer Concert Office) (26 August 2011); Interview with Maire Pulkkinen (worked for Fazer Concert Office) (August 2011). Both used to work for the Fazer Concert Office that was the primary Finnish partner used by the Soviet concert organizer Goskontsert. Pulkkinen had been in close contact with top Soviet artists since early 1950s, looking after their concert tours and arrangements in Finland. Furthermore, interviews with Finnish guides that took care of Soviet groups in Finland seem to indicate that despite having tight pro-

grams, there was always room for private enterprise and detours. Interviews from Memory Archives of Central Finland (January-February 2012).

12. For examples of how the system of Soviet artistic profession came to be controlled by the Communist Party both by giving out privileges and through coercion, see Kirill Tomoff, *Creative Union*; Simo Mikkonen, *Music and Power in the Soviet 1930s: A History of Composers' Bureaucracy* (New York: Edwin Mellen, 2009).

13. A peace treaty with the Soviet Union included an article demanding that every Soviet citizen had to be repatriated. In practice, only Finnish citizens were allowed to defect to Finland from the Soviet Union. Jussi Pekkarinen and Juha Pohjonen, *Ei armoa Suomen selkänahasta. Ihmisluovutukset Neuvostoliittoon* 1944–1981 (Helsinki: Otava, 2005).

14. Tourism to Finland increased practically throughout the Soviet era, topping in 1990 at 343000 visitors. Finland was the major tourist spot for Soviet tourists in the West. See Alexei Golubev, "Neuvostoturismin ja läntisen kulutuskulttuurin kohtaaminen Suomessa" [Meeting of Soviet Tourism and Western consumerism in Finland] in *Finnish Historical Journal* 4/2011, 412–425.

15. Simo Mikkonen, "The Finnish-Soviet Society: From Political to Cultural Connections." In Rosa Magnusdottir and Valur Ingimundarsson (eds) *Nordic Cold War Cultures: Ideologies, Exchanges, Representations* (Helsinki: Kikimora, 2015).

16. Vladislav Zubok has emphasized that even those considered loyal by the Party often experienced their first encounters with the West as transformative moments. Zubok, *Zhivago's Children*, 91.

17. Zubok quotes the Manege affair of late 1962 as the symbolic occasion when Khrushchev "destroyed a chance for a common cause" with a new generation that was ready to reform the Soviet project. Zubok, *Zhivago's Children*, 195.

18. Zubok refers to backlash of the KGB and the Party on liberal thinking and even minor signs of protest in the latter half of the 1960s, continuing with what he calls "The Long Decline" of Soviet intelligentsia, dissidence and emigration. Zubok, *Zhivago's Children*, 290–295,

19. Iu.V.Aksiutin, *Khrushchevskaia "Ottepel" i obshchestvennaye nastroeniia v SSSR v 1953–1964 gg.* (Moscow: Rosspen, 2010); Cynthia Hooper, "What Can and Cannot Be Said: Between the Stalinist Past and New Soviet Future," *Slavonic and East European Review* 86 (2008), no 3, 306–327; Karl E. Loewenstein, "Re-Emergence of Public Opinion in the Soviet Union: Khrushchev and Responses to the Secret Speech," *Europe-Asia Studies* 58 (2006), no 8, 1329–1345; Polly Jones, "From Secret Speech to the Burial of Stalin: Real and Ideal Responses to De-Stalinization," Polly Jones (ed) *The Dilemmas of De-Stalinization: Negotiating Cultural and Social Change in the Khrushchev Era* (London: Routledge, 2006).

20. Michael David-Fox, "The Implications of Transnationalism," in *Kritika* vol 12, 4 (Fall 2011): 885–904.

21. Gorsuch, *All This Is Your World;* Caute, *The Dancer Defects;* Susan E. Reid, "Who Will Beat Whom? Soviet Popular Reception of the American National Exhibition in Moscow," 1959, *Kritika* 9 (2008), no 4, 855–904; David Hoffman, *Cultivating the Masses: Modern State Practices and Soviet Socialism, 1917–1939* (Ithaca, NY: Cornell University Press, 2011); Katerina Clark, *Moscow, The Fourth Rome: Stalinism, Cosmopolitanism, and the Evolution of Soviet Culture, 1931–1941* (Cambridge, MA: Harvard University Press, 2011).

22. See e.g. AHR Conversation: On Transnational History, *American Historical Review* 111 (2006), no 5, 1140–1165. Here, transnational approach is seen as reach beyond the focus that was typically fixed within the confines of a nation-state.

23. György Péteri, "Nylon Curtain: Transnational and Transsystemic Tendencies in the Cultural Life of State-Socialist Russia and East-Central Europe," *Slavonica* vol 10, 2 (2004): 113–123; imagined borders and differences are core theme for the volume by Peter Romjin, Giles Scott-Smith and Joes Segal, *Divided Dreamworlds: The Cultural Cold War in East and West* (Amsterdam: Amsterdam University press, 2012).

24. Akira Iriye, *Cultural Internationalism and World Order* (Washington DC: Johns Hopkins UP, 1997), 15–16.

25. This can be confirmed in a number of archival sources, see e.g.: O perestroika VOKSa, TsK KPSS, 5 September 1957. RGANI f. 89, per. 55, d. 21, l. 2; also, see Mikkonen, Winning Hearts and Minds.

26. Surroundings of the 22nd Party Congress illustrate that ideas about bringing the Communist Part closer to the people and enhancing of democracy were topical in the early 1960s. See e.g. Elena Zubkova, *Obshchestvo i reform 1945–1964* (Moscow: Rossiia Molodaia, 1993), 171–174. Also, Zubok presents an interesting picture of reform-minded Soviet intelligentsia in the 1950s and 1960s in his *Zhivago's Children*. He see this generation as socially diverse group that was connected by a belief in the socialism with a human-face, in de-Stalinization, but were socialists and Soviet patriots altogether.

27. Some works that address impact of the West and western connections in the Soviet Union include Robert English, *Russia and the Idea of the West: Gorbachev, Intellectuals, and the End of the Cold War* (New York: Columbia University Press, 2000); Gerd-Rainer Horn & Kenney Padraic (eds), *Transnational Moments of Change. Europe 1945, 1968, 1989* (Oxford: Rowman&Littlefield, 2004); Yurchak, *Everything Was Forever;* Sergei Zhuk, *Rock and Roll in the Rocket City. The West, identity, and ideology in Soviet Dniepropetrovsk, 1960–1985* (Washington: Wilson Center Press, 2010); György Peteri (ed), *Imagining the West in Eastern Europe and the Soviet Union* (Pittsburgh: University of Pittsburgh Press, 2010); Sari Autio-Sarasmo & Katalin Miklossy (eds), *Reassessing Cold War Europe* (London: Routledge, 2010).

28. David-Fox, Showcasing the Great Experiment, 247–249; Clark, *Moscow, the Fourth Rome*, 38–41.

29. O perestroike VOKSa, Sekretariat TsK, 5 Sept 1957. RGANI f. 89, per. 55, d. 21, ll. 3–5; ibid. RGANI f. 89, per. 46, d. 28, ll. 1–3.

30. See e.g. Memoranda Zhukova v TsK KPSS, 16 July 1959. RGANI f. 5, op. 30, d. 304, ll. 78–84; more in detail about GKKS, see Gould-Davies, "Logic of Soviet Cultural Diplomacy"; Mikkonen "Winning Hearts and Minds".

31. Frederick Barghoorn, *Soviet cultural offensive:* the role of cultural diplomacy in Soviet foreign policy (Westport, CO: Greenwood Press, 1960), 11.

32. Relationship of the peaceful coexistence with US-Soviet agreement on cultural exchange has been examined by Rósa Magnusdóttir, Be careful in America, 109–130.

33. Memorandum Zhukova o dogovorokh mezhdu sovetskogo soiuza s zapadnym Evropam i SShA, 28 November 1961. RGANI f. 5, op. 30, d. 370, ll. 74–76.

34. In 1958, head of goskontsert, G.G. Vladimirov recommended that they should work with western concert organizations rather than with western governments. This recommendation was since followed by Goskontsert. RGALI f. 2329, op. 35, dd. 2–9 Dos'e o kulturnoi zhizni SShA v 1959–1980 gg. Memo by Vladimirov from 4.5.1958, see ll. 59–67.

35. Caute for one records the gradually freezing development from 1963 onwards, Caute, *Dancer Defects*, 30–32; also, Zubok, *Zhivago's Children*, 193–225; Susan Reid, "In the name of the People."

36. His resignation was apparently connected to internal power struggle with the Ministry of Foreign Affairs. Before GKKS he had been Deputy Chief-Editor of Pravda, and correspondent in France before that. After GKKS he assumed the position of vice-head of Soviet Peace Committee and other less-influential positions.

37. Zapiska Ministerstva kul'tury SSSR v TsK KPSS o kul'turnykh sviazakh s SShA, 19 April 1972. RGANI f. 5, op. 64, d. 126, ll. 11–19.

38. In Finland, Finnish-Soviet Society is often equated with later political finlandization (Finnish political subjugation to Soviet foreign policy). Mikkonen, The Finnish-Soviet Society; Sonja Grossman, "Dealing with 'Friends': Soviet Friendship Societies in Western Europe as a Challenge for Western Diplomacy." In Simo Mikkonen and Pia Koivunen (eds), *Beyond the Curtain: Entangled Histories of Cold War Europe* (New York: Berghahn, 2015), 196–216.

39. Suomi-Neuvostoliittoseuran toimintakertomus [Annual report of the Finnish-Soviet Society for 1945] (Helsinki: SN-seura, 1946), 6, 15.

40. One example is the correspondence between Finnish-Soviet and Soviet-Finnish societies that was active in the late 1950s and along the 1960s, but became less frequent (and unsubstantial) by the 1970s. See Finnish National Archives, Finnish-Soviet Society, Box 88. By the 1970s, correspondence with Soviet embassy in Finland (and with Soviet ambassador Stepanov) grew accordingly. See, Box 85.

41. Interview with Leena Nivanka (interpreter and PR officer from the Finnish National Opera) (August 2013); Interview with Juhani Laurila (rector of Jyväskylä conservatory) (March 2012); Interview with Onni Kelo (conductor and musical administrator) (December 2011). Soviet interviewees do not indicate that Finnish-Soviet society would have been involved in exchanges in any way. Head of Estonian opera, Arne Mikk (interviewed in August 2013), for example did not see society playing any kind of important role. It has to be assumed that the society played a bridge building role primarily toward Soviet bureaucracy.

42. Interview with Arne Mikk (August 2013). Although Porgy and Bess had been performed in the Soviet Union by Everyman Opera in 1956, the score was not available. Yet, the very fact that it had been performed, made it possible to perform it again. Staging of previously unseen works in the Soviet Union was always very difficult.

43. Interview with Märta Gartz-Kuokkanen (August 2011); Interview with Maire Pulkkinen (August 2011).

44. Gorsuch, All This is Your World, 117–125.

45. Studies about Soviet travel to the West point out that the political motives and foreign policy objectives of the Party were quickly forgotten, and travelers' own objectives took the forefront. Golubev, "Neuvostoturismin;" Aleksei Popov, "Sovetskie turisty za rubezhom: ideologiia, kommunikatsiia, emotsii (po otchetam rukovoditelei turistskikh grupp)" *Istorichna panorama* 6, 49–56. Also, about tourism to Finland in particular, see: Aleksandr Chistikov, Sovetskii turist v Finliandii v seredine 1950-kh—seredine 1960-kh godov, *Noveishaia istoriia Rossii: vremia, sobytiia, ljudi. Sbornik statei i vospominanii* (St. Petersburg: Fora-Print, 2010), 384–392.

46. Letter of Toivo Karvonen (Chair of Finnish-Soviet Society) to Soviet Ministry of Culture concerning Soviet artistic visits to Finland, 25 November, 1964. Finnish National Archives, Finnish-Soviet Society, Box 85.

47. Zubok, Zhivago's Children, 259–296.

48. Interview with Onni Kelo (December 2011).

49. For official correspondence, see Finnish National Archives "Soviet-Finnish Society" Box 85, Letters from Onni Kelo to Soviet Finnish Society in June 1967; also interview with Onni Kelo (December 2011).

50. Interview with Erkki Palola (violinist) (December 2011); Interview with Päivyt Meller (violinist) (December 2012); interview with Juhani Laurila (March 2012).

51. Interview with Onni Kelo (December 2011); see also e.g. letter of Christina Porkkala (Chairwoman of Finnish-Soviet Society) to the Soviet Ministry of Culture concerning sending of piano pedagogue to Jyväskylä, 11 January 1974; Letter of Laurila (rector of Jyväskylä Conservatory) to Soviet Ministry of Culture concerning sending of piano pedagogue to Jyväskylä, 2 January 1974. Finnish National Archives, box 85; Interview with Juhani Laurila (March 2012).

52. Interview with Onni Kelo (December 2011); interview with Juhani Laurila (March 2012).

53. Interview with Onni Kelo (December 2011).

54. There were no persons of African origin in Finland and few people had ever seen African Americans apart from books. Negro was a generally used concept in Finland at the time.

55. Letter of Finnish-Soviet Society to VOKS on 12 January 1948, Finnish National Archives "Soviet-Finnish Society" Box 85.

56. E.g. Letter of VOKS (L. Kislova) to Finnish-Soviet society (Karvonen) on 25 October 1948, Finnish National Archives "Soviet-Finnish Society" Box 88.

57. Interview with Onni Kelo (December 2011).

58. Interview with Onni Kelo (December 2011); Interview with Märta Gartz-Kuokkanen (August 2011); Interview with Maire Pulkkinen (August 2011).

59. Exchanges increased along the 1960s at least based on the correspondence facilitated by the Finnish-Soviet Society between Soviet Ministry of Culture, Soviet Goskontsert and Finnish festivals and concert organizers. See, Finnish National Archives, Finnish-Soviet Society, boxes 85 and 88.

60. More about the Richter case, see Mikkonen, "Winning Hearts and Minds?"; Meri Herrala, "Pianist Sviatoslav Richter: Soviet Union launches 'cultural Sputnik' to the United States in 1960," in Mikkonen & Suutari, *Music, Art and Diplomacy*.

61. Interview with Mikael Hintze (September 2011); Interview with Juhani Laurila (March 2012).

62. Interview with Mikael Hintze (musician, son of Dmitry Hintze who arranged Soviet musicians to Jyväskylä in the 1960s and 1970s) (September 2011); Interview with Maire Pulkkinen (August 2011); Interview with Leena Nivanka (May 2013); interview with Aulis Sallinen (composer) (October 2013).

63. For correspondence of Finnish festivals with Soviet organizations facilitated by Soviet-Finnish Society, see for example Finnish National Archives "Soviet-Finnish Society" Box 88. Turku festival organized visits by Soviet artists already in 1959, Jyväskylä Summer Festival was very active along the 1960s. Letters can also be found in RGALI (Moscow) in the files of Ministry of Culture (f. 2329, op., as well as Goskontsert (f. 3162).

64. Mikkonen, "Winning Hearts and Minds."

65. Interview with Juhani Laurila (March 2012).

66. Märta Gartz-Kuokkanen, Interview with author, 26 August 2011; Maire Pulkkinen, Interview with author, 27 August 2011.

67. Interview with Erkki Palola (December 2011); Interview with Juhani Laurila (March 2012).

68. Abundant correspondence between Finnish Society of Music teachers and numerous Finnish summer festivals with Soviet organizations via Finnish-Soviet Society point to this direction. See Finnish National Archives "Soviet-Finnish Society" Box 85.

69. Interview with Märta Gartz-Kuokkanen (August 2011); Interview with Maire Pulkkinen (August 2011).

Bibliography

XXVII Party Congress of the CPSU, vol.1 (Moscow: Politizdat, 1986)

Adamsky, Dima P. "Through the Looking Glass: The Soviet Military-Technical Revolution and the American Revolution in Military Affairs" *Journal of Strategic Studies*, Volume 31, Issue 2, 2008 (257-294)

Adamsky, Dima P. *The Culture of Military Innovation: The Impact of Cultural Factors on the Revolution in Military Affairs in Russia, the US, and Israel* (Stanford: Stanford University Press, 2010)

Aksiutin, Iu.V. *Khrushchevskaia "Ottepel" i obshchestvennaye nastroeniia v SSSR v 1953-1964 gg*. (Moscow : Rosspen, 2010).

Amerongen, O. W., *Der Weg nach Osten. Vierzig Jahre Brückenbau für die deutsche Wirtshaft*. (München, Droemer Knaur, 1992).

Arbatov, Georgii. *Chelovek sistemy* (Moscow: Vagrius, 2002)

Autio-Sarasmo, S. and Miklóssy, K. eds., *Reassessing Cold War Europe*. (Abingdon: Routledge, 2011).

Bacon, Edwin, and Sandle, Mark, eds., *Brezhnev Reconsidered* (New York: Palgrave Macmillan, 2002)

Baibakov, N. K. *Ot Stalina do El'tsina* (Moscow: GazOil press, 1998).

Baigell, Renee and Baigell, Matthew. *Soviet Dissident Artists: Interviews after Perestroika*, ed. (New Brunswick: Rutgers University Press, 1995)

Bange, Oliver and Niedhart,Gottfried, eds., *Helsinki 1975 and the Transformation of Europe*. (New York Berghahn Books, 2008).

Barghoorn, Frederick C. "Trends in Top Political Leadership in USSR' in *Leadership in East European Communism, 1945-1970*," ed. by R. Barry Farrell (Chicago: Aldine Publishing, 1970).

Barghoorn, Frederick. *Soviet cultural offensive:* the role of cultural diplomacy in Soviet foreign policy (Westport, CO: Greenwood Press, 1960).

Barsukov, M.I., ed., *Ocherki istorii zdravoohraneniia SSSR: 1917-1956*, (Moskva: Medgiz, 1957).

Bart, John. *Friday Book: Essays and Other Non-Fiction* (London: The Johns Hopkins University Press, 1984).

Barthes, Roland. *The Rustle of Language* (Berkeley and Los Angeles: University of California Press, 1989).

Bittner, Steven V. *The Many Lives of Khrushchev's Thaw: Experience and Memory in Moscow's Arbat* (Ithaca, NY: Cornell University Press, 2008).

Blokhina, N. G. *Akademik Nikolai Nikolaievich Blokhin: vrach i chelovek*. (Moskva: Meditsina, 2001).

Boldin, Valerii. *Krusheniia Pedestala: shtrikhi k portretu M.S. Gorbacheva* (Moscow: Respublika, 1995)

Boym, Svetlana. *Common Places: Mythologies of Everyday Life in Russia* (Cambridge, Mass: Harvard University Press, 1994).

Bozo, Frédéric at al., eds.,*Europe and the End of the Cold War, A Reappraisal* (Abingdon: Routledge, n 2008).

Bradley, Joseph. *Muzhik and Muscovite: Urbanization in Late Imperial Russia* (Berkeley: University of California Press, 1985).

Brezhneva, L. *The World I Left Behind: Pieces of a Past*, (New York: Random House, 1980).

Brown, Archie and Kaser, Michael. *The Soviet Union Since the Fall of Khrushchev* 2nd edition, (London: Macmillan, 1978).
Brezhneva, L. *The World I Left Behind: Pieces of a Past,* (New York: Random House, 1980).
Buckley, Cynthia. "The Myth of Managed Migration: Migration Control and Market in the Soviet Period," *Slavic Review,* vol. 54, no. 4 (1995): 896-916.
Bushnell, John. *Moscow Graffiti: Language and Subculture* (Boston: Taylor and Francis, 1990).
Bystrova, I. V., *Sovetskii voenno-prmyshlennoi kompleks: problemy stanovleniia i razvitiia (1930-1980-e gody).* (Moscow: Rossiiskaja Akademiia Nauk: Institut Rossiiskii istorii, 2006).
Caute, David. *The Dancer Defects: The Struggle for Cultural Supremacy during the Cold War* (Oxford: Oxford University Press, 2003).
Chernyaev, Anatoly. *Sovmestnii iskhod: dnevnik dvukh epokh, 1972-1991* (Moscow: ROSS-PEN, 2008).
Chernyshova, Natalya. *Soviet Consumer Culture in the Brezhnev Era* (London: Routledge, 2013)
Clark, Katerina. *Moscow, the Fourth Rome: Stalinism, Cosmopolitanism, and the Evolution of Soviet Culture, 1931-1941* (Cambridge, MA: Harvard University Press, 2011).
Cohen, Stephen F. *Bukharin and the Bolshevik Revolution: A Political Biography, 1888-1938* (Oxford: OUP, 1971, 1980)
Cohen, Stephen F. *Soviet Fates and Lost Alternatives: From Stalinism to the New Cold War,* (New York: Columbia University Press, 2009
Cohen, Stephen F., and Vanden Heuvel, Katrina. *Voices of Glasnost: Interviews with Gorbachev's Reformers* (New York: Norton & Co., 1989)
Cohen, Stephen F., Rabinowitch, Alexander, and Sharlet, Robert, eds. *The Soviet Union Since Stalin* (Basingstoke: Macmillan, 1980)
Cooper, J. 'Research, development and innovation in the Soviet Union' in Economic development in The Soviet Union and Eastern Europe, Volume 1. Reforms, technology and Income Distribution. ed. by Zbigniew M. Fallenbuchl. (New York: Praeger Pubvlushers, 1975).
Conroy, Mary Schaeffer. "The Soviet Pharmaceutical Industry and Dispensing: 1945-1953," *Europe-Asia Studies,* Vol. 56, No. 7 (Nov., 2004), pp. 963-991.
Crowley, David and Reid, Susan E. eds., *Socialist spaces: Sites of everyday life in the Eastern Bloc* (Oxford: Berg, 2002)
Davidovich, Ia. A., Kosaev, A. G., and Podol'naia, M. N. "Privlechenie i ratsional'noe ispol'zovanie inogorodnikh rabochikh," *Sotsiologicheskie issledovaniia,* no. 4 (1981): 123-28.
David-Fox, Michael. *Showcasing the great experiment: cultural diplomacy and western visitors to the Soviet Union, 1921-1941* (Oxford: Oxford University Press, 2012).
De Grazia, Victoria, *Irresistible Empire: America's Advance through Twentieth-Century Europe* (Cambridge, Mass: Belknap Press, 2005)
Denisova, Liubov. *Rural Women in the Soviet Union and Post-Soviet Russia,* ed. and trans. Irina Mukhina (London: Routledge, 2010).
Dobson, Miriam. *Khrushchev's Cold Summer: Gulag Returnees, Crime, and the Fate of Reform after Stalin* (Ithaca: Cornell University Press, 2009).
Dodge, Norton. "Notes on Collecting Soviet Nonconformist Art," in Alla Rosenfeld and Norton Dodge, eds., *Gulag to Glasnost: Nonconformist Art from the Soviet Union* (New York: Thames and Hudson, 1995).
Dodge, Norton. *Women in the Soviet Economy: Their Role in Economic, Scientific, and Technical Development* (Baltimore: Johns Hopkins Press, 1966).
Dodge, Norton and Tsuchigane, Robert. *Economic Discrimination against Women in the United States: Measures and Changes* (Lexington, MA: Lexington Books, 1974).
Engel, Barbara *Between the Fields and the City: Women, Work and Family in Russia, 1861-1914* (Cambridge: Cambridge University Press, 1994).

English, Robert D. *Russia and the Idea of the West: Gorbachev, Intellectuals, and the End of the Cold War* (New York: Columbia University Press, 2000)

Esakov, V.D. and Levina, E.S. *Stalinskie 'Sudy Chesti': delo 'KR,'* (Moscow: Nauka, 2005).

Fain, Aleksandr. *Eta neponiatnaia molodezh': Problemy neforma'nykh molodezhnykh ob'edinenii* (Moscow, Profizdat, 1990).

Fainberg, Dina 'Notes from the Rotten west, Stories from the Backward East: Soviet and American Foreign Correspondents in the Cold War, 1945-1985' Unpublished PhD Dissertation, Rutgers, 2012.

Fairclough, Pauline, ed. *Twentieth- Century Music and Politics* (Farnham: Ashgate, 2013).

Favarel-Garrigues, G. *Policing Economic Crime in Russia. From Soviet Planned Economy to Privatisation*, trans. R. Leverdier, (London: Hurst and Company, 2011).

Field, Mark G.*Soviet Socialized Medicine: An Introduction*, (New York: The Free Press, 1967).

Fitzpatrick, S. *Everyday Stalinism: Ordinary Life in Extraordinary Times* (Oxford: Oxford University Press, 1999).

Fitzpatrick, Sheila. *The Russian Revolution* 3rd ed. (Oxford: Oxford University Press, 2008)

French, Mary-Catherine. 'Reporting Socialism: Soviet Journalism and the Journalists' Union, 1955-1966'. Unpublished PhD Dissertation, University of Pennsylvania, 2014.

Friedman, Thomas L. *The Lexus and the Olive Tree* (New York: Anchor Books, 2000).

Gerd-Rainer Horn & Kenney, Padraic (eds), Transnational Moments of Change. Europe 1945, 1968, 1989 (Oxford: Rowman&Littlefield, 2004).

Gorbachev, O. V. *Na Puti k gorodu: sel'skaia migratsiia v Tsentral'noi Rossii (1946-1985 gg.) i sovetskaia model' urbanizatsii* (Moscow: MPGU, 2002).

Gorsuch, Anne. *All this is Your World. Soviet Tourism at Home and Abroad after Stalin* (Oxford: Oxford University Press, 2011).

Grandstaff, Peter. *Interregional Migration in the USSR: Economic Aspects, 1959-1970* (Durham: Duke University Press, 1980).

Grushin, B.A. *Chetyre zhizni Rossii v zerkale obshestvennogo mneniia. Epokha Brezhneva chast' 1,* (Moscow: Progress-Traditsiia, 2003), 136-176.

Gumeniuk, A. A. "Chelovek i reformy v SSSR v 1953--1985 gody (po materialam Saratovskoi oblasti)," *Izvestiia Saratovskogo universiteta*, vol. 9, no. 2, 2009.

Henningsen, Monika. *Der Freizeit- und Fremdenverkehr in der (ehemaligen) Sowjetunion unter besonderer Berücksichtigung des Baltischen Raumes* , (Frankfurt: Peter Lang, 1994).

Hanson, P., *The Rise and Fall of the Soviet Economy. An Economic History of the USSR from 1945*, (LondonL Longman, 2003).

Hanson, P., *Trade and Technology in Soviet-Western Relations* , (London: Macmillan, 1981).

Hixson, Walter L. *Parting the Curtain: Propaganda, Culture, and the Cold War, 1945-1961* (New York: St. Martin's Press, 1997).

Hochstadt, Stephen. *Mobility and Modernity: Migration in Germany, 1809-1989* (Ann Arbor: University of Michigan Press, 1999).

Hoffmann, David. *Peasant Metropolis: Social Identities in Moscow, 1929-1941* (Ithaca: Cornell University Press, 1994).

Hooper, Cynthia "What Can and Cannot Be Said : Between the Stalinist Past and New Soviet Future," Slavonic and East European Review 86 (2008), no 3, 306-327.

Hoptman, Laura and Pospiszyl, Tomás, eds. *Primary Documents: A Sourceook for Eastern and Central European Art since the 1950s*, (New York: Museum of Modern Art, 2002)

Hughes, R. G., Britain, Germany and the Cold War. The Search for a European Détente 1949–1967. (Abingdon: Routledge, 2007).

Huxtable, Simon. "In Search of the Soviet Reader: The Kosygin Reforms, Sociology, and Changing Concepts of Soviet Society, 1964-1970", *Cahiers du Monde russe*, 55/3-4 (2013), 623-642.

Huxtable, Simon. "Shortcomings: Soviet Journalists and the Changing Role of Press Criticism after the Twentieth Party Congress", in *De-Stalinisation Reconsidered: Persistence and Change in the Soviet Union*, ed. by Thomas M. Bohm, Rayk Einax, Michel Abesser (Frankfurt-am-Main: Campus, 2014).

Iriye, Akira. Cultural Internationalism and World Order (Washington DC: Johns Hopkins UP, 1997).

Jackson, I., *The Economic Cold War. America, Britain and East–West Trade, 1948-1963* , (New York: Palgrave, 2001).

Jackson, Matthew Jesse. *The Experimental Group: Ilya Kabakov, Moscow Conceptualism, Soviet Avant-Gardes* (Chicago: University of Chicago Press, 2010).

Johnson, Robert E. *Peasant and Proletarian: The Working Class of Moscow in the Late Nineteenth Century* (New Brunswick: Rutgers University Press, 1979).

Jones, Polly, ed. The Dilemmas of De-Stalinization: Negotiating Cultural and Social Change in the Khrushchev Era (London: Routledge, 2006).

Kagarlitsky, Boris. *The Thinking Reed: Intellectuals and the Soviet State, 1917 to the Present. Trans. Brian Pearce* (London: Verso, 1988)

Kaje M. and Niitamo, O., 'Scientific and Technical Cooperation between a Small Capitalist Country and Big Socialist Country' in *Finnish-Soviet Economic Relations.* Möttölä, Bykov and Korolev (Eds.) (London: Macmillan Press 1983).

Kelly, Catriona and Shepherd, David., eds. Russian Cultural Studies: An Introduction (Oxford, 1998)

Kessler, Gijs. "The Peasant and the Town: Rural-Urban Migration in the Soviet Union, 1929-40," 2 vols. Doctoral Dissertation, European University Institute, 2001.

Koenker, Diane P. "Whose Right to Rest? Contesting the Family Vacation in the Postwar Soviet Union," Comparative Studies in Society and History 51,2 (2009), 401-425.

Kornienko, Gerogii and Akhromeev, Sergei. *Glazami Marshala i Diplomata* (Moscow: Mezhdunarodnye otnosheniia, 1992)

Kotkin, Stephen. (with a contribution by Jan T. Gross) *Uncivil Society: 1989 and the Implosion of the Communist Establishment* (New York: Modern Library, 2009).

Kotkin, Stephen. *Armageddon Averted: The Soviet Collapse, 1970-2000* (Oxford: Oxford University Press, 2001).

Kozlov, Denis . *The Readers of Novyi Mir: Coming to Terms with the Stalinist Past* (Cambridge: Harvard University Press, 2013).

Kozlov, Denis and Gilburd, Eleonory, eds. *The Thaw: Soviet Society and Culture during the 1950s and 1960s* (Toronto: University of Toronto Press, 2013).

Krementsov, Nikolai. *The Cure: A story of cancer and politics from the Annals of the Cold War*, (Chicago: The University of Chicago Press, 2002).

Kudriashov, S, ed. *General'nyi sekretar' L. I. Brezhnev, 1964-1982*, (Moscow: Arkhiv Prezidenta Rossiiskoi Federatsii, 2006).

Kulakov, A. A. and Sakharov, A. N. et al. (eds), *Obshchestvo i vlast'. Rossiiskaia provintsiia, 1917-1980-e gody (po materialam nizhegorodskikh arkhivov)*, vol. 5, 1965-1980, (Moscow: Institut Rossiiskoi istorii RAN, 2008).

Laclau, Ernesto and Mouffe, Chantal. *Hegemony and Socialist Strategy* (London and New York: Verso, 1985).

Ledeneva, A. *Russia's Economy of Favours. Blat, Networking and Informal Exchange*, (Cambridge: Cambridge University Press, 1998).

Levykin, I. T. and Pokrovskaia, M. V. "Problemy urovnia i kachestva zhizni sovetskikh liudei", in I. T. Levykin and A. A. Voz'mitel' (eds), *Sovetskii obraz zhizni: sostoianie, mneniia i otsenki sovetskikh liudei*, Moscow: ISI AN SSSR, 1984

Lewin, Moshe and Elliott, Gregory. *The Soviet Century* (London: Verso, 2005)

Lewis, Philippa. "Peasant Nostalgia in Contemporary Russian Literature," *Soviet Studies*, vol. 28, no. 4 (1976).

Loeber, Dietrich Andre. "Limitchiki: On the Legal Status of Migrant Workers in Large Soviet Cities," *The Soviet and Post-Soviet Review*, vol. 11, nos. 1-3 (1984): 301-08.

Loewenstein, Karl E. "Re-Emergence of Public Opinion in the Soviet Union: Khrushchev and Responses to the Secret Speech," Europe-Asia Studies 58 (2006), no 8, 1329-1345.

Ludlow, N. Piers, ed., *European Integration and the Cold War: Ostpolitik, 1965-1973* (Abingdon: Routledge, 2007).

Magnusdottir, Rosa. "Be careful in America, Premier Khrushchev!" Soviet perceptions of peaceful coexistence with the United States in 1959." *Cahiers du monde Russe* 47 (2006).

Magnusdottir, Rosa and Ingimundarsson, Valur, eds., *Nordic Cold War Cultures: Ideologies, Exchanges, Representations* (Helsinki: Kikimora, 2015).

Matthews, Mervyn. *The Passport Society: Controlling Movement in Russia and the USSR* (Boulder: Westview, 1993).

Mikkonen, Simo. *Music and Power in the Soviet 1930s: A History of Composers' Bureaucracy* (New York: Edwin Mellen, 2009).

Mikkonen, Simo and Koivunen,Pia. Beyond the Divide: Entangled Histories of Cold War Europe (New York: Berghahn Books, 2015).

Mikkonen, Simo & Suutari, Pekka (eds) *Music, Art and Diplomacy: East-West Cultural Exchanges and the Cold War* (Farnham: Ashgate, 2016).

Millar, J. R. 'The Little Deal: Brezhnev's Contribution to Acquisitive Socialism', *Slavic Review*, vol. 44, no. 4, 1985, pp. 694-706.

Mirskii, M.B. *Meditsina Rossii X-XX vekov: ocherki istorii*, (Moskva: Rosspen, 2005)

Moch, Leslie Page. *Paths to the City: (Regional Migration in Nineteenth-Century France* (Beverly Hills: Sage, 1983).

Moch, Leslie Page. *Moving Europeans: Migration in Western Europe since 1650* (Bloomington: Indiana University Press, 2003).

Nathans, Benjamin and Platt, Kevin. 'Socialist in Form, Indeterminate in Content: The Ins and Outs of Late Soviet Culture', *Ab Imperio* Nr. 2, 2011.

Noack, Christian. " Mighty Weapon in the Class War: Proletarian Values, Tourism and Mass Mobilisation in Stalin's Time", *Journal of Modern European History* 10,2 (2012) 233-256.

Noack, Christian. "Building Tourism in One Country?: The Sovietization of Vacationing, 1917-41", in Eric G. Zuelov (ed.) *Touring Beyond the Nation : A Transnational Approach to European Tourism History* (Farnham: Ashgate, 2011) 171-195.

Orlov, Igor and Iurchikova, Elena. *Massovyi turizm v stalinskoi povsednevnosti*, (Moscow: 2010).

Paperny, Vladimir. *Architecture in the Age of Stalin: Culture Two* (Cambridge University Press, 2011).

Parfenov, L. *Namedni. Nasha Era. 1971-1980*, (Moscow: KoLibri, 2010)

Péteri, György, ed. *Imagining the West in Eastern Europe and the Soviet Union* (Pittsburgh: University of Pittsburgh Press, 2010).

Péteri, György. "Nylon Curtain: Transnational and Transsystemic Tendencies in the Cultural Life of State-Socialist Russia and East-Central Europe," *Slavonica* vol 10, 2 (2004): 113-123.

Pilkington, Hilary. "'For the Sake of the Children': Gender and Migration in the Former Soviet Union," in *Post-Soviet Women from the Baltic to Central Asia*, ed. Mary Buckley (Cambridge: Cambridge University Press, 1997).

Pilkington, Hilary. *Russia's Youth: A Nation's Constructors and Constructed* (London: Routledge, 1994).

Plisetskaia, M. *Ia, Maiia Plisetskaia*, (Moscow: Izdatel'stvo 'Novosti', 1994).

Priestland, David . "Stalin as Bolshevik Romantic" in *Stalin: A New History* , ed. Sarah Davies and James Harris (Cambridge: Cambridge University Press, 2005) .

Prokhorov, Aleksandr. *Unasledovannyi diskurs: paradigm stalinskoi kultury v literature i kinematografe ottepeli* (St. Petersburg: Akademicheskii proekt, 2008).

Raleigh, Don. *Soviet Baby Boomers: An oral history of Russia's Cold war Generation* (Oxford: Oxford University Press, 2012).
Richmond, Yale. *Cultural Exchange and the Cold War: Raising the Iron Curtain* (University Park: Penn State Press, 2003).
Reid, Susan. "Communist Comfort: Socialist modernism and the Making of Cozy Homes in the Khrushchev-Era Soviet Union," *Gender and History* 21:3 (2009).
Reid, Susan. "In the Name of the People: The Manege Affair Revisited," Kritika 6:4 (2005), 673-716.
Reid, Susan E. "Who will beat Whom? Soviet Popular Reception of the American National Exhibit in Moscow, 1959," Kritika 4 (Fall 2008), 855-904.
Reid, Susan and Crowley, David. *Style and Socialism: Modernity and Material Culture in Post-War Eastern Europe,* (Oxford: Berg, 2000).
Reynolds, David. "Science, Technology and the Cold War," in *The Cambridge History of the Cold War. Volume III, Endings*, ed. Melvin P. Leffler and Odd Arne Westad (Cambridge University Press, 2010).
Risch, William. "Soviet 'Flower Children': Hippies and the Youth Counter-Culture in 1970s L'viv." *Journal of Contemporary History* 40.3 (July 2005): 565-584.
Romjin, Peter, Scott-Smith, Giles and Segal, Joes. Divided Dreamworlds: The Cultural Cold War in East and West (Amsterdam: Amsterdam University press, 2012).
Rosenberg, Victor. *Soviet-American Relations, 1953–1960: Diplomacy and Cultural Exchange During the Eisenhower Presidency* (Jefferson: McFarland & Co. 2005).
Rosenberg, William G., and Siegelbaum, Lewis H. *Social Dimensions of Soviet Industrialization*, ed (Bloomington: Indiana University Press, 1993).
Rosental, Paul-André., *Les sentiers invisibles: Espace, familles, et migrations dans la France du 19e siècle* (Paris: Ecole des Hautes études en Sciences Sociales, 1999).
Rozin, M. 'The psychology of Soviet hippies', *Soviet Sociology* 2 (1), 1999, 44-72.
Ryan, Michael, *Doctors and the State in the Soviet Union*, (New York: St. Martin's Press, 1990).
Rudolph, K., Wirtshaftsdiplomatie im Kalten Krieg. Die Ostpolitik der Westdeutschen Groβindustrie 1945–1991, (Frankfurt, Campus, 2004).
Shepanskaia, Tat'iana. *Sistema: Teksty i traditsii subkul'tury* (Moscow, 2004).
Shipler, David. *Russia: Broken Idols, Solemn Dreams* (New York, New York: Times Books, 1983)
Shlapentokh, Vladimir. *Public and Private Life of the Soviet People. Changing Values in Post-Stalin Russia* (New York and Oxford: Oxford University Press, 1989).
Siegelbaum, Lewis H. ed., *Borders of Socialism: Private Spheres of Soviet Russia* (New York: Palgrave Macmillan, 2006).
Smolkin-Rothrock, Victoria. "The Ticket to the Soviet Soul: Science, Religion, and the Spiritual Crisis of Late Soviet Atheism," The Russian Review 73 (April 2014), 171-197.
Solomon, Susan Gross ed., *Doing Medicine Together: Germany and Russia Between the Wars* (Toronto: University of Toronto Press, 2006).
Spechler, Dina R. *Permitted Dissent in the USSR:* Novyi mir *and the Soviet Regime* (New York: Praeger, 1982).
Star, Susan and Griesemer, James, "Institutional Ecology, 'Translations' and Boundary Objects: Amateurs and Professionals in Berkeley's Museum of Vertebrate Zoology, 1907-39," *Social Studies of Science* (1989),19/3: 387–420
Starks, Tricia. *The Body Soviet: Propaganda, Hygiene, and the Revolutionary State*, (Madison, WI: The University of Wisconsin Press, 2008).
Starodubtseva, Zinaida ed. *Russkoe ART zarubezh'e, vtoraia polovina XX-nachalo XXI veka*, ed (Moscow: Gosudarstvennyi Tsentr Sovremennogo iskussva, 2010).
Strovskii, D.L. *Istoriia otechestvennoi zhurnalistiki noveishego perioda* (Ekaterinburg: Izd. Ural'skogo universiteta, 1998)
Stuart, Robert C. and Gregory, Paul R. "A Model of Soviet Rural-Urban Migration," *Economic Development and Cultural Change*, vol. 26, no. 1 (1977).

Suri, Jeremy. "The Promise and Failure of 'Developed Socialism': The Soviet 'Thaw' and the Crucible of the Prague Spring, 1964–1972," *Contemporary European History*, 15, 2, 2006

Tatu, Michel. *Power in the Kremlin* (London: Collins, 1969).

Tomoff, Kirill. *Creative Union: The Professional Organization of Soviet Composers, 1939-1953* (Cornell University Press, 2006).

Troitsky, Artemy. *Back in the USSR: The True Story of Rock in Russian* (London, 1987).

Vail', Petr and Genis, Aleksandr. *60-e: Mir sovetskogo cheloveka. 2-e izd.* (Moscow: Novoe literaturnoe obozrenie, 1998).

Venediktov, D.D., *Sovetsko-Amerikanskoe sotrudnichestvo v oblasti zdravoohraneniia*, (Moscow: Meditsina 1977)

Vinogradov, Alexey and Pleysier, Albert, eds., *The Women of Izmaelovka, a Soviet Union Collective Farm in Siberia*, (Lantham: University Press of America, 2007).

Ward, Christopher. *Brezhnev's Folly: The Building of BAM and late Soviet socialism* (Pittsburgh, 2009).

Wenger, Andreas et al., eds., *Origins of the European Security System*, (Abingdon: Routledge, 2007).

Willis, David K. *Klass: How Russians Really Live* (New York: Avon Books, 1987)

Wolfe, Thomas C. *Governing Soviet Journalism: The Press and the Socialist Person after Stalin* (Bloomington, IN: Indiana University Press, 2005).

Yakovlev, Aleksadndr. *Sumerki*, (Moscow: Materik, 2005)

Yurchak, Alexei. *Everything was Forever, until it was no more: the Last Soviet Generation* (Princeton University Press, 2006)

Zaslavsky, Victor. *The Neo-Stalinist State* (Armonk, NY: M. E. Sharpe, 1981).

Zezina, M.R. *Sovetskaia khoudozhestvennaia intelligentsia i vlast' v 1950-e – 60-e gody* (Moscow: Dialog-MGU, 1999)

Zhuk, Sergei. *Rock and Roll in the Rocket City: The West, Identity, and Ideology in Soviet Dniepropetrovsk, 1960-1985* (Baltimore: John Hopkins's University Press, 2010).

Zubok, Vladislav M. *A Failed Empire: The Soviet Union In the Cold War from Stalin to Gorbachev* (Chapel Hill: University of North Carolina Press, 2007).

Zubok, Vladislav. *Zhivago's Children: The Last Russian Intelligentsia* (Oxford: Harvard University Press, 2009).

Index

About the Editors and Contributors

EDITORS

Dina Fainberg is assistant professor of East European Studies at the University of Amsterdam. Her research explores the intersection between history, mass media, and foreign relations, focusing on the relationship between Russia and the West. Dina's work has been published in *Cold War History, Journalism Histor,* and a number of edited collections. Currently she is completing a manuscript which follows the work and the private lives of Soviet and American foreign correspondents in the Cold War.

Artemy M. Kalinovsky is Assistant Professor of East European Studies at the University of Amsterdam. He is the author of *A Long Goodbye: The Soviet Withdrawal from Afghanistan* (Harvard University Press, 2011), and coeditor of *The End of the Cold War and the Third World* (Routledge: 2011) and *The Routledge Handbook of the Cold War* (2014). Artemy's writing has also appeared in *Foreign Policy,* the *National Journal, Foreign Affairs,* and the *Washington Post.* His current research is focused on the politics and practices of development and modernization in Tajikistan.

CONTRIBUTORS

Sari Autio-Sarasmo works as a senior researcher and research coordinator at the Finnish Centre of Excellence in Russian Studies coordinated by the Aleksantari Institute, University of Helsinki, Finland. Her research interest focuses on East-West technology and knowledge transfer and the economic modernization of the Soviet Union and Russia. She has published widely about the multilevel East-West interaction during the Cold War. She is the coeditor of *Reassessing Cold War Europe* and her latest contribution to the topic is *Technological Modernization in the Soviet Union and Post-Soviet Russian: Practices and Continuities.*

Natalya Chernyshova is Senior Lecturer in Modern History at the University of Winchester, UK. She is the author of *Soviet Consumer Culture in the Brezhnev Era* (Routledge, 2013), which explores the political, social, and cultural consequences of the relative prosperity under 'developed socialism.' Chernyshova is currently working on a political biography of Piotr Masherau, the charismatic leader of the Belorussian Communist Party during the Brezhnev years.

Courtney Doucette completed her B.A. in history and Russian language at Lawrence University (Appleton, WI) in 2004 and received an M.A. at the European University at St. Petersburg (Russia) in 2005. She is now a doctoral candidate in modern European history, with an emphasis on the Soviet Union, at Rutgers University. Her research interests span the twentieth century, though her current work focuses on the Gorbachev era, the last six years of Soviet history. Looking at Soviet history from its end, her dissertation investigates reformers' attempts to reinvigorate socialism and how Soviet people across the social spectrum engaged their attempts. Under the auspices of the Social Science Research Council's International Dissertation Research Fellowship, she completed twelve months of dissertation research in Russia and is currently writing up her thesis.

Juliane Fürst is a Senior Lecturer in Modern European History at the University of Bristol. She is the author of *Stalin's Last Generation: Soviet Post-War Youth and the Emergence of Mature Socialism* (Oxford University Press, 2010) and the editor of *Late Stalinist Russia: Society Between Reconstruction and Reinvention* (Routledge, 2006). She is currently writing a monograph *Flowers through Concrete: The World of Soviet Hippies*, which will come out with Oxford University Press in 2017. She is also working on an exhibition on Soviet hippies in collaboration with the Wende Museum in Los Angeles.

Anna Geltzer is a Visiting Scholar in the Science in Society Program at Wesleyan University, where she has taught for the past several years. She holds a PhD in Science & Technology Studies from Cornell University, and is working on a manuscript titled "Surrogate Virtues: The Transition from Soviet to Russian Biomedicine."

Simon Huxtable is a Research Associate at Loughborough University. Simon's research focuses on mass media in the Soviet Union. He is preparing a monograph on the Soviet press after 1945, based on his doctoral research. Simon is currently working on the 'Screening Socialism' project, a five-country comparative study of television under socialism, and is co-writing a volume on television and everyday life under socialism with Sabina Mihelj.

Simo Mikkonen is Research Fellow of the Academy of Finland and an adjunct professor of Russian history at the University of Jyväskylä, Finland. His primary research interests include the cultural, international, and transnational relations of the Soviet Union, especially with the West. He has previously published *State Composers and the Red Courtiers. Music, Ideology and Politics in the Soviet 1930s* (Mellen, 2009); edited *Beyond the Divide: Entangled Histories of Cold War Europe* (Berghahn, 2015), and *Music, Art and Diplomacy: East-West Cultural Interactions and the Cold War* (Ashgate, 2016); and written a number of articles to journals such as *Kritika, Journal of Cold War Studies*, and *Journal of Scandinavian History*, as well as in several edited volumes.

Christian Noack is a trained historian and currently Associate Professor of European Studies at the University of Amsterdam. His research focuses on the late Soviet period. He is also interested in the past and present of Muslims in the post-Soviet space and in the politics of memory in different parts of Europe. Recent publications include (with S.A. Dudoignon, eds.) *Allah's Kolkhozes. Migration, De-Stalinisation, Privatisation and the New Muslim congregations in the Soviet Realm (1950s-2000s)*, (Berlin: Klaus Schwarz, 2014); "Songs from the Wood, Love from the Fields: The Soviet Tourist Song Movement." In A.E. Gorsuch & D.P. Koenker (Eds.), *The Socialist Sixties: Crossing Borders in the Second World* (pp. 167-192). Bloomington: Indiana University Press, 2013 and (with T.A. Dooley), "Ot aristokraticheskogo proshlogo k publichnogo naslediiu. Sravnitel'noe issledovanie russkikh i irlandskikh usadeb posle revoliutsiei." In A.B. Sokolov (Ed.), *Na peresecheniiakh Britanskoi istorii.* (Yaroslavl: Izdatelstvo YaGPU, 2013).

Andrey Shcherbenok has a PhD in Russian Literature from St. Petersburg State University and a PhD in Rhetoric with a Designated Emphasis in Film Studies from UC Berkeley. Andrey is professor of practice at Skolkovo Business School in Moscow where he deals with strategic governance and change management of research universities. He was a Mellon postdoctoral fellow in the Society of Fellows in the Humanities at Columbia University and Newton international research fellow of the British Academy at the University of Sheffield. He has authored works on literature, film, trauma theory, historical memory, and ideology.

Lewis H. Siegelbaum is the Jack and Margaret Sweet Professor of History at Michigan State University, where he has taught since 1983. He received his D.Phil. from Oxford University in 1976 and taught for seven years in Melbourne, Australia. He is the author of books on the Stakhanovite movement of the 1930s (1988), the Soviet state and society in the 1920s (1994), and the award-winning *Cars for Comrades* (2008). He has edited and coedited books on disability in the Soviet Union, Soviet industrialization, Soviet working-class formation, coal miners in late- and post-Soviet Ukraine, private spheres in post-Stalinist Soviet Russia, and the automobile in the Eastern Bloc. He coauthored with Jim von Geldern the award-winning website "Seventeen Moments in Soviet History," an online sourcebook used extensively to teach Soviet history. Until recently, his work was animated by his interest in technology, ideology, and material culture, but recently he published with Leslie Page Moch *Broad Is My Native Land: Repertoires and Regimes of Migration in Russia's Twentieth Century* (Cornell University Press, 2014).

Lightning Source UK Ltd.
Milton Keynes UK
UKOW02n0706281016
286364UK00010B/224/P

9 781498 529938